Two Go to Italy

Exploring Italy by Motorhome

John Laidler

By the same author

"Two Go to Spain"

Available on Amazon as an ebook and paperback.

Cover: Ragusa, Sicily

www.john-laidler.co.uk

Copyright

Published by: Swallow Books (Devon)

ISBN 978-0-9956514-3-2

Contents

The Second Journey
We Go to Sicily

Introduction

Two Go to Spain was my first book and in it I described two journeys into Spain by motorhome. For our third venture into Europe we decided to go somewhere different. Not because we were bored with Spain, we had deliberately left out some of the best bits such as Cordoba and Granada on our first trips to give us good reasons to return. I love Spain but because there is so much more in Europe to see we decided to go to Croatia.

So here is my account of a journey which started for Croatia and is called Two Go to Italy. We were seduced by Italy, swung south instead of continuing east and ended up in Puglia and almost as far south as you can go on mainland Italy. We started the journey with a broken down ferry, landing unexpectedly in France and the dog chewed up one of our guidebooks. We didn't go to Croatia the following year either, we returned to Italy and drove to the tip of the toe and across the Straits of Messina into Sicily. So like the last book this one is about two journeys of discovery and having failed to reach Croatia it is about our discoveries in Italy.

This isn't a comprehensive guidebook. It is an account of our journeys and my aim is to give you an impression of what we saw so if you go yourself you might have a better idea what to expect, what to miss out and where to go. The latter list no doubt including all the popular places we didn't visit such as Venice, Rome and Florence. But we went to Sicily and it was magical.

The wrinkled old man standing on a steaming volcano in the image on the next page is the author. I thought I would put this right at the beginning. The images get better and less frightening the further you go into the book.

Free ebook

Apart from my dishevelled appearance there is another disappointing aspect to the above photograph. Sadly, the cost of colour printing would have made this book at least four times more expensive to produce so I have enrolled it in Kindle Matchbook which lets you to download the ebook version of this book for free. The ebook has a few more photographs (for example the one of a green orchid against a green background which *really* didn't look good in black and white) but all of them are in colour and can be viewed on a tablet, PC/Mac or even a smart phone with the free Kindle app.

The First Journey

We Aim for Croatia and Miss it

May to July, 2016

Where Shall We Go?

Towards the end of 2015 we gave serious thought to where we might go for the following year. You could spend a lifetime touring the UK and many do, Norway has always drawn me but southern Europe has a variety unmatched almost anywhere. So southern Europe it would be.

As Christmas approached there wasn't much of a plan in place so I thought I should book the ferry to put a stake in the ground. This would establish the dates of sailing which I hoped would encourage me to decide later on where to go between the landing and the returning.

We live close to Plymouth and don't enjoy the long drive across the south coast of England to reach ports like Newhaven or Dover where the crossings are cheaper so a departure from our local port was a given. There are two options from Plymouth, landing in France at Roscoff or taking the longer ferry to Santander in Spain. As we were heading for southern Europe I thought it would help if we started as far south as possible. So I booked the Santander ferry for the first week of May. This was later than I would have liked but I was organising a motorhome rally for the Murvi Owners' Club in Cornwall at the end of April.

Until we bought a motorhome we would never have described ourselves as "rally people". When we owned a caravan many years ago going on a rally with it was a repellent idea. Wind the clock forward several decades and after buying our Murvi motorhome we were soon on a rally and thoroughly enjoyed it. We went on several, including a memorable one to the east coast of Scotland where we saw the value of local knowledge in introducing folk to areas they might not otherwise go to on their own.

We had been several times to a campsite outside Portscatho on the Roseland Peninsula in Cornwall and enjoyed good times there so it seemed only fair to share the place with others. So I organised a rally so successfully I did it again the following year. Both times we were lucky with the weather, it wasn't warm but it stayed dry for the feast around a fire I arranged at the campsite when the Hidden Hut came to cook us delicious paella. The Hidden Hut is nationally famous and based at Porthcurnick Beach near Portscatho. They are open every day in summer for lunches and two or three times a month for evening "feasts" which are hugely popular. Tickets for the feasts sell out in moments when they are offered for sale online, a culinary equivalent of ticket sales for Glastonbury though being next to a sandy beach there is less mud when it rains. They will if you have enough people in your group come to the campsite if you ask nicely and cook a meal using their mobile kitchen. So we asked, they came, they cooked and we all ate around a big log fire.

The meal and weather aspects of this second rally had been a success but on the last night our heater started making a noise like a jet engine. It refused to be turned off when the usual buttons provided for turning it off were pressed and I resorted to pulling out fuses to make it silent. This happened at about two o'clock in the morning so we went back to bed afterwards and would worry about it the following day.

The heater blows hot air into the motorhome and also supplies hot water. We were leaving for Spain in another week and no heater meant no showers or no hot showers anyway. This was not a good prospect for an early May departure even if we were planning on heading towards sunshine and warmth.

The same heater unit is fitted in boats and Plymouth being well supplied with companies supporting the boating industry I booked it in with a local agent to be inspected.

Many years ago if a motorhome was fitted with a heater it would have run off gas and been simple in design and construction. Our heater runs on diesel and is a fearsomely complex beast. The first thing the expert did was to plug it into a laptop computer which told him not just how many hours it had been run, but pages of other information too including how long I spent under it in the shower and what tunes I had been singing.

The good news was the heater-doctor could find nothing wrong with the thing and whatever we witnessed was as isolated incident best forgotten about. I'm not sure this was entirely reassuring only a few days left before we left friendly shores but it was good news for my wallet. In fact my wallet was so relieved I went into the chandlery section of the place and bought a large brass ship's clock to mount inside the motorhome. I'm still saving for the matching barometer.

By this stage I had a detailed plan for what we might do when we got to Croatia, in the sense I had a list of places we wanted to see when we got there but missing from this plan was any detail on what to do between landing in Spain and arriving in Croatia. The only fixed point was a visit to my cousin who lives in France for six months each year. So their house would be somewhere to aim for and afterwards we would make it up as we went along.

If this gives the impression we didn't have a clue it would only be partly right. I had been reading guidebooks and looking at maps so I had an idea of the regions we would visit, what I didn't have was a precise route worked out in advance with daily schedules and overnight halts all mapped out. Some people do this and if your plan is to reach a specific destination in a reasonably quick time then this is a sensible strategy. For us, where the travelling is more important than the arriving it would be too confining. In my first book I mentioned the tyranny of the satnav or GPS. This is a condition where having selected a destination you slavishly follow its directions, staring forward through the windscreen until you arrive. As a navigation tool it can be useful but as a way to ensure you won't see or appreciate the countryside you pass through on your way it has no equal.

There is also the great unknown of the weather. Our attempts to explore the Pyrenees on our first visit to Spain had been thwarted by it but I wanted to give them another chance although this early in the year we couldn't rely on finding sunshine and clear skies. So I formed a plan or to be more accurate a general line of intention rather than a detailed itinerary, which saw us sneak around the north end of the Pyrenees, take a swerve near Toulouse to stay a few days with my cousin then head east, keeping the sea on our right and eventually exploring the Croatian coast and visiting one or two islands. What could go wrong?

Plymouth, We Have a Problem

We had booked the Brittany Ferries' *Pont Aven*, a ship we have used several times before. This runs on the route between the UK and Spain, alternating between Plymouth to Santander and Portsmouth to Bilbao. It also makes an occasional run between Ireland and France and two days before we were due to board her something went wrong. While sailing between Cork and Roscoff the ship experienced a major technical problem. Although detail was missing at first on how bad it was the ship was towed into Brest by a tug which didn't sound promising.

What followed over the next few days was an emerging picture of the vessel not going anywhere quickly as it became clear there were major problems with one of her propeller shafts. Brittany Ferries were good during this time, issuing email updates on the situation but trying to contact them was tricky as their telephone lines were understandably busy. The *Pont Aven* can take over two thousand passengers but it wasn't only the passengers on our trip affected, those booked on subsequent voyages had to revise their travel plans.

The solution for getting updates came from an unexpected source, or at least it was an unexpected source for me, though no doubt this would be the first place many others would have turned to and this was Twitter.

I owned a Twitter account but I didn't know how to contact anyone on it. Google found me the method and I quickly received a response from someone in Brittany Ferries. It was a revelation; Twitter was useful beyond letting people know what you planned to eat for lunch.

The outcome of this Twittering was we accepted the offer of a ferry from Plymouth to Roscoff landing us in France a few days later than we originally planned to arrive in Spain. While this was going on the *Pont Aven* was transferred to a dry dock in Brest where it remained for several weeks so I think we can say we had a successful outcome. Brittany Ferries reimbursed us the difference between the two tickets and contributed to the cost of driving through France and several weeks later they gave us a voucher towards our next crossing with them. The breakdown of the *Pont Aven* must have cost them a great deal money both in repairs to the ship and the cost of the cancelled and rescheduled bookings but you could not have accused them of not trying hard to compensate the displaced passengers.

I mentioned earlier buying a clock to go inside our motorhome but there was something else new to take with us this year. Charlie the Border Terrier/Jack Russell cross was a new member of the family, filling the vacancy created by the loss of Bertie the aged Jack Russell. Charlie was eight months old but working hard on trying to stay around the age of eight weeks and somehow he must have picked up on the delayed departure and took it out on a pair of shrubs in the garden when we were not looking. The first to go was a *camellia* in full flower. The stump of what remained afterwards we covered with an upturned bucket to protect it so he turned his attentions to an evergreen *clematis*, something else coming into bloom. This plant grew on a trellis in front of our oil tank and did a reasonable job of trying to make attractive a feature otherwise simply functional. After Charlie's horticultural contributions the oil tank became more visible but the plant suffered no fatal damage, unlike the *camellia* which went into a terminal decline and was replaced later in the year.

Despite our plan to sail to Spain the first week of May in ruins, like the *Pont Aven's* propeller shaft and the *camellia*, we were excited with finally getting away on an overnight ferry to Roscoff. From Charlie's point of view the rescheduled ferry was a bonus though he was unaware he had escaped a day-long confinement in a metal kennel. Our crossing was on the *Amorique* which doesn't have on board kennels and dogs remain in your vehicle. So when we drove on at ten in the evening we closed all the blinds in the motorhome and left Charlie to go to sleep for the night. Subsequent experience suggests our actions were a shade on the reckless side. Charlie was a new dog who had not been left alone in the motorhome before so what we would find left of the interior the next morning was something we would just have to wait to discover.

Disembarkation was at eight o'clock and we found everything undamaged inside the motorhome when we went to the car deck. I suspect we even woke Charlie when we unlocked the vehicle and the lack of anything shredded inside strongly suggested he enjoyed a sound night's sleep.

Because of the early arrival time we postponed breakfast until after we landed in France, so as soon as we cleared immigration we headed for one of the parking areas inside the port. We knew from previous visits motorhomes could stay here overnight, though a port isn't somewhere we would willingly choose for a quiet night's sleep but for breakfast it was ideal. After a quick dog walk and a full fried breakfast (we *were* on holiday) the next important event of the day was shopping. For me this was primarily wine but inevitably a few domestic necessities like food would be added to the purchases.

Our experience in Spain has been supermarkets are good places to buy cheap wine, less than one euro a litre if you choose the cartons or "bricks" as they are known. I wasn't expecting the same here in France and cheap wine wasn't on offer. This was no great disappointment, such wines can unremarkable but there was a surprising range of boxed wines. The last few years have witnessed a change in the drinking habits of the French. Though they seem as a nation to be solid in their rejection of the screw cap wine bottle they have embraced boxed wines and we found a wide selection in three and five litre sizes for sale in the Super U supermarket near the centre of Saint Pol de Léon.

This town is close to Roscoff and is well worth a visit and not only for shopping. Like the old part of Roscoff it is too easy to drive past it heading into rest of France but Saint Pol de Léon is worth exploring if only to see the flying Cornish pasty. The centre of the city is dominated by the cathedral with its twin towers and like any old church there are numerous tombs of the great and good dotted around inside it and one caught my eye.

I may not be the first to let my imagination dwell on this carving. The prosaic mind will identify it as a dragon shaped foot-warmer for the late departed bishop whose mortal remains dwell within the tomb. To my eye the lumpy back of the creature looks identical to the crust of a Cornish pasty and having made this connection the fact it has the head of a cow suggests it can only be a beef pasty and a flying one too as it has wings.

South of the cathedral is another building worth wandering around inside; the Chapelle du Kreisker. This has a single tower, the tallest in Brittany and visible from a great distance away and long an important navigational mark for shipping. The tower is supported on four slender pillars above the centre of the chapel and as you walk under them it is hard not to imagine the great mass of the structure above your head. Like the towers of the cathedral the tower is surmounted by a slender spire with many piercings or openings in it to reduce the buffeting of the wind. They were clever folk long ago.

South Through France

After purchasing wine, fruit and cheese we set out on the long journey through France. Our plan to reach the south was to take an inland route. We had time to follow the west coast but having cycled this way a few years ago I knew it had long stretches which were busy, boring or not attractive and in a few places all three. So the interior it was and we were not disappointed.

France is referred to as "motorhome heaven" and touring through France in a motorhome is a lot easier than doing the same in the UK. France has about the same population as the UK but twice the land mass so it is easy to find roads free of traffic. What makes motorhoming especially easy in France are the *aires*. These can be a source of confusion, as the term is used in different ways, for example *aires de service* are service areas on the motorways and these are not recommended for overnight halts. The *aires* motorhomers use in France are typically provided by the local council and offer overnight parking, often together with fresh water and waste disposal facilities. It is free to park in many of them although there may be a charge for fresh water.

Pouencé is a small town midway between Rennes and Angers and here we would spend our first night in France. The *aire* in Pouencé is beside an attractive lake and is one of those where all the services are free.

It was only later I learned Pouencé has an interesting old castle built along the classic round-turret-at-every-corner model. As we hadn't anticipated coming this way I had done little research on what we might see so we missed an opportunity to visit it, but this incident highlighted how much there is to see in France if you seek it out.

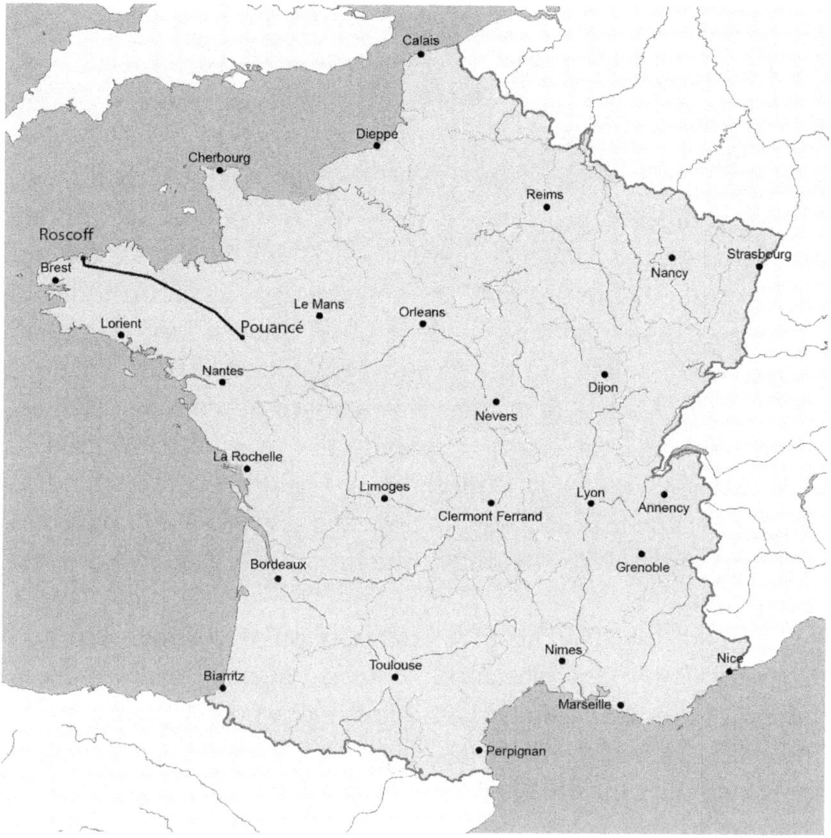

It was early afternoon when we arrived so we ate a late lunch. This was to be the pattern of a normal day. Drive during the morning doing any shopping required then pull into wherever would be the halt for the night for a late lunch. Afterwards, we would explore our surroundings on foot.

Not planning to drive again today I could enjoy a Pelforth Blonde beer with my lunch of cold meats and cheese. I am a late convert to French beers, having been more inclined towards their wines but the small bottles of beer are pleasant well chilled even when it isn't blazing hot outside. These beers are stronger than we are used to in the UK so coming in small bottles is sensible but it isn't only France where the beer comes in small bottles. I am fond of Grimbergen beers and at a liver-shrivelling 6% or more in strength only to be drunk sparingly. Beers are like cars these days. The name on the label is not always much of a hint where it comes from or even who made it. Grimbergen is a beer originally made by monks at the Norbertine Abbey at Grimbergen in Belgium who built a brewery soon after the founding of the Abbey in 1128. The monks developed a reputation for their hospitality though their kindness to strangers did not prevent the Wars of Grimbergen in the late Twelfth Century. However, years later their product attracted the interests of the big brewers and the legal position today is curious. Grimbergen sold in Belgium is brewed by a company owned by Heineken but the Grimbergen found outside Belgium is brewed by Carlsberg at their Kronenbourg brewery in France. To add a further layer of complexity the Grimbergen found in Belgium is marketed by Grolsch but it is not brewed by them. It is hard not to suspect these arrangements were only arrived at following enthusiastic tasting of the product during an extended lunch break.

The lake besides the *aire* was a popular fishing lake and there were marked places, or "swims" as anglers call them, dotted all around it. Many were built like wooden piers, jutting out into the water to clear the marginal reeds. A few were converted agricultural trailers or carts with large metal wheels fitted to an axle below the platform and reached by a walkway hung between the cart and the shore. In the UK the fishing season would not have started this early in the year as coarse fish breed in the spring but here in France they seem to have a different timetable. Two anglers were busy below the *aire* and as we didn't see them catch anything any breeding probably remained undisturbed. We walked around the lake keeping Charlie on a long lead and giving him just enough room to chase back into the water the numerous frogs basking around the lake margin. The weather was warm with blue skies and we experienced little difficulty settling into a relaxing mood.

We were parked on grass and we set up a pen for Charlie on it. The pen was a purpose made folding thing and it allowed him to be off the lead and looked dog-proof. We were to be proved wrong before too long as Charlie, a growing puppy, soon learned to clear the side of the pen from a standing start. We left the pen folded up beside a dustbin a few days later.

I was wrong about the weather because the next day we saw little sign of blue skies and drove through intermittent heavy rain to Nieuil l'Espoir, a few miles southeast of Poitiers where we stayed at another *aire* close to the town centre. The *aire* here was free to stay but water required a token or *jeton* available from the town hall. However, we had enough water on board to last us until the next day so we didn't need to fill up.

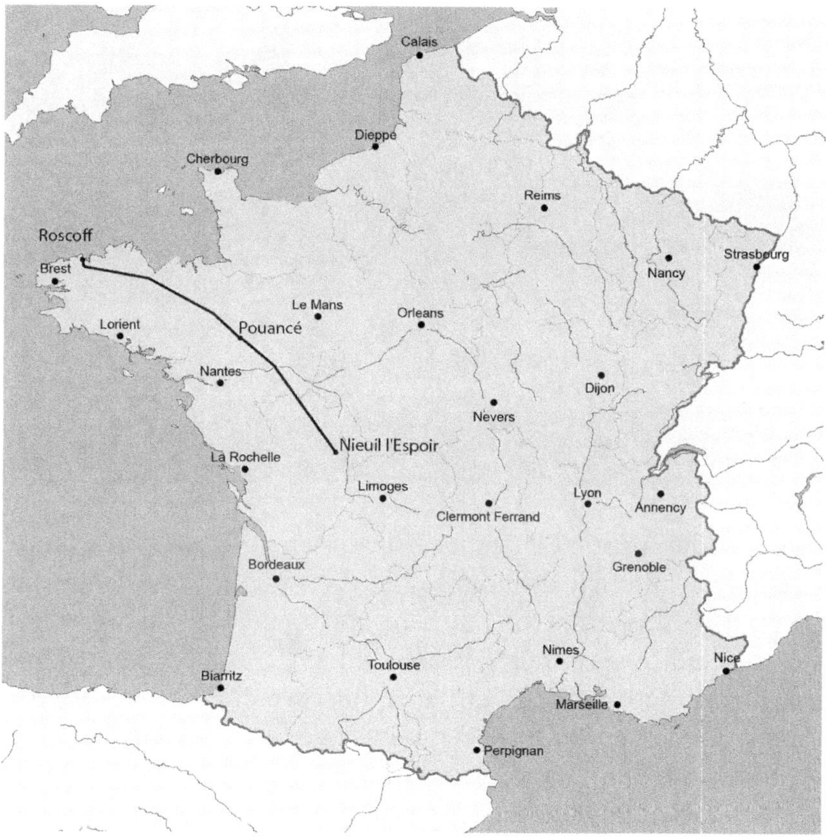

The city of Poitiers has a battle from the Hundred Years' War named after it though the battle took place some distance from the city. A little background to the Hundred Years' War and a description of the Battle of Poitiers can be found in Appendix 4.

To find the site of this battle we headed about four kilometres northwest from Nieuil l'Espoir to the village of Nouaillé-Maupertuis. I didn't know what to expect here so we headed into the centre and followed the signs for the Office of Tourism which was, as they always seem to be, shut, but next to it was a an old abbey with a moat and turrets.

This was the fortified abbey of Nouaillé founded in the seventh century and though the interior of the building was following the lead of the Office of Tourism and firmly closed we could walk around the grounds. This we did as it stopped raining and was an attractive place. Little of its seventh century origins remain and the abbey has been rebuilt and extended over a long period before falling into disuse in the eighteenth century but it is worth a visit and at other times of the year I am sure it can be found open. The grounds are scattered with several plaques describing in both French and English the history and features of the abbey, including the "squinches" of the tower decorated with the twenty four Old Men of the Apocalypse. This alone must justify a visit if only to see a squinch.

After walking around the abbey we drove back to the centre of the village and followed the signs to the "Champ de Bataille". The battle site was not marked on Google maps, an omission now corrected after I submitted an edit to Google, so we were driving on dead reckoning as I only knew roughly where to look. This is why we momentarily stopped at the Omme ford because I mistook it to be the site of the battle as a plaque was fixed to a post beside the road. However, it was the site of a former long established tile and brick works instead. The ford still had a link to the Battle of Poitiers because it was in the marshes around it the English or to be more precise the Anglo-Gascon forces were delayed in their flight. This allowed the French forces to catch up and as they say in military parlance "close with them".

We found the battle site memorial further up the road and fortunately had the place to ourselves as parking spaces were limited. After over five hundred years you can't expect there to be much evidence left of a major battle and there isn't. The main woods are where they were at the time and the course of the river hasn't moved a lot but otherwise any reconstruction on the ground must inevitably involve conjecture. The French have done a good job and the site, admittedly a small site, has stands with plaques you work your way around and read a potted history of the battle. It is only a memorial; the actual battle must have been held over a much wider area than this little lumpy field.

Afterwards we drove into the Limousin, stopping west of Limoges at the Parc Verger campsite beside the village of Champagnac-la-Rivière. Here we planned to stay two days, catch up on the laundry and do some walking.

This is a site with a strong UK following having been run originally by a British couple as a stopover for RVs (large US manufactured motorhomes) but it had recently been taken over by a new British couple who were investing money into expanding its facilities and number of pitches.

It is a good site but we failed to see it at its best. It didn't pour down all the time and when it rained it was a *light* rain but the weather remained overcast and sunless throughout our stay.

During a longer than usual break in the damp weather we walked the four kilometres along a disused railway track to the nearby town of Oradour sur Vayres. I am not a great fan of walking on old railway tracks or even cycling on them. The main problems with old railway lines are first when they are not sunk into a cutting they are often lined by trees as was the case here, both situations reduce the view of the countryside you are walking through. The second problem is railway lines skirt anywhere interesting unless it is a major town. I first noticed this when cycling in France on the old line running south from Morlaix in Brittany. This takes most of a day to complete but you see little of Brittany from it. Canal tow paths sometimes have the same issues with the added fun they can prescribe long loops around hills, adding to the length of your journey.

Oradour sur Vayres in the light rain wasn't inspiring but it was memorable for the price of the tomatoes, lettuce and courgettes we bought at a green grocers. There is a supermarket but we forgot to get directions to it before leaving the campsite. If anyone retraces our steps the supermarket is nowhere near the old railway line.

From Champagnac-la-Rivière we continued south to visit a few more French villages. The first stop was Saint Jean de Cole just inside the northern boundary of the Dordogne region. It is easy to become blasé about French villages with their narrow streets,

and châteaux,

watermills,

bridges and impressive doors.

But we spent an enjoyable hour wandering around before moving on to the much more popular Brantôme.

Perhaps because it was a Saturday and it was no longer raining Brantôme was busy. There is a lot to see here but after squeezing into a car park by the river Dronne for lunch we decided not to linger and the troglodyte caves with the rock carving of the Last Supper where the first monks of the abbey used to live will have to wait for another visit at a quieter time.

Continuing our gentle southeasterly direction we drove on further before stopping for the night at an *aire* at Sainte Alvère, yet another attractive little French village and one we could explore on foot and in sunshine for a change.

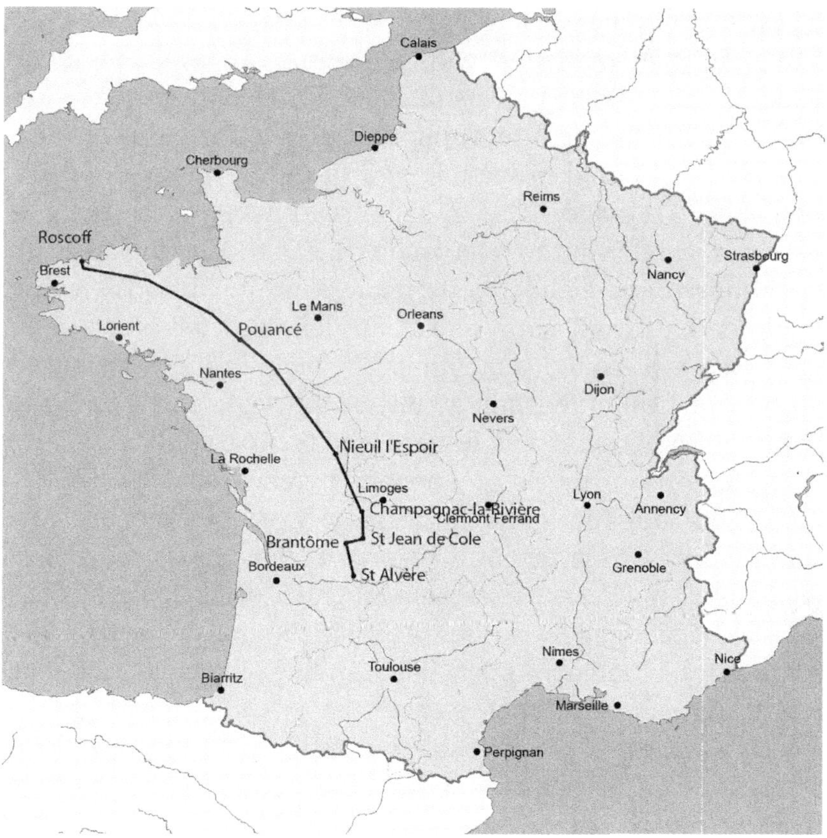

Sainte Alvère is a place about which little information seems to be available, possibly because there are so many other places in the Dordogne region to compete against, but it is worth visiting. There are the remains of a castle and ruined tower we poked around and in one of the narrow streets we found an intriguing structure. What at first glance looked like a well was a device or more accurately an engine for replacing the shoes on cattle or as the sign said "*ferrer leurs bœffs*". Iron shoes are not normally fitted to cattle but they can be when the animals are used to pull ploughs and carts. The device worked by passing two ropes under the animal which were then tightened with a windlass to support the beast while the farriers completed their work. A sign explained why it was needed with the phrase: "*contrairement aux chevaux, les bœves ne savent pas tenir debout sur trois pattes*." Which translates to: "unlike horses, the cattle could not learn to stand on three legs".

We finished our walk with a beer at a pavement table, relaxing and enjoying the sunshine. From Sainte Alvère we headed south the next morning but after a short distance we stopped as I wanted to see the view of the Dordogne from the Cingle de Trémolat. This is an escarpment overlooking a massive meander in the river where the Dordogne makes a full one hundred and eighty degree change in direction. The name Cingle derives from Latin and is an old word for a belt or to "gird" or wrap around something. The bend in the river looked impressive from the photographs in our guidebook but the reality on the ground was less so. The photographs must have been taken from the air or someone perched on a tall ladder. For us on foot the view of the river were blocked by trees growing on the escarpment. I suspect the guidebook must have been edited by someone who moonlighted on their days off as an estate agent selling houses where a glimpse of water in the far distance, obtainable only while standing on a table, would be described as a house possessing "sea views". This might be slightly unjust as we didn't walk far on the path running along the escarpment. It is possible a better viewing point could be reached but I was concerned about the security of the motorhome. This risk had not troubled me on previous journeys but it was something which returned several times during this one. So much so once we returned to the UK I arranged for an alarm to be fitted. However, we didn't have one and leaving the vehicle too long unattended in a remote and largely deserted car park worried me so we returned to it.

The Dordogne is an area long known to British tourists and we came here in the motorhome on our first trip outside the UK, stopping for several days at a campsite close to the Cingle beside the village of Limeuil. Limeuil is another claimant to the title of "prettiest village in France" and is worth a visit, something you must do on foot. Limeuil is built on a steep hillside with narrow streets and if you meet anyone there you might find it easier to communicate in English as you probably both share it as a mother tongue. There is at least one village in the Dordogne, or Dordogneshire, where there are more British than French. The invasion started in the Seventies and rapidly gathered momentum.

Leaving the Anglo-French region of the Dordogne we travelled slowly on minor roads into the Gers, the least populated of all the French Departments. Gers is unknown to many in the UK. It lies immediately to the west of Toulouse but viewed on a map it has no major towns other than in its centre Auch, pronounced "Osh". Gers includes much of Gascony although of the wines made here perhaps only Côtes de Gascogne is well known in the UK. Much more well-known is another local product, Armagnac brandy, regarded as the oldest brandy in France with a first mention in 1310 in a treatise on medicine by Prior Vital Dufour. In this work he laid out the forty virtues of the liqueur:

"*This water, if taken medically and soberly, is said to have forty virtues. It enlivens the spirit, if taken in moderation, recalls the past to memory, renders men joyous, preserves youth and delays senility.*"

The Prior goes on to say Armagnac "*restores the paralysed member by massage*" but I cannot attest to this as the effect on me is usually the opposite although he stated the virtues are only released if "*partaken in moderation*". I must work on this aspect if I wish to avoid paralysis of any members so we bought a bottle of Armagnac in a supermarket to practice on.

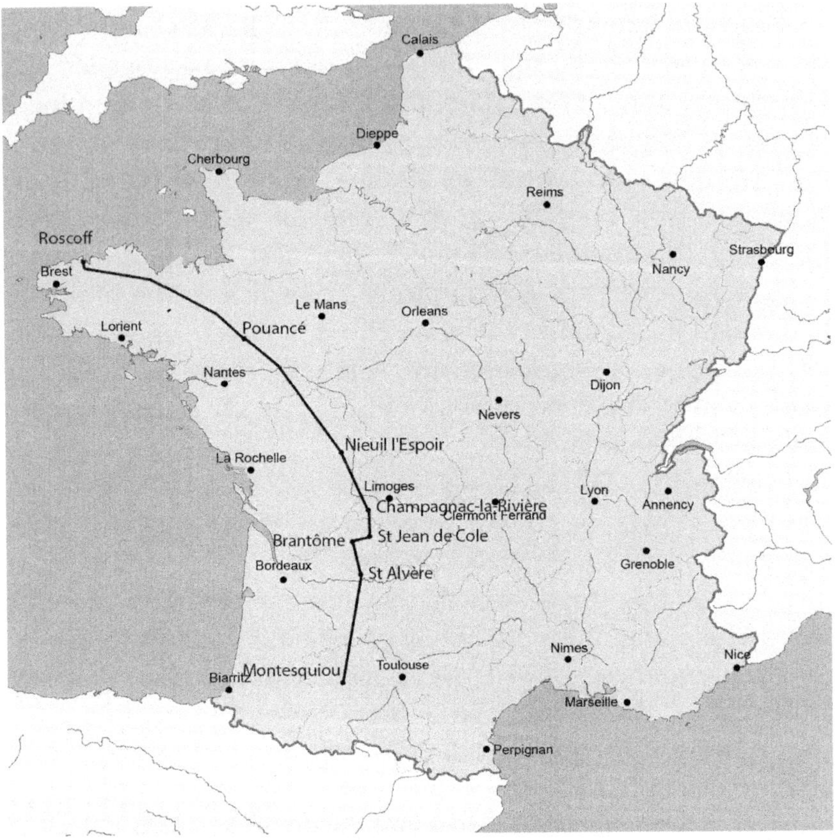

Our home for the next couple of nights was a house outside the little village of Montesquiou, west of Auch, where a cousin of mine and her husband live during the summer. I hadn't seen them for decades and we only made contact again at the funeral of her brother earlier in the year. It was a strange meeting as we started chatting away as though the intervening thirty years had never taken place.

They live an idyllic life at Montesquiou with two large rescue dogs Charlie made a great fuss over and received only the odd growl in return for his annoying attentions.

The first morning after we arrived we went with them to the market at nearby Mirande to buy tomato plants and a few other vegetable seedlings including cucumber. The varieties were unknown to me although the one called "cerise" was a cherry tomato from the name but the rest were a mystery. We did our shopping in a large and busy open-air market. The customers at the market were all local apart from ourselves and only the occasional expat voice was heard. Tourists seemed unknown or at least rare around here.

The phrase "*France profonde*" is sometimes encountered. It translates as profoundly French but it means something more subtle. A French lady I know describes it as follows.

"When we use this expression it means the real France. Places that haven't changed for decades or nearly. Places where you don't fear to take your children to the school. No gun, no pestering, normal and peaceful life with lots of walking in the woods with Dad. Gardening, baking with Mum, pottering about, climbing trees, pulling the cat's tail, running after the hens, building huts in the wood or up in the trees. Places where the school yard is used at weekends to play football.... It's where you feel a bit out of time and at the same time.... you ....breathe again! This is what France Profonde is."

Montesquiou is *France profonde* and for lunch we walked into the village, going part of the way along one of the paths used by pilgrims going to Santiago de Compostela. Although the main pilgrimage route runs east to west across the top of Spain there are innumerable starting points where pilgrims can join it, both within Spain and in France and beyond. The path running through Montesquiou starts at Arles crossing the Pyrenees at the Col de Pourtalet and then to Jaca in Spain. From Jaca it joins the main route passing through Burgos, León and by way of Cape Finisterre, if you want to burn your socks, to Santiago de Compostela. The sock burning refers to the tradition of before entering Santiago de Compostela pilgrims would burn their old clothes at Cape Finisterre and put on new ones for the last leg of the journey. The tradition is maintained and you can find small fires on the rocks around the Cape though now pilgrims just burn a symbolic sock or two.

Lunch in Montesquiou was at a restaurant called L'auberge de Montesquiou and a place which doesn't need to advertise. It is at the end of a narrow side street with no signs pointing to it from the main road. Even if you look down the side street from the main road you will not see it because the little sign hanging above the door is obscured by the branch of a tree the proprietors feel no inclination to prune.

There were only a few copies of the handwritten menus so we shared one. Today was Whit Monday with a special €23 menu; normally it is €15 for four courses. Throwing animal welfare out of the window three out of the four of us ordered *foie gras* as a starter and very good it was too. The menu was a challenge even to my fluent French speaking cousin, mainly because she hadn't brought her reading glasses but there were also some unusual words on the menu. "*Cayette*" in the dish "*cayette aux olives*" was a female duck or more specifically the leg of one. I had the more familiar "*magret*" of duck breast. It was served rare and perhaps for symmetry came from a male duck although I suspect if all the legs were used in the *cayette aux olives* then a use for other parts of the female ducks needed to be found.

The restaurant has a strong local following and you would never find it unless by a lucky accident. It is only open for lunches and the owners make a living from it even with such reduced hours. Testimony of its popularity and success derived from the quality of the food.

After lunch we sobered up by walking gently around the village, the old part of which is built on a low hill. Though there do not appear to be any signs of the village ever having a wall around it the old buildings on one side are all joined together so their outer walls blend together to form a curve like a wall. There were a few windows in these buildings but they were small and placed high up. Montesquiou, whilst not a fortified village had its way in days past of keeping out the unwelcome. In England during the Middle Ages it was necessary to seek a license to "*crenelate*" or build fortifications around your home or castle. It is possible the same applied in France and the permission of the local baron was needed before you could construct a wall around your village. I would assume permission was only granted to those who were deemed loyal to the king or other personage who was deputed to issue such licenses such as bishops. Otherwise, the fortifications could be used to keep out those such as tax collectors whose comings (unwelcome) and goings (most welcome) were something the ruling classes wished to see continue. Whether Montesquiou earned the opprobrium of their local landlord or more likely they lacked the funds to build a wall we shall never know.

Returning to my cousin's house by the local branch of the Way of Saint James we passed a farm with several hundred ducks running free in a field. Inevitably destined for the table but whether as *foie gras*, which I should point out translates as "fat liver" so there is no ambiguity, or they were being reared for meat I could not tell. Geese are the traditional bird used for *foie gras* today but they account for only 5% of French production and specially selected breeds of duck are used for the rest. *Foie gras* production is highly controversial because the birds are force fed, a process known as *gavage*. A word I find curiously apt for the process of force feeding simply because of the sound of it. Some countries have banned the importation or sale of *foie gras* on animal welfare grounds but the Chinese have developed a taste for it and as a result business is booming in France, who produce 75% of the world's supply.

Heading East

We left my cousin and her husband enjoying their delightful house near Montesquiou and continued our journey, this time with an eastwards aspect to our direction. To reach where we were we had travelled south from Roscoff but our destination at this stage of the trip (it was to change later) was much further to the east. So we needed to turn left somewhere and this is where we did it. If I hadn't gone to see my cousin we might have cut diagonally across France from Roscoff or even headed for Germany and then through Austria but from southwest France the way east was clear. The only choice to be made was whether to keep inland or have a look at the coast. This was a decision we could postpone for a while because we didn't do much driving each day and we had to get around Toulouse first.

Toulouse is the fourth largest city in France and I suspect at the wrong time of day it has epic traffic jams, but travelling in the middle of the day the roads, while busy were free flowing. We avoided the *péage* although this will be worth taking during the rush hour. As a measure of how rural Gers is, Toulouse alone has a population five times greater than the population of the whole of the Gers department.

After squeezing around Toulouse we drove southeast before stopping at a campsite in the village of Sorèze at the western edge of the Montagne Noire, a group of low mountains north of Carcassonne. This is another largely unknown French backwater and our first impression of the campsite was the singular lack of dog walking facilities. We were on the edge of the village but there were no convenient paths other than one going around the outside of the local cemetery. There were no complaints from the residents to our presence as I walked Charlie there but on the other side of the cemetery an actual burial was being held. I don't know who it was they were interring but the grave diggers outnumbered the mourners so it was a lonely farewell for someone.

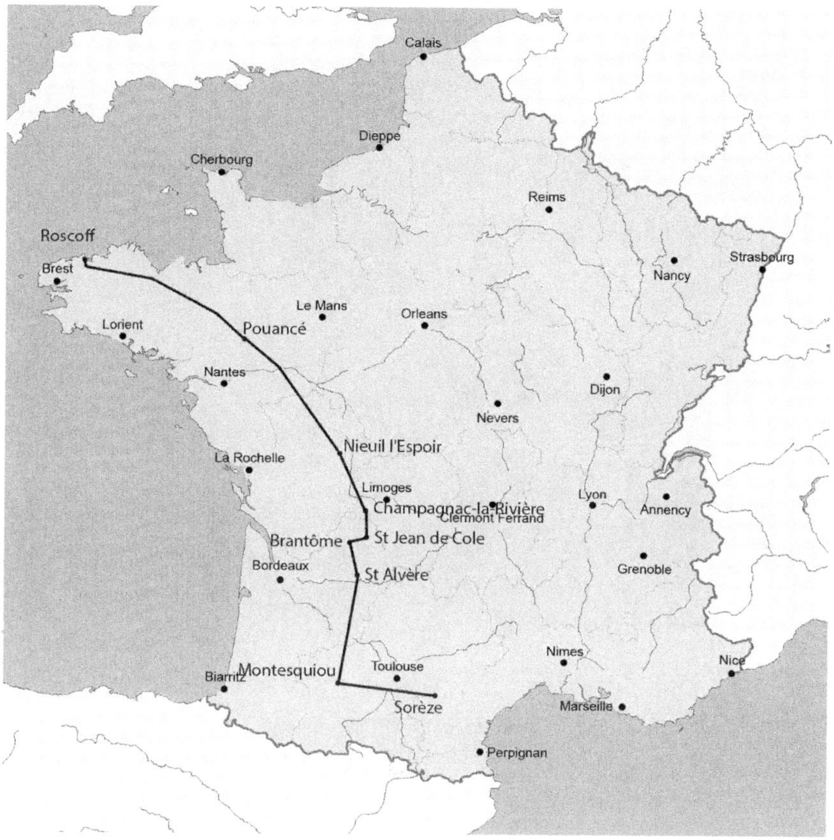

On a cheerier note I found it was warm enough to put on a pair of shorts, an act marking for me the official start of British Holiday Time. The five minute bell having been sounded when we sat outside in sunshine a few days earlier with cold beers in front of us. We intended to stay two nights at Sorèze but despite a grass pitch and a few British neighbours to chat to the limited dog walking persuaded us to move on the next day. By now we had a plan, though it wasn't to survive long after contact with the Mediterranean.

The next morning we left dog-limited Sorèze and headed towards the sea, as the Mediterranean wasn't too far away. Our route soon took us through the little village of Durfort where we spotted a good *aire* close to a village well furnished with bars and a restaurant from what we could see as we drove past. This *aire* wasn't in my online guide (CamperContact - see Appendix 2) otherwise we would have chosen it over the campsite, but it is somewhere to note should we (or you) come this way again.

After driving on narrow roads across a corner of the heavily wooded Montagne Noir we headed towards Carcassonne, going past the village of Salsigne where there used to be a major gold mine, now worked out but according to local gossip you can still scratch the odd flake of gold out of the river Orbiel.

We were on the edge of the Haut Languedoc, the southwestern corner of the Languedoc-Roussillon, an area well known for its wine production. The name Languedoc derives from the language once spoken in a broad band stretching from northeast Spain, through southern France and Monaco and into Italy. In France, which always had the largest number of speakers of Occitan it has been supplanted by French but it remains an official language of Catalonia in Spain although even here Catalan, a close relative of Occitan, is more widely spoken. Despite a concerted attempt in the nineteenth century in France to stamp out the local patois to unify the population it persists in one form or another in local dialects. For example, as *Provençal* in Provence and if you ever hear it being spoken, cherish the moment as it features in the UNESCO Red Book of Endangered Languages.

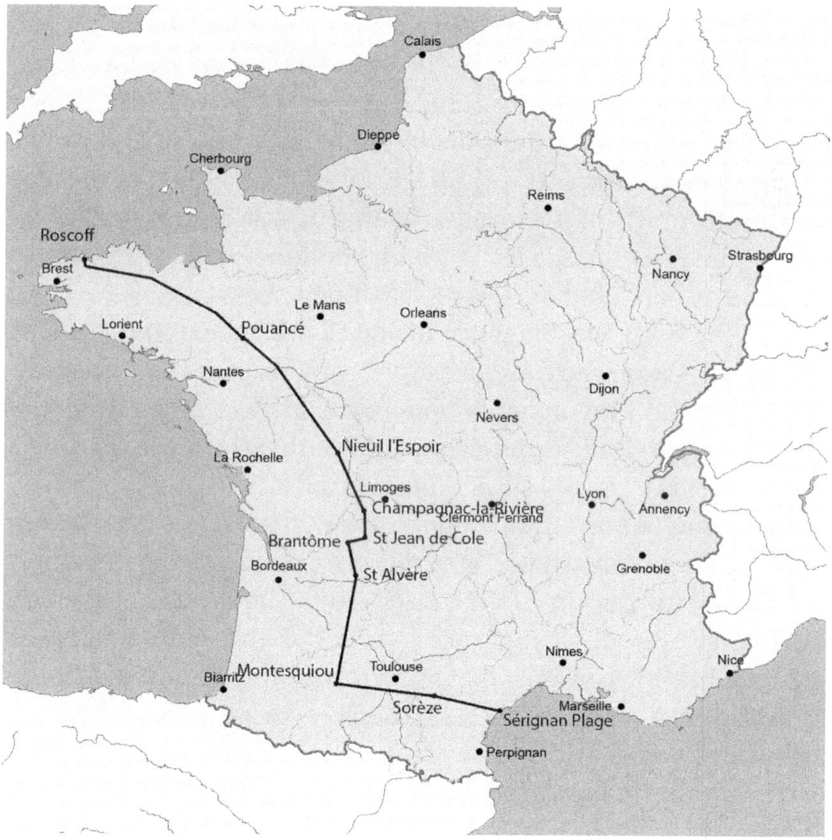

Our seaside destination was a campsite at Sérignan Plage, south of Béziers. Sadly we found seaside weather here, *British* seaside weather. It was chilly, intermittently raining and gales were forecast for the next day. It was a busy but soulless site and we decided almost immediately to move to somewhere more interesting the next day. I half expected this part of the coast to be not for us and so it turned out. Live and learn or rather live and re-learn because we keep doing this and as things turned out we kept doing it and were to repeat this mistake again. The tell-tale signs are obvious from the map. If the coastline is smooth and there are no hills near the coast then you can expect flat, featureless beaches with modern resort towns. The original inhabitants were not so daft they would live amongst the mosquito ridden marshes often backing these types of coast. The main cities on this stretch, Narbonne, Béziers and Montpellier, are all set well back and above the coastal lands. Defence was a major factor in siting these cities. Even the Vikings reached as far as Sicily but pirates from North Africa regularly predated on shipping in the Mediterranean and would readily take captives to sell on as slaves. These factors did not encourage much of a building boom for seaside properties so what there is by the sea is invariably modern except where there is a natural sheltered harbour for fishing boats.

Leaving Sérignan Plage we headed back inland and straight into countryside where we felt more comfortable; the Cévennes. These are the first uplands you reach driving away from the Mediterranean and form part of the southeastern corner of the Massif Central, the raised middle of France.

I first took notice of this region a few years ago when cycling from Aix Les Bains (near Geneva) to Avignon with my brother. We were staying in hotels each night and at La Bastide Puylaurent we only just got a room in the only hotel open as it was late in the year. As we arrived it was already rapidly filling up with walkers and we soon learned they were all following the Stevenson Trail.

The walk follows the path of the writer Robert Louis Stevenson who in 1878 accompanied by a donkey called Modestine travelled from Le Puy en Velay to St Jean du Gard. His journey took him through the only remaining part of France where Protestantism prevailed. The route has since been reconstructed from his writings as far as possible for the present day and many organised groups, as we met in Puy en Velay, plus many others doing it unsupported on their own, complete it every year. Stevenson described his experiences in a book, Travels with a Donkey in the Cévennes, and the trail takes about 14 days. The organised tours will even carry your luggage to the next hotel if you want to give it a go. It is even possible to hire a donkey if you insist on being authentic but this takes more planning as the hotels don't offer the stabling they once did in Stevenson's day.

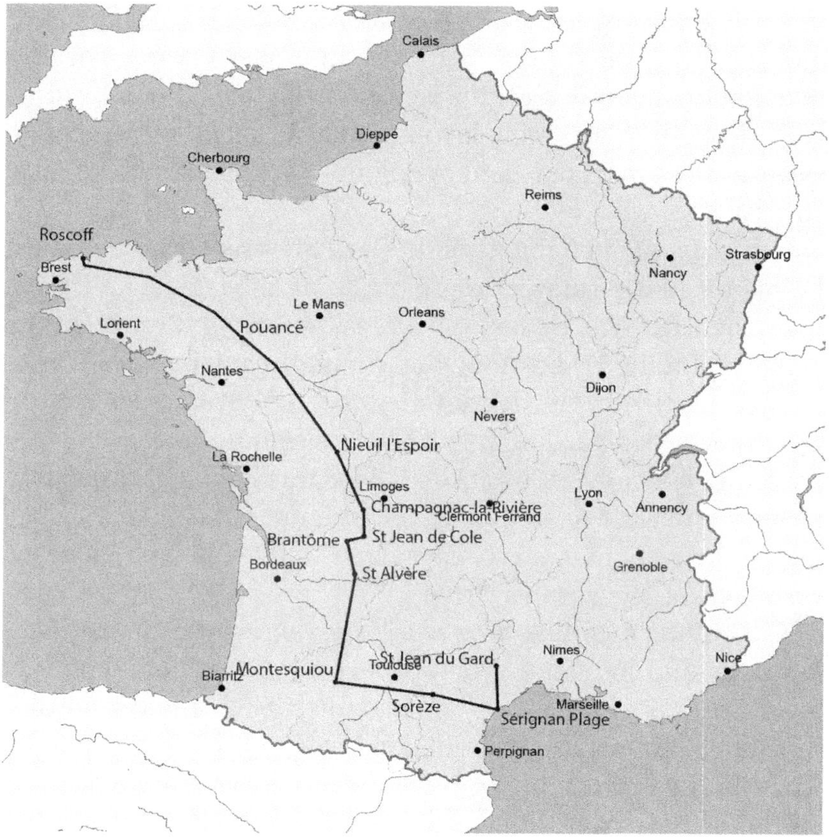

By a strange stroke of symmetrical fate our destination in the Cevennes was Saint Jean du Gard, where Stevenson finished. Having stumbled by accident on the middle of the walk while cycling we now found ourselves at the end of it in a motorhome.

Saint Jean du Gard is the end of another route, a heritage railway running beside the river from Anduze. When we arrived at the *aire* in the station car park the *train à vapeur* (steam train) was sitting in the station vapourating and whistling intermittently. Sadly, by the time I got my camera out it was gone and I had missed the train again.

Stevenson did not plan to end his journey at Saint Jean du Gard; he only stopped here because Modestine the donkey suffered an injury and needed rest. So the author sold the animal together with fittings for "five and thirty francs". Stevenson was keen to get to "Alais" to pick up his post, so he proceeded onwards in a coach or more precisely a "*diligence*". The Alais he headed to is spelt Alés on modern maps. Locally, they don't make much of this aspect of the tale. If *you* lived in Saint Jean du Gard would you want the place remembered because of a spavined donkey? Better to concentrate on the author.

While staying in Saint Jean du Gard Stevenson was asked by the town's Marie (mayor) to help a local lady translate letters from agencies in London. The area remained Protestant in largely Catholic France and the common religion made it a popular place for the recruitment by the British of French governesses. After helping with the translation Stevenson gave the young lady advice, what the advice was is not recorded but Stevenson felt the quality of it "...struck me as being excellent." His donkey might have been called Modestine but modesty wasn't one of Stevenson's virtues.

The author recorded how *phylloxera* destroyed the region's vineyards and he met a group of labourers crushing apples to make cider. They remarked "It's like this, just like in the north." This was a reference to cider making being hitherto a pursuit of places in the north of France. The inference was the world was mad. France's loss was the making of the Spanish wine industry as *phylloxera* did not travel south of the Pyrenees and the vineyards of Rioja flourished in the extra demand. The disease is caused by a sap-sucking aphid native to North America but introduced to Europe by gardeners keen to try North American vines. The solution to the disease also came from North America because there the native vines exhibited tolerance to the aphid and so it is almost universal vines grown in Europe are grafted onto rootstocks originating from North America. Perhaps more surprising even today there is no effective treatment for phylloxera other than the growing of resistant plants.

I attempted to photograph the steam train later in the day when we returned to the station after walking around Saint Jean du Gard and discovering it was a busy town filled with lots of bars and restaurants catering for the tourists and walkers. I saw the train in the distance coming towards me, throwing smoke and steam up into the air above it. As I stood ready to take a photograph it suddenly veered off at a set of points and disappeared into an engine shed never to be seen again.

Before we left the following morning we walked over the bridge to the supermarket for a few essentials like wine. We were surviving well on boxed wines costing from about €10 to €15 for 3 litres. Cheaper wines were available, €9.50 for 5 litres in plastic barrels for example, but the 3 litre boxes were good quality.

Supermarket shopping in France is painless and no one should be worried about travelling in France or anywhere in Europe providing they can find a supermarket. No language skills are needed although in France it is wise to look out for the word "*Cheval*" on the meat counter though there will be an accompanying picture of a horse's head to ensure no errors of identification. Horse meat won't poison anyone and horse meat burgers were sold recently in the UK for some time before it was noticed but eating it should be a matter of choice not accident.

The important thing to remember is in several supermarkets you must weigh your vegetables before taking them to the checkout. We have learned to look for the tell-tale weighing machines by the fruit and vegetable counters but it is easy to be caught out and this is a memorable way to get an introduction to the French language as the queue grinds to a halt at the checkout as you present your unweighed and unpriced produce.

The photograph above illustrates an interesting and at the moment topical point. Apart from the Chinese cabbages and the asparagus there is no plastic packaging visible. In the UK these are usually stripped of their outer leaves and then put in a plastic bag. The French way isn't more environmentally friendly than ours; the produce may be displayed loose and without packaging but to purchase it you have to put it in a plastic bag from a roll.

We left Saint Jean du Gard without seeing the steam train again and drove around a busy Alés to the village of Chusclan, close to the Rhône and north of Avignon.

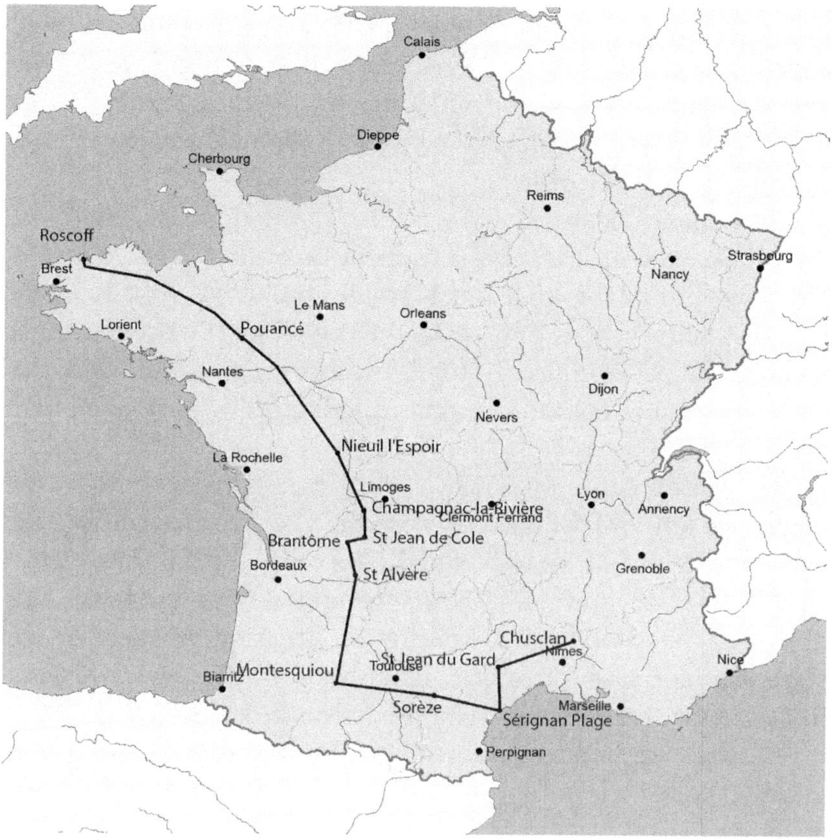

Here there is a free *aire* owned by the Vignerons de Chusclan. It is a large car park opposite a big wine cooperative and surrounded by vines and with the sun shining we had a relaxing lunch then went for a walk around the village. One of the first things we saw was a sign describing the "mystery of the arches". Chusclan we discovered as we explored its streets has many arches. There are fourteen remaining around the old centre although once there were apparently many more. Their purpose seems obscure but it is likely a few were entrances and others were opening to allow rainwater to drain away. Some of the arches had rooms built over them but others were just openings in walls.

We finished our exploration of Chusclan (it doesn't take long) with a glass of local wine at an outside table in the village centre. Chusclan, apart from the arches, is a typical French village with the only businesses in the centre being the holy trinity of post office, pharmacy, bread shop and the bar/restaurant where we drank our wine. Which numbers four but it is a Douglas Adams' trinity of four or even five if you include the mayor's office.

They have been making well regarded wines here at Chusclan since at least the seventeenth century. It is mainly a red wine producing area but a small amount of rosé is made from the same grapes they make the red with. The trick, using a method called *saignée*, is to draw the grape juice from the pressing leaving behind the skins and from this pink juice rosé is made.

We visited the co-operative wine *caves* opposite the *aire* before we left and found they were busy with locals turning up with big plastic bottles to be filled. You could try the wines, Côte de Rhone, but there was a queue and it was 09:30 in the morning. We didn't fancy waiting or drinking so early so we bought a half case for later consumption of the rare rosé (less than five percent of production) and set off for the day.

We had one hundred and thirty kilometres to go on a route taking us over Mont Ventoux but the legendary Tour de France peak turned out not to be the greatest hazard of the day. We were starting to the west of the Rhône and the options for crossing it at this point without involving busy cities are limited. The satnav took us through the city of Orange without problems until on the east side of the city, at a point when I thought the worst of any problems would be behind us, I suddenly saw the road ahead dipping under a railway with a 2.3m headroom warning sign and 0.4m lower than we were. There was just time to swing right into a car park where we turned round after a considerable amount of backward and forward shuffling as the car park had height barriers at the entrance. It was an entirely avoidable incident as the Michelin road atlas shows the height restriction but to see this obstacle one must check the map before starting the day's journey. Another lesson re-learned.

Our route over Ventoux was almost the reverse of the one taken by my brother and I when we cycled up it, this time we ascended the north side, which seems the steepest.

The traffic going up was light with cyclists outnumbering cars and motorcycles by a considerable margin. Ventoux is a magnet for two wheelers of all description but some don't make it. On the approach to the mountain I slowed as a car in front reduced speed to turn right into a narrow gate. The car behind us slowed as well but the motorcycle behind him decided to overtake us all. This was on a long sweeping right-hand bend so the motorcyclist couldn't have seen the car coming the other way. There was just room for him between the oncoming car and the one turning right but a change of underwear may have been needed later.

Further on we came to light-controlled roadworks where there people were milling around. A motorcycle was wedged under the rear corner of a car but the rider was sitting nearby with his helmet off and looked unscathed if not unshaken. He may have jumped or rolled sideways before his machine tried to do its disappearing trick.

All this was before we even *got* to Mont Ventoux. It is not obligatory to drive over Mont Ventoux and anyone in a hurry would be strongly advised not to and go around it instead. But the mountain (technically part of the Alps but sitting apart from them like a naughty child) had been placed in eons past right in the way we were heading, so going over it was the obvious thing to do.

For those unfamiliar with Ventoux it is notable for being almost two different mountains. As you ascend it you pass through forests interspersed with meadows where at this time of year a profusion of cowslips were growing. After twenty kilometres of ascent you emerge into a treeless landscape of bare, shattered rock. The name Ventoux is derived from the French for "windy" but we were fortunate in having perfect conditions. In the distance I could see the snow covered Alps although I avoided mentioning them because this was the way we would head and Mary isn't a great fan of the cold.

The route up was quiet in terms of motorised transport but even the numerous cyclists were outnumbered a million to one by the flies as we approached the end of the tree line. The air was thick with small brownish flies and it must have been horrendous to cycle through them. They were only on the north side and seemed to prefer shade as the warmer south side of was free of them. There is in theory parking at the top but it was packed with people, parked cars and those cyclists enjoying the moment of their victory and escape from the flies. Stopping at the summit wasn't an option but there were places to pull off the road afterwards. The picture below was taken a little beyond the Simpson memorial which I confess I missed while looking for a parking place.

Behind our motorhome you can see a parked car and a few figures. They are visiting the Simpson Memorial, erected at the spot where Tom Simpson collapsed and died aged 29 in 1967. Simpson was at the time Britain's most successful cyclist but he raced when the use of drugs was both widespread and considered almost essential by those who wished to win races.

At his post mortem his blood was found to contain traces of amphetamines and alcohol, the latter apparently from brandy mixed with water in his water bottle. Simpson's tragic death on the thirteenth stage of the Tour on a blisteringly hot day was a factor leading to mandatory testing of athletes for banned substances. Tests were conducted for the first time at the Giro d'Italia and the Olympics in Mexico the following year.

Descending carefully from the 1912m summit in low gear we were overtaken in the upper stretches several times by cyclists. It was predominantly second or third gear all the way but I needed first gear *and* brakes on the steepest bit below the summit. Going up had been second or third gear as well but I often changed into first gear to follow cyclists until we reached a point on the twisty road where I could see whether it was clear to overtake. The road is reasonably wide but near the top there is no white line in the middle of the road and you have to be careful overtaking the cyclists as traffic is coming quickly towards you from the opposite direction.

The road is well graded, averaging around 10% or 11% almost all the way except for the summit section. My brother and I found cycling up it not too strenuous if you selected your lowest gear but the biggest surprise of our ride was the descent. In the shade of the northern side the cold after cycling up in sunshine was bitter and soon penetrated our windproof clothing. We were forced to stop several times to defrost our fingers and wiggle our toes to encourage the circulation. In our motorhome there were no such problems but I felt envy for the riders because I remember the tremendous sense of achievement we felt after summiting the "Beast of Provence".

A Pause for Cheese

Our destination after Ventoux was the small mountain town of Banon in the Alps de Haute Provence and alarmingly when we arrived the *aire* was full. It was early afternoon and time for lunch so we pulled up on hardstanding below the *aire* to take stock and decide what to do if we couldn't find anywhere to stay. While we were eating lunch two French motorhomes turned up and parked beside us. One owner wound out his awning and got the chairs out and from him I learned a *féte du fromàge* was to be held the next day in the village. This explained why the *aire* was full. Not only filled with French motorhome owners but French motorhome owners who liked cheese.

They were swiftly joined by others and soon we were all but boxed in by a wall of French motorhomes and leaving was no longer an option but we needed no encouragement to stay and visit a cheese festival.

After lunch we explored the village. Compared to other remote French towns Banon was thriving. There was a wide variety of shops including that endangered species, the *alimentación* or general grocery store which have been almost eradicated by competition from supermarkets.

Our walk ended with the customary drink at an outside table at a bar. This time rosé for both of us.

The photograph below shows the motorhomes clustered around the covered market below the official *aire*. Any gaps you can see were later all filled by new arrivals. We are to the right in this shot, out of sight behind the covered market building. It must be an approved place to park because a man with a receipt book came round in the evening and charged us €4. This is the first of a few photographs I have included in this section because there was a lot to see in Banon.

During the afternoon and evening numerous stalls and traffic management systems were erected in the village and the following day with the streets packed with people we went on a cheese hunt.

Several stalls sold different goats' cheeses. Banon itself has a local *fromage de chevre* wrapped in sweet chestnut leaves.

There were expensive cheeses on sale, this slightly villainous pair sold multi-coloured cheeses at up to nearly €40 a kilogram although this did not stop us buying a slice of their "red" cheese which contained roasted garlic. The red colour coming from tomatoes according to the label although it was hard not to suspect a food dye might have been involved but we could not deny the result was delicious.

Cheese wasn't the only thing on offer, a wide variety of cured meats were available.

We bought a curious looking sausage from this lady. It was delicious and we later regretted not buying more of them. Other stalls included cookery demonstrations.

Refreshments were freely available as witnessed by the wine glass held by the gentleman in the photograph above. The dish being made below is *tartiflette*, made from potatoes and cheese and is a speciality of the Savoy region of France. The Savoy is an area north and east of where we were and borders Switzerland and Italy. The name of the company, *Poêle Géante*, means "large stove" and theirs was a big one.

Away from the main food area there were many stalls selling the usual stuff you see at craft fairs but a few selling the more unusual items, such as cow bells in different sizes including one large one priced at over five hundred euros. More practical but no cheaper was a composting toilet. Every allotment should have one.

Returning to our vehicle with a tasty smelling shopping bag Mary prepared lunch while I watched activities in the field below us where they were setting up for a demonstration of *chiens de troupeaux* or sheepdogs.

Our pre-lunch drink was the Côtes du Rhone rosé we bought at Chusclan. It had an interesting label.

For lunch we sampled one of the local goats' cheeses plus a cured sausage encrusted with herbs. We ate them with a salad and bread made with olive oil. We thought it would be like *focaccia* but it lacked the salt and was slightly sweet, but not unpleasantly so, more like a dense croissant.

The demonstration of sheep wrangling started with a mounted shepherd who showed how the sheep could be ushered around the ring.

The horse was good at standing on its hind legs but the shepherding significance of this escaped me. It looked impressive anyway. Then it was the dogs' turn.

The shepherd had a long whip and he used it occasionally like a shepherd's crook to direct the sheep in the desired direction. Intriguingly, the commands to the dog seemed to be normal French, in the sense of the French words for left, right and stop. There seemed to be no equivalent of “come bye” or “away” used by our shepherds.

Up into the Mountains

Leaving Banon I wanted to fill up with fuel as we would soon enter less populated regions so after buying food for three days I drove around to the supermarket pumps only to discover they were out of diesel. The next town had a filling station with fuel and a queue for it. I filled the one hundred and twenty litre tank up to the top and by doing so contributed to the wave of panic buying sweeping through France and causing pumps to run dry. A national strike was forecast over reforms to labour laws and fuel shortages were expected. My excuse for taking so much was we were leaving France and I am sure they would not have wanted to delay our departure.

We crossed the Durance, a major tributary of the Rhone and on the far bank entered Les Mées. This may sounds like a mis-spelt musical but it is famous for another kind of rock. The "*Penitents des Mées*" are a cliff of conical shapes overlooking the town.

Their shape gives rise to the legend they are the remains of local monks who were literally petrified by Saint Donat because they fell in love with a young Arab lady (or ladies) a local lord brought back from a crusade. In these less imaginative times we think the shape may be due to weathering of a conglomerate of bedrock from the Valensole stratum dating from the late Miocene and Pliocene epochs. However, the monks are apparently still able to throw a rock or two onto you if you wander too close.

Not long after passing through Les Mées we came upon the back of a queue following a circus on the move and there we stayed for the next hour as overtaking wasn't possible until we eventually came to a stretch of dual carriageway. Our night halt was an *aire* at Annot strewn with litter and discarded BBQ charcoal Charlie tried to eat if we didn't watch him closely. It was also cold and windy. The thermometer barely rose above 12°C all day but the forecast was for an improvement and so we looked forward to saying goodbye to the depressingly cold northern blast. I learned the reason for the litter afterwards; the *aire* had been reserved for use during the recent village fête. This was a week-long affair and it was used as a campground for vendors.

We explored the old part of Annot, entering the village over a 17th Century bridge, possibly reconstructed as it looked in too good a state of repair.

Like other old places it was hard to work out what the village might have looked like in the past as there had been so much rebuilding and reuse and reconfiguration of existing buildings over the centuries. Annot is built amongst and in places *into* the mountains as bits of the bedrock protrude up into the village in places.

This street on the following page may well have been a model for Diagon Alley from the Harry Potter books.

As with many old villages we have walked through there was no lack of interest for the old door enthusiast. One even had an intriguing early cat flap built into it.

We ended our walk around Annot in the customary manner with a glass of wine at an outside table sheltered from the wind. Very full measures were being dispensed, perhaps as an attempt by the proprietor to ward off the cold.

Our evening meal fitted the climate; boiled potatoes with a thick slice of ham with asparagus spears. The white form is the commonest available although you can find the green type we prefer at home. The difference is only how it is cultivated but given we were in France we went for the white. The ham was from the cold meat counter of the supermarket (without diesel) and was excellent with a strong smell and flavour of garlic. We finished with a slice of the red cheese bought from the villainous looking cheesemongers of Banon. At €38 a kilogramme we only allowed ourselves a small portion but with butter and cheese biscuits it was most enjoyable. Not so enjoyable but still interesting were our observations later on the after effects of the consumption of asparagus. Apparently asparagus acid is converted into sulphur containing chemicals in the body and subsequently expelled in the urine. The effect has long been known about. The Scottish mathematician, physician and satirist John Arbuthnot wrote about it in 1731. Later, Benjamin Franklin wrote in 1781 to the Royal Academy of Brussels; "*A few Stems of Asparagus eaten, shall give our Urine a disagreeable Odour*". Franklin was at the time trying to persuade the academy to discover a drug to make "*the natural Discharges of Wind from our Bodies, not only inoffensive, but agreeable as Perfumes*". Sadly this is something even modern medicine has not yet achieved. However, science has identified the issues around "asparagus pee". It had long been known not everybody seemed to be afflicted by the smell to the same degree. A debate ensued over whether this was because not everyone produced it or was it because not everyone could smell it? It seems both theories are true. The primary reason is not everyone can smell the sulphur in their urine but there are a few who do not produce the malodorous chemicals. By such small steps Mankind advances.

From Annot the main road runs east but it soon turns south and heads for the coast at Nice. This was an area we wanted to avoid as inevitably the stretch of coast running through and beside the French Riviera and Monaco carries a lot of traffic. So perversely, instead of going east from Annot we turned and into the Gorges de Daluis. The website www.dangerousroads.org describes this road with phrases such as "an adrenaline-pumping journey....not for the faint of heart...the road is difficult and a nightmare in the wet or dark".

The route through the gorge is a balcony road. A term used to describe a road with a steep drop on one side and not much of a barrier between users of the road and a sudden and fatal experiment with gravity. The river Var flow through the gorge and the entrance to it looks innocent enough but soon the road climbs up far above the river.

The barrier on the edge of the road is less than knee high. The drop may not look far in the photograph but this is misleading. It is a *very* long way to the bottom.

Although on paper there was only about forty kilometres to do this day it took over four hours, partly because this was not a road you would willingly rush along but we stopped at least half a dozen times for roadworks. These were repairs to crumbling edges or work to prevent stones falling from above. It was reassuring they were doing this work but it might have been even more reassuring if they had finished before our arrival.

Should you ever find yourself in these parts I recommend the Gorges de Daluis and if you have time a look at the nearby Gorges du Cians. This has numerous tunnels cut through red sandstone but it has a 3.1m height limit so you would need to take care in a big motorhome. Before the attempt you may wish to refer to the Dangerous Roads website description of the Gorges du Cians: "The road is in dreadful condition and requires strong nerves to negotiate. Any barriers along the edge afford little more than token protection; large stretches should be taken at a snail's pace and a lookout kept for vehicles coming from the opposite direction." I suggest this information is best not shared with your passengers in advance.

After escaping unscathed and unplummeted from the Gorges du Daluis we turned east again and crossed over the 1,678m Col de la Cuillole before stopping near the mountain village of Roubion, pictured below from the free *aire*.

The only problem with the *aire* was the fresh water connection was of a type unknown to motorhomers including even a French one which arrived after us. We had plenty of water on board and could easily manage another night before needing to refill. We always carry several bottles of drinking water and if we were careful when washing up and not flushed the toilet too often we could have stayed a second night if we wanted.

A more major setback was the refrigerator stopped working on gas, which is how we run it when there is no electrical supply and on *aires*. It had been reluctant to run on gas for some time but now seemed to have gone on strike. Perhaps after being so long in France it picked up the national mood? The gas would light, you could hear the "*whoomph*" as it lit, but it would not stay alight. It had been troublesome for a while but we always got it going after a few attempts. I knew the burner was clean as I cleaned before we left the UK so the problem was something more serious than soot in the wrong place. However, we possessed a good electric coolbox, a fearsomely expensive compressor model and this could be used for critical things like meat, milk and wine. Stuff like salads and butter would stay in the broken refrigerator. There was only another nine weeks to go and we would be fine on campsites with electric hook ups.

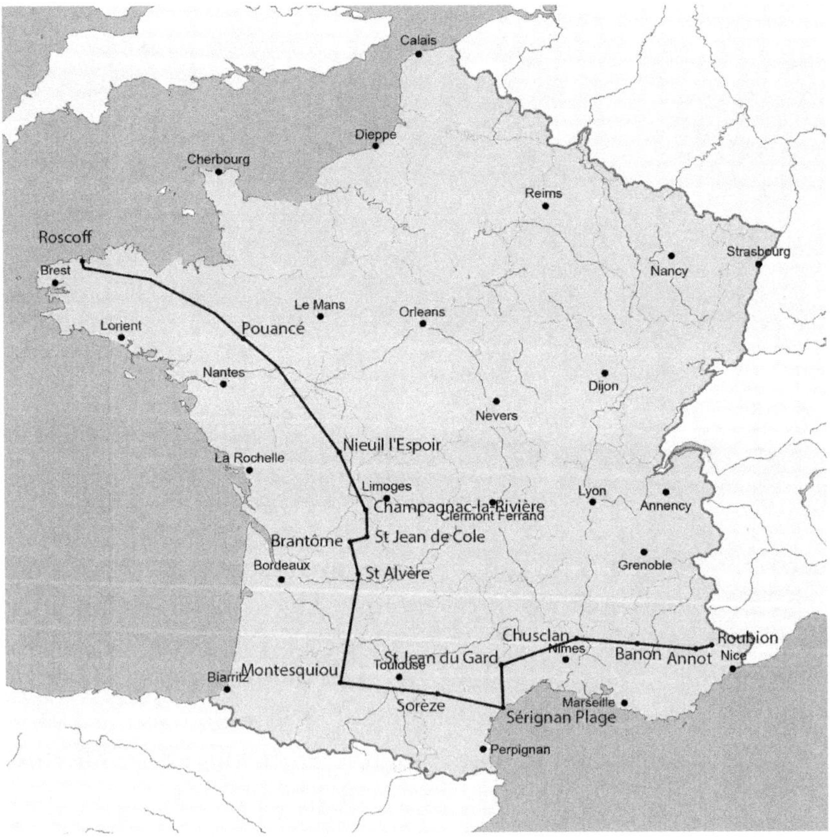

From the map you can see we were close to the Mediterranean coast, but it is a different France up in the mountains compared to the hustle and bustle of the coast. It is a lot cooler here and this can be a great relief in summer if you ever find yourself cooking on a beach. You don't have to go far inland from Nice before you climb into the hills and the temperatures become much more pleasant.

On the following morning, possibly sensing we would leave France soon, the refrigerator worked. It may have been Mary's magic touch but more likely it was because it had all cooled. Subsequently, we found it was much easier to light and keep alight if we waited half an hour at the end of each day's driving before trying it on gas. Back in the UK the main control valve was subsequently changed and this seemed to cure it but for the moment and halfway up a French alp we found cursing reasonably effective. In fact, the same problem reoccurred the following year but by then we were masters in the art of getting it to stay alight.

By one of those curious twists of fate the problems with the refrigerator coincided with a planned route taking us over one of the highest roads in Europe and a place where keeping things cool would not be a problem. Today we would go over the Col de la Bonette. At 2,715m it isn't the highest pass in the Alps, there are three more higher, the highest being the Col de l'Iseran at 2,764m. Despite this there is a sign on the Col de la Bonette mentioning "the highest road in Europe". This is artistic licence as it refers to a two kilometre scenic route they have built starting at the Col then looping around the Cime de la Bonette peak and arriving back close to where it started. This loop reaches 2,802m at the highest point so it beats the other three cols but only on a technicality as the road is a short loop going nowhere but it can claim to be the highest asphalted road in the Alps. The highest road in Europe is not in the Alps, where you might expect it but in the south of Spain. In the Sierra Nevada the road to Veleta is much higher at 3,392m but the road is a dead-end and no longer open to the public so the Alpine cols remain the highest through roads in Europe.

As we ascended, going north now, we soon left the trees and entered a barren and snowy landscape. Alpine Marmots were running over the snow and in and out of their burrows.

The views from the Col were impressive.

The temperature at the top was about 9°C and there was no wind. We saw less than a dozen cars and a few cyclists and motorcycles. The road is easy driving and could be done by any size of motorhome I think although those with a large overhang at the rear would need to be careful of grounding on the inside of the hairpin bends. The melting snow and recent rain had washed little and not so little stones onto the road near the summit. These would have been puncture inducing for those on two wheels but not too bad for us.

It had been a grand day out as Wallace might describe it and descending from the Col de la Bonette we headed for an *aire* on the outskirts of Jausiers. The coordinates took us to the *aire* service point but this was in a layby off a road running beside a river with nowhere to park overnight. If you have a sharp-eyed co-pilot as I do they will at this point spot the parked motorhomes on the other side of the river. Having been unable to fill with water at Roubion because of the unique water connection we were in need of a refill so we drove a few kilometres to Barcelonnette where there was another *aire* with a similar card machine but this time with instructions in several languages including English. The downside was it cost us €8 for two *jetons* and a receipt to put in the window if we wanted to stay overnight which we didn't as the *aire* was beside some noisy sports pitches. So back we went to the riverside *aire* at Jausiers where we enjoyed a quiet night.

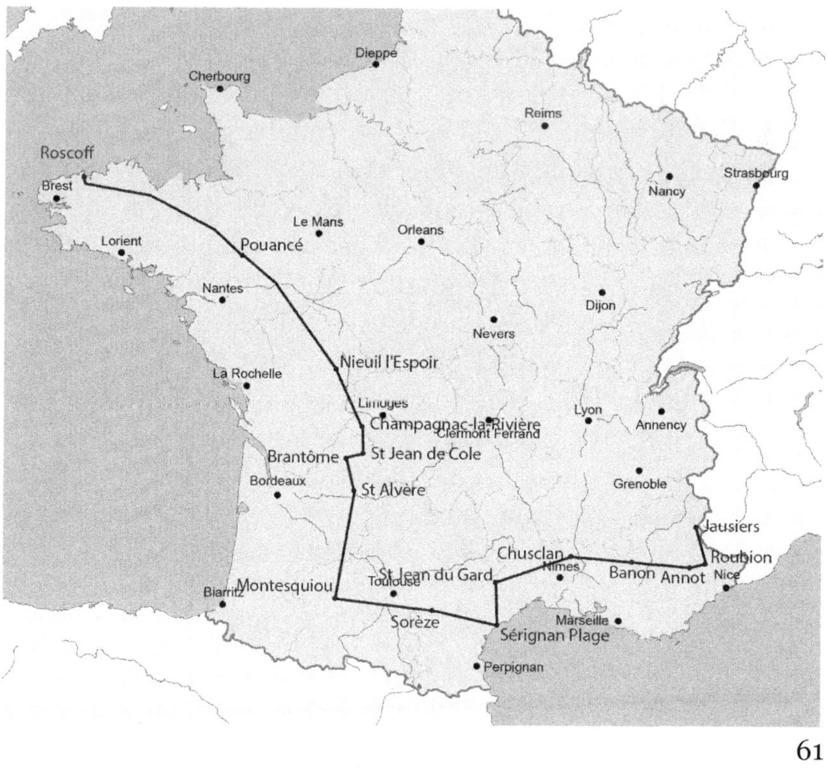

Into Italy

Leaving Jausiers we made another diversion to the Barcelonnette *aire* to spend our second *jeton* on water and then headed east to leave France for Italy by way of the Col de Larche (1948m) or Colle della Maddalena as the Italians call it.

The summit is the border between the two countries and immediately after it the road descended rapidly through about twenty hairpin bends. These are not shown on the Michelin atlas as they are so closely packed together, but it was an impressive zig-zag drop into Italy, made more entertaining by huge trucks coming towards us. These I soon learned gave no quarter. The road surface was also poorer here than on the French side.

Not long afterwards we went through a village with lights to control the traffic in the narrow village centre. The lights were on the outside of the town on the west side, where we were coming from, but the matching lights facing the oncoming traffic were almost in the centre of the village and there were other tight spots beyond them. In was in these we encountered traffic chaos for several minutes as huge trucks squeezed passed each other through the gaps, with us clutching to the coat tails of the truck in front. The deterioration of the road and the manic traffic were a sure reminder we were in Italy but this entrance into Italy was only a feint because soon afterwards we drove back into France through the three kilometre long Tunnel de Tende, a light controlled single track tunnel with long queues either side but we waited only fifteen minutes before being given our green light. The tunnel is stone lined having been opened in 1882. Work is underway to create a second tunnel and widen the original but it will not be completed for several years I suspect. What you can enjoy now are another impressive series of steep hairpins straight after you exit the tunnel.

Then it was back into Italy yet again where just over the border we stopped at a campsite near Olivetta San Michele. This was built on abandoned olive terraces and it was doing a good job of imitating an abandoned campsite too as it was deserted.

The site was a pleasant and tranquil location but the route up to it was steep and narrow and there was a fearsome hump at the entrance we got over with only an inch to spare underneath.

We still hadn't seen the owner when we came to leave so with fingers and everything else crossed we slid over the hump at the entrance again with fittings like steps and exhaust pipe remaining intact. The service point, which was outside the entrance, doubled as a black waste orifice so all unwanted liquids went into it. A one euro coin released the fresh water at a rather feeble pressure. A notice said we would get 50 to 80 litres for our coin but I doubt even the lower figure dribbled in but it was enough to keep us going for the day.

Another notice said there was a charge of two euros for "discharge" and to "put it through the letterbox" if no one was in the office. Someone cursed with literalism might take them at their word and do this but I think they meant only the money should go into the letterbox and the waste should be consigned to the multi-purpose opening. Being an honest bloke I put €2 into the office though I suspect many wouldn't and my honesty did not extend to following the first offering up with another eight for the overnight stay. My excuse before Saint Peter will be the letterbox didn't give change and I didn't have enough coins to post the full amount. A weak excuse but it was true and so might save me from the fires.

I must also confess to a little pillaging from the place besides short changing them on the full residential fee. On one of the lower terraces of the olive grove I found wild strawberries growing and they were the sweetest I've ever tasted. These foraged delights subsequently went well with the morning's muesli. In hindsight I shouldn't have added the banana as its strong flavour overpowered the strawberries but they were still excellent and all the more so for being free.

To head east, as was our intention, there isn't much choice of routes from where we were. There are only two options, the inland *autostrada* toll road or the coastal road going through all the towns. We followed the latter which was a mistake though one worth making once if only for the invaluable experience of Italian driving styles it affords. If your intention is to learn how to drive like an Italian and I think you should if visiting the country to preserve your sanity I can recommend this route. I even think I could pass an Italian driving test, so adapt did I become at pulling out in front of other vehicles at junctions and I'm unfazed by being undertaken by scooters while being closely tailgated by a Fiat 500. The Italians have a natural aptitude for mortal combat on the road, otherwise known as "normal driving for Italy".

It was coming up to a weekend so we headed for a campsite with washing machines on the coast at Pietro Ligure. This was in most respects a good site except for mean token operated showers giving you about thirty seconds of hot water before they turned cold. It wasn't a cheap site but coin operated showers seem to be something the Italians are keen on and we were to find many others.

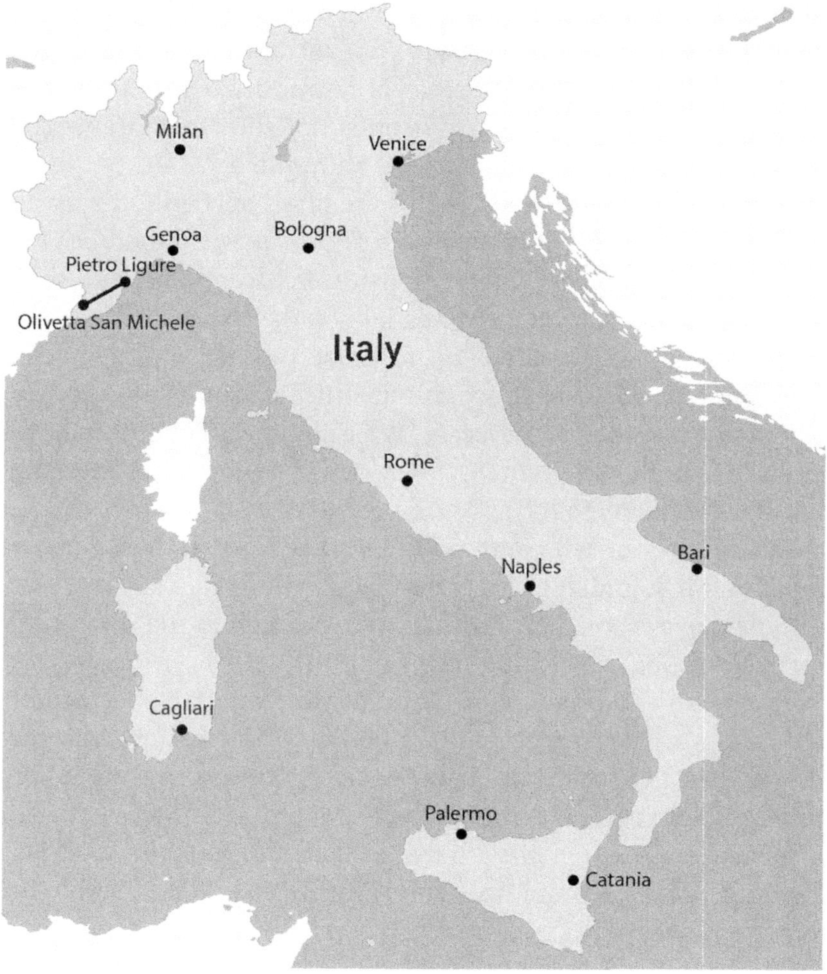

There was a pleasant bar near the entrance where we could sit outside in the evening, and you needed to sit when the bill arrived, nearly €8 for one large and one small beer.

Our first night here was illuminated (literally) by a little magic I stumbled across when I took Charlie for his last walk before bed. There were fireflies in amongst the bushes and trees. Charlie saw them first, little twinkling lights flying around us like fairies with intermittently faulty torches. I'd only seen fireflies once before, in Provence when camping as a child and I was surprised to see them here as I thought they would have preferred somewhere darker but they were under trees so they must have been able to find each other in what darkness there was. The local lonely hearts' pages must have many messages on variations of "single light seeks other for brief encounter."

Despite the name they are beetles not flies, but firebeetles lacks something both poetically and alliteratively.

After a relaxing weekend at the site plans needed to be made about the coming week because the Thursday was Republic Day and a public holiday. The campsite we were on said they expected to be busy so we headed further south where the weather might be better. The forecast was for a changeable week here in the northwest but further south, Rome for example, sunshine was forecast. We didn't at this point plan to go so far south but the closer we got to Rome the better the weather was likely to be.

Tuscany, even with our poor knowledge of Italy we knew about and it sounded like a good place to head for. Tuscany has a shape like a whole ham, with a broad section in the south and a narrower "leg" stretching into the north. Much of the narrow section is the Garfagnana Valley, inland from the spectacular and therefore massively popular and busy Cinque Terre villages on the coast. The valley looked perfect for sitting out the public holiday. It was some distance from the sea and there were no lakes nearby which might otherwise attract local families taking the day off or combining the Thursday holiday with the weekend and making a short break of it.

After a warm final night at Pietro Ligure we headed along the coast road. This stayed close to the sea with tunnels to be negotiated as it cut through headlands. We had two things to do, find a supermarket for shopping and an ATM for cash and in both aims we failed. We didn't see a single supermarket and though the satnav told me there were ATMs in the villages and little towns parking spaces anywhere near them were non-existent. Eventually we joined the *autostrada* outside Savona after a mildly disconcerting moment when a front wheel suddenly skidded as we climbed a slope before joining the main road. I'm not sure what it was, spilt diesel or a slippery surface from the rain.

Joining the *autostrada*, a toll road here, entailed collecting a ticket from an automated booth. There were no instructions visible, other than a cartoon hand pointing to a large red button. The phrase “don't press the button” came into my head but I pressed it anyway and won a strip of thin card like an oversized bus ticket.

I expected the *autostrada* to be like a UK motorway or a French *péage* and a lot less fraught than our Italian driving experience so far, but I can’t say it was.

Trucks didn't stay in the often narrow lanes and the slip roads where traffic entered the *autostrada* were short to non-existent. There were remarkably tight bends all made more exciting than usual because the road surface was damp from the recent rain.

We skirted around Genoa, seeing the evocative sign to the port where we could have taken a ferry to Sicily. As well as food and cash we needed diesel and gas and from a website I saw there were motorway services with gas just before we were due to leave the *autostrada*. Here I stopped for diesel and put one €100 worth in. It would have taken more but the price for the fuel was higher than I saw away from the *autostrada* but a nearly full tank was one less thing to worry about. Unfortunately, we were less successful with the gas.

At the manned gas pump I was told the gas was for “traction” only but I could get gas for “cooking” in nearby Sarzana. I’d heard of this problem before but hoped we would be lucky and get served, but it was not to be. Motorway services won't fill vehicles with gas unless the vehicle is adapted to run on gas and though we have a built in gas tank with external filler this cut no ice with the pump attendant.

Fortuitously, the Sarzana turnoff was the one we wanted anyway though first we needed to agree terms with an automated toll booth reluctant to wake and allow us to proceed. The problem was solved, after head scratching, by driving forward far enough for the camera on the booth to recognise it had a customer. At this point the until then entirely mute and lifeless payment machine sprang into life and devoured a €20 note before spitting out a small amount of change.

Sarzana is a reasonably large town we entered blindly, looking for the mystic source of "cooking" gas. We found a supermarket first with the added attraction of lots of parking so we stopped there to take on supplies for the next few days. Consulting the internet after our shopping expedition I identified and found a garage stocking LPG close by but by the time we got there the pump operator had retired for a long lunch and was not expected back until much later.

As we weren't critical on gas we left and drove on to Agriturismo dei Peri near the hilltop village of Castelnuovo Magra. This was a smallholding with olives and vines. Products from both they apparently sold although we were never to discover how or where from due to the conspicuous absence of the owner apart from a few fleeting appearances when she would shout at sundry workers and passing tradesmen from her metal garden gate. In France this would be called an *aire* but here in Italy the word used is *sosta*.

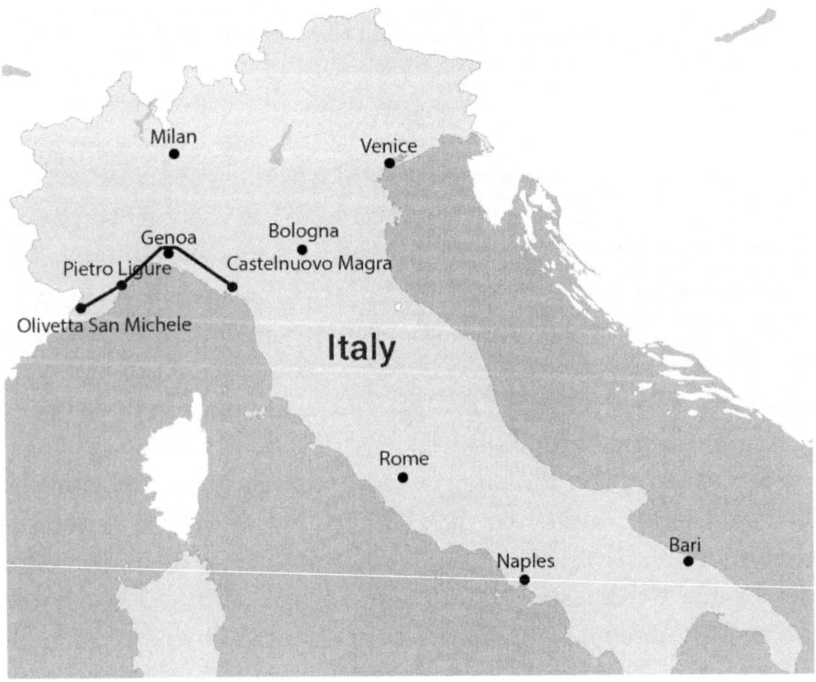

Once parked we tried exploring the little vineyard after lunch and came across a compound in the middle of it filled with two large and noisy dogs placed there as intruder alerts. We hastily retreated, dragging Charlie with us who was determined to meet the dogs and pulled hard on the lead to get near them. As a puppy he was naive about the intentions of guard dogs. Instead we went out of the sosta entrance and walked for a while on the road until the threat of rain suggested a second withdrawal was prudent. We had gone far enough on the road to realise walking to nearby Castelnuovo Magra was possible so we planned to do this the following day. We returned to the motorhome for the usual late afternoon mug of Earl Grey, drank while listening to the rain falling on the roof.

Geographically we were in the foothills of the Alpi Apuane, part of the Apennines. The Apennines form a spine of mountains running much of the length of Italy. The Alpi Apuane or Apuan Alps are the source of Carrara marble, a pale stone much sought after for buildings, monuments and sculpture. The Parthenon, Michelangelo's David, Marble Arch and on a smaller scale the statue of Robbie Burns in Dumfries are all made from Carrara marble. The region was a cradle of anarchism at the end of the nineteenth century, partly because the work in the quarries was so demanding and harsh the quarry owners would use anyone willing to work in them and no questions were asked on an individual's background. As a result ex-convicts and fugitives including people from outside Italy came to work here and radical ideas grew, fuelled by the neglect the quarry owners showed for their employees.

My reason for coming to this region was not driven by any admiration for anarchy but by my love for the writing of Eric Newby who owned a house in the area. Newby's first book, The Last Grain Race recounts his voyage on the last sailing clipper to Australia before the Second World War. During the war he served in the SBS before being captured following a raid on Sicily when they failed to rendezvous with a submarine and were picked up by a fishing boat instead. Newby was held prisoner in an old orphanage near Parma where he met his future wife Wanda, who taught him Italian. He was released from prison after the armistice between Italy and the Allied Forces in 1943 but the Germans together with Fascist sympathisers were in control of the country and Newby was secretly, and at great risk to his helpers taken into the mountains, spending several months at one point living in a cave surrounded by snow. In *Love and War in the Apennines* Newby describes how he was sheltered and fed here by the local people but his liberty did not last long and he was eventually recaptured, apparently betrayed by Fascist sympathisers. In the mountains it seemed no secret could be kept for long and the news a British officer was in hiding became almost common knowledge. Newby returned to the region after the war and he and Wanda were married in 1946. Twenty years later they bought a tumbledown house near the village of Fosdinovo, which was only about two kilometres away from where we were parked. Their experiences at Fosdinovo are recounted in *A Small Place in Italy* a book much more about the local people than it is about buying and renovating a house in Italy, a theme well worked to death in other lesser accounts.

If Eric Newby is unknown to you as a writer then you should correct this. His best known book and a work reliably included in almost anyone's list of the top ten best travel books ever written, *A Short Walk in the Hindu Kush* is not to be missed.

Despite grey and threatening skies we walked the following day, as we promised ourselves, to the local village of Castelnuovo Magra which overlooks the *sosta*. This took us about half hour of gentle uphill walking.

Castelnuovo Magra, a name translating literally as "slim new castle" sits on a hilltop overlooking the valley of the river Magra. While we were walking we could hear distant rumblings, it was too early to be my stomach and it didn't sound like the thunder forecast for later so it could only have been blasting at the marble quarries.

As an aside at this point, have you ever wondered why marbles (the little round things) are called marbles? It is because the earliest found, dating back several thousand years were made from marble. Modern "marbles" are made from glass using a process invented in Ohio in 1915 where a blob of glass runs down a pair of rollers, rotating and cooling before dropping off at the end as a solid sphere.

Our route to the village I plotted using Google Maps on my mobile 'phone. Passing between terraces of olives, interspersed with a scattering of cherries, plum and níspero or loquat we first encountered in Spain the previous year. These small orange coloured fruit, like misshapen peaches, are often used as an additive to other preserves as they are high in pectin.

In the town several buildings were painted in the traditional pink/red known locally as *sangue di bue* or oxblood. Eric Newby observed in the sixties, when he came here all the houses were this colour but since then Mr Dulux has been busy selling many different colours.

Any wash cycle you want as long as it is cold - the village laundry above.

On our walk to the village we had a good view looking west towards the sea. In the far distance were the hills backing the Cinque Terre villages. However, the plain between them and where we were has an interesting history. Here is Eric Newby on the subject, describing his journey as they entered this region from the north.

"Here we entered the Plain of Luni, the site of what had been Luna, an important Etruscan city and seaport which Livy described as being 'the first city of Etruria' and Strabo as having one of the finest and largest harbours in the world, much of its prosperity being because of the marble trade. But in the fourth century AD its decline began, brought on by the malaria which eventually rendered it more or less uninhabitable. It was subsequently sacked many times: by the Lombards, by the Normans in the ninth century and by the Arabs, who finally destroyed it and carried its inhabitants into captivity in 1016. Both city and seaport disappeared from history some time in the twelfth century, killed off by the

malarial mosquitoes, and became an area largely populated by ghosts and goats. Now all that remained of it was an amphitheatre that once seated six thousand spectators and a theatre. It was Luna that gave its name to what is now the present region of Lunigiana, although originally it was much larger."

As Mary reacts badly to mosquito bites I kept quiet about this being close to a malarial hot-spot. And I didn't mention the ghosts though there were more fireflies amongst the olive trees. Or what I took to be fireflies but may have been wandering spirits.

It rained during the night but it faired up long enough for us to pack and pay. The *sosta* was a rum place. When we arrived there was no one to be seen but I searched around until I found the lady owner and we booked in. They couldn't be faulted on the recycling though with bins for paper, food waste, glass, general rubbish, metals and plastic.

The only odd thing was a notice stating toilet discharge may only be made if it was treated with a "disruptive chemical". Presumably it went into some large underground tank to be emptied periodically because if it went into the local sewer system or a septic tank chemicals would not be desirable, especially not disruptive ones.

The elderly lady owner was working out the bill when what I think was her daughter turned up, she had some English, better than my Italian and from her I heard they had a washing machine and a shower. We hadn't used these, not knowing they were available but they asked because they wanted to include them on the bill if we had. I subsequently put a review online about our stay suggesting it was a place which could be better. For example, some and more information about what facilities were available. A map of local walks would have been handy too. Months later they must have found the review and replied in what can only be considered as uncompromising terms. We won't be welcomed there again I think. A pity as it was otherwise an excellent place.

The rain began again the next day as we drove into Sarzana, going first to the filling station we found when we first arrived. There no qualms from the operator when we wanted "cooking" gas and not "traction" gas. After stocking up at the supermarket we went on another ATM hunt. This time they weren't too hard to find as there were several banks in the same area but parking anywhere near was again virtually non-existent. We found somewhere eventually and walked back to the bank (a Barclays of all things) and extracted money from the ATM. This was all done while it rained heavily with large puddles everywhere to paddle through.

Our destination was the free *sosta* in San Romano or to give it its full name San Romano in Garfagnana. As the crow flies and they have hooded ones here it wasn't far but the route was a hilly one. The satnav first took us on a real back road to Fosdinovo, the nearest village to Eric Newby's house, but we saw little of the village as by then were driving in cloud. What we did see was intriguing with a hint of a town wall glimpsed through the murk.

What we also didn't see was the amphitheatre of Luni. It was on the day's plan but the rain was so heavy and unceasing we decided to abandon the idea.

From Fosdinovo we crossed over into the Garfagnana Valley and wriggled up the road to San Romano, narrowly missing a huge tanker at one point belting around a corner towards us and causing sharp braking by both parties. It was not the first such incident in Italy and wasn't to be the last. There is a well understood hierarchy of vehicles in the country and on mountain roads with hairpin bends large trucks have the absolute right to use the full width of the road. Drivers from outside Italy need to learn this unpublicised rule quickly if they are to avoid coming to harm.

The *sosta* at San Romano in Garfagnana (that really is its Italian name and not an Anglicisation) is beside a football pitch but it seemed quiet and remained so throughout our stay.

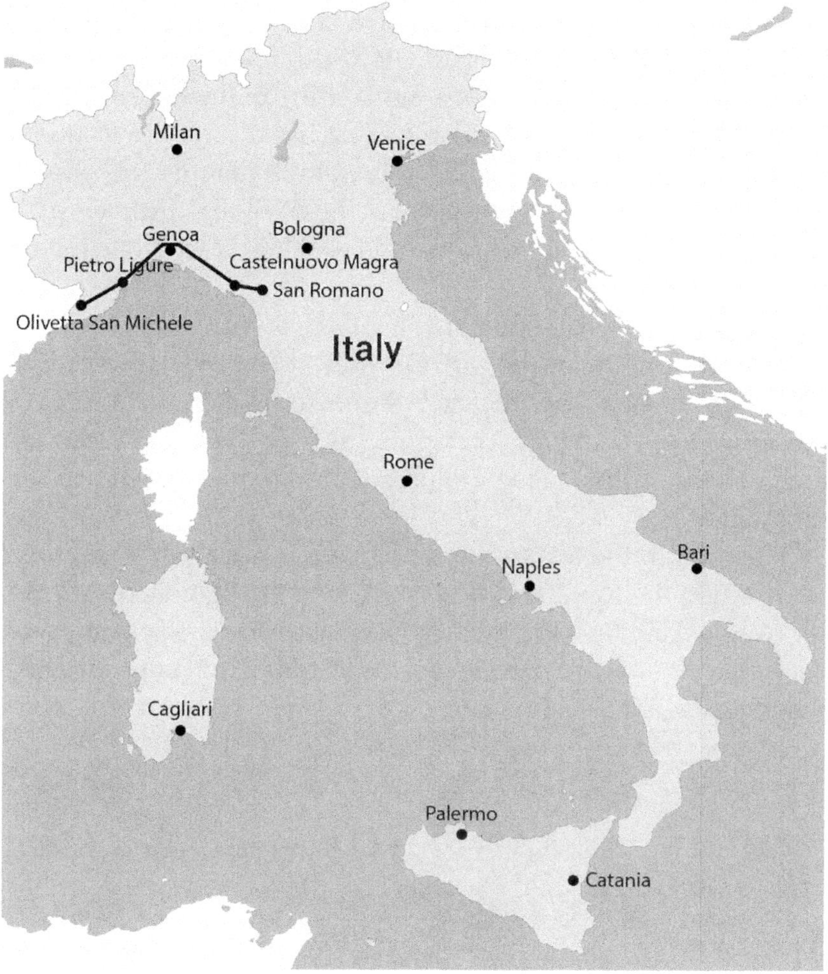

We woke the next morning to see the hills around us covered in cloud but it wasn't raining so things looked promising for a walk.

Next to the *sosta* was an entrance to an adventure park, it seemed in good repair but remained deserted all the time we were there.

A notice inside the entrance showed a thirty minute walk to the Fortress of Verrucole. This was a well-marked and easy GR path with the familiar red and white markings showing the way. The GR or Grande Randonnée paths are found all over Europe and are usually well marked. The red and white stripes painted on a post or boulder identifies them and they can be relied upon to give you a good walk. The GR 20, for example, traverses Corsica and is one of the most demanding paths in Europe but hopefully this one would prove less taxing. I have yet to find a map showing all the GR paths so I couldn't identify the one we were on but it is likely it was part of the long distance path starting at the top of Norway and ending in southern Italy known as the E1.

The path we took ended at the village of Verrucole, a village dominated by the little fortress and its rebuilt tower. The village, for fans of TripAdvisor, is home to the best restaurant in the area, the Ostaria le Verrucole, but we were too early for lunch although this being a public holiday we were later to see them busy.

The path to the fortress was steep and we feared by the time we reached the top it might be shut on a public holiday but we received a friendly welcome from a fluent English speaking lady who was dressed in period costume under an appropriately thatched shelter.

The fortress had a replica catapult, but deactivated so we couldn't play with it and see how far a dog could be hurled (see later for explanation).

In the small herb or physic garden all the plants were labelled but unfortunately all the labels were neatly stacked in an alcove. Note the ones with the skulls.

The picture below, showing part of the castle wall and the tower, was taken from the veranda of a bar called the "Warrior Rat". I have not been to a castle with a bar before and can commend the idea to English Heritage. If they can sanction the carving of a Disney figure on Tintagel what's stopping them building more bars?

Exploring the fortress didn't take long and afterwards we retired to castle bar which was tended by another fluently English speaking young lady in medieval costume. Here we shared a bottle of a refreshing 7% cider they were promoting. I forgot to photograph the bottle (it was 7% in my defence) but it appeared from what I could decipher from the label honey was involved in its brewing. It was a potent little drink on an empty stomach and I was soon musing over whether the costumed ladies were wearing wimples. I've no idea what a wimple looks like but something in my memory suggested medieval ladies wore them.

What we did deliberately miss was the tour of the tower (try saying that after a few glasses) because although it was "in several languages" it lasted an hour and Charlie's attention span is measured in seconds. He had already disgraced us at the moment of our entrance to the castle. While I was talking to the lady in the thatched reception hut Charlie jumped up to see what was happening and left muddy paw prints on her immaculately clean tablecloth. Luckily for Charlie we found no stocks for dogs on our exploration either, the catapult being deactivated as mentioned.

Later in the day, when the rain which started after lunch ended, we explored San Romano. As expected it was fully of narrow streets, but curiously no shops or bars except a few around the edges and there were few people. So rare were the local folk I took a picture of one of the few I saw. The tall bell tower on the next page is a separate building to the church, with a small piazza between the two.

There were the usual old doors and over one was carved the inscription: "SANCTUM ET TERRIBILE". This isn't as fearsome as it might seem on first reading. If images of sadistic nuns come to mind put them aside because it is part of Psalm 111 "*Sanctum et terribile nomen ejus*" translates as "holy and reverend is his Name". How "terrible" in Latin became what we understand by the word today is a mystery.

After exhausting the compact pleasures of San Romano in Garfagnana we repaired to the “Rewind Bar and Pizzeria” (6 out of 8 on TripAdvisor) for a (German) beer.

Tuscany was growing on me and if a place looks good in the rain it suggests it might have something going for it. Tomorrow we would edge further south.

We’d been in Tuscany for several days but the photographs may not match everyone’s idea of what Tuscany is supposed to look like. Where were the rolling hills with pencil slim trees on the horizon?

We left San Romano with the low clouds almost bumping our heads and drove down the valley of the river Serchio. The rain was constant all morning and fell as a steady drizzle.

On the way we stumbled across a big supermarket called Esselunga. It didn't look like a supermarket from the outside but on the inside it was by far the most impressive one we had found so far in Italy. The fruit and vegetable section was enormous but the wine section was upmarket with a resident sommelier. Very much a first for a supermarket and the gentleman took his duties seriously if his girth and red nose were any sign.

As you might expect wine prices were upmarket with shelf after shelf of €10+ wines but with diligent searching we did find a few under €4, twice our normal budget and we bought a €6 bottle of Prosecco (reduced to €4) to celebrate another day survived on the roads of Italy. So if in Italy and you see an Esselunga or "Essex unmanageable" as my spell checker wants to correct it to, have a rummage around inside for their wines.

What the shop wasn't good for were towels. We previously travelled with big fluffy bath towels but they took a long time to dry after washing so we brought with us two microfibre towels instead. These weren't cheap, £24 each from a company whose main selling point was the towels contained a special silver odour control. But why should you need odour control on a towel?

What we found after a few days of use was these special towels needed the dour control best obtained with a blow lamp.

Despite regular washing they stank even moments after being used.

The problem I think is the microfibres trap minute bits of skin and this is what you can smell, or rather you can smell the flatulent bacteria feeding on your discarded epidermis. So we decided to discard the space age towels and buy big fluffy bath towels just like the ones we left behind at home. Unfortunately, Senor Esselunga only sold tiny towels you would be hard pressed to dry your hands on.

So toweless we pushed on and headed towards Lucca but turned before we reached it and went cross country on minor roads to finish mid-way between Pisa and Florence at Camping Toscana Village at Montopoli in Val d'Arno.

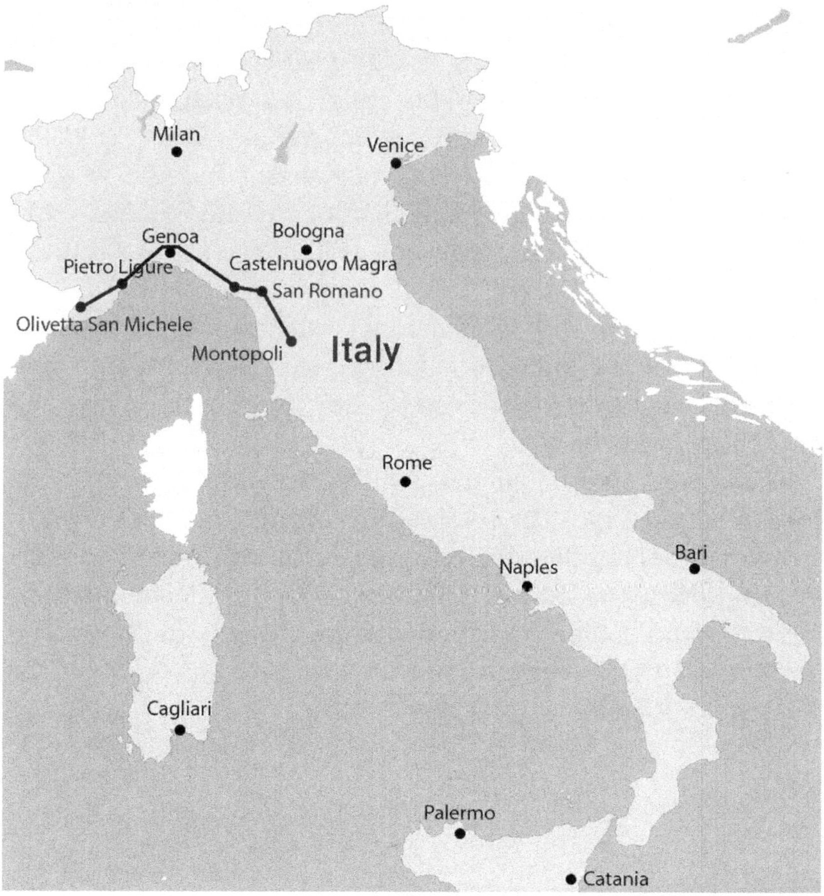

We were well settled into our routine of finding a campsite each weekend. This afforded us the opportunity to do the laundry and give the motorhome a good clean, weather permitting. From the forecast it was expected to the sun would arrive on Sunday and stay for at least the following week. Sun might also help the smelly towels too, UV does wonders for killing bugs. New towels would be better, large fluffy ones if possible but these were proving harder to find than the sun.

The campsite was quiet but it had a bar and a restaurant serving upmarket food. A set meal for two with steak and a bottle of Chianti headlined the menu at €80 and the price might explain the lack of customers. Less rarefied, a first course of antipasto was a "mere" €12 though the dishes we saw being served looked good.

Our plan on the Saturday was to visit the weekly open air market in the local village but this was postponed to the afternoon as it rained constantly all morning. It wasn't cold and with virtually no wind it wasn't unpleasant but the weather wasn't what we expected of Italy in June. By the time we got to the village after lunch the market was long departed as it was a Saturday *morning* market.

Montopoli even without a market is worth a wander round as it has several old buildings dating from the thirteenth and fourteenth centuries including a tall bell tower in the centre and a watchtower on the edge.

There were the usual narrow streets and views over the Tuscan countryside. The tall building rising above the town in the photograph on the following page is the bell tower and sadly for Montopoli the builders of the tower got the foundations correct. If only they had followed the designs of those who constructed the Leaning Tower of Pisa. The town would be much more famous.

Deeper into Tuscany

From Montopoli we headed southeast into Chianti country. Skirting round the south of Florence and from here onwards the landscape looked like the Tuscany I expected, pencil slim cypress trees everywhere and hilltop villages.

We were aiming for one such village, Volpaia, in the Monti de Chianti and they do make a big thing of the name here. Everywhere seems to find a way of working “Chianti” into their name, well almost everything. I don't remember seeing a “Chianti laundrette” though there may well be one somewhere and the use of the name hasn’t done them any harm. This was a prosperous area with well-maintained houses and busy restaurants in every village, plus the manicured wine estates. It was like parts of France I thought. Not all was upper class though and we found a Lidl with limited stock and curiously no lemons for our Earl Grey tea. They did have 1.5 litre bricks of wine for less than €2 instead so we bought a pink and red purely in the interests of research. In Spain these brick wines all taste the same irrespective of colour after they have been well chilled, which is essential. The local Chianti in bottles wasn’t cheap, with nothing on offer under €6 even in Lidl.

After our shopping we made for the *sosta* at Volpaia, a small hill top village where we planned to stay overnight if it looked suitable. Unfortunately, the *sosta* was a car park on the edge of the village next to a busy and popular restaurant. All the cars of the customers were in the same car park. I expected it could be noisy in the evening with the coming and going of clientele not only for the nearest restaurant but the other one in the village too because the *sosta* doubled as the car park for the whole village.

We lunched here anyway and were only disturbed by American tourists, one of whom made a big fuss over Charlie, cheering him up no end. Afterwards we made our usual exploration of narrow village streets. Volpaia has a good collection and some intriguing passages.

We ended the day not far from Volpaia at a luxurious campsite with no less than three swimming pools. It was next to the Parco Naturale Cavriglia, an oak forest with good opportunities for walking and getting lost.

Despite having been in Italy for nearly two weeks we had not yet eaten any pasta so I corrected this by cooking spaghetti for supper. I cooked this as I do at home and it is a wonder the sky did not fall in on me. When we were later to have pasta in an Italian restaurant I suddenly realised I have been over-cooking pasta all my life.

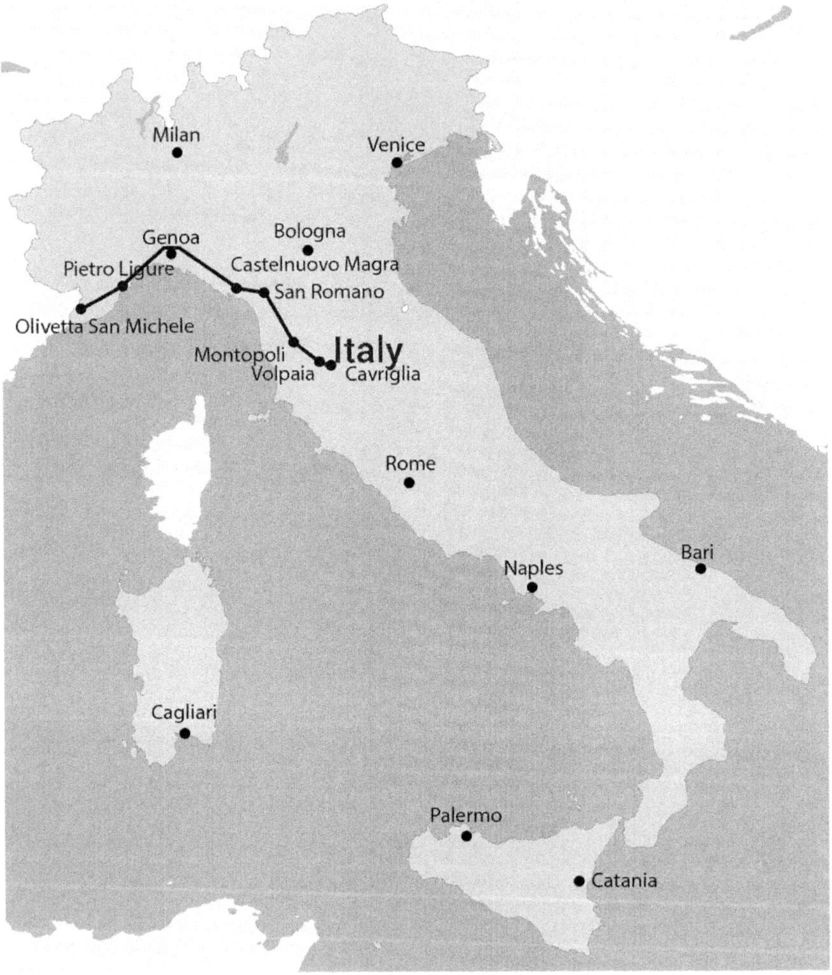

At the campsite reception office, where the largely Dutch staff spoke near perfect English was a folder showing walks from the campsite. We chose the shortest, appropriately called *Senterio #1* and they kindly printed a colour copy of the map for us. This made a pleasant contrast with our first Italian campsite with its mean coin-operated showers.

The walk, despite being at the junior end of the spectrum of routes on offer was 6.7 km long and with application it could be made considerably longer as we were to discover.

The route was a loop around a hill but with a detour to see the remains of a castle before you retraced your steps back to the loopy bit. The first half of the walk to the castle was on a track, with many muddy sections where we could see recent hoof prints of wild boar. The honey-like scent from the broom was strong.

The castle, when we reached it was a ruin and its decrepitude an ongoing project. Signs warned us to keep away from the walls by at least a metre and a half. We opted for a greater measure of caution.

After the castle we walked back to the main trail to continue the loop around the hill but soon afterwards I made a wrong turning. In my defence the waymarks for the walk were grey circles painted on the tree trunks with, on this route, a black number 1 painted in the circle. They were infrequent and given the trunks of the trees were also grey and black they were remarkably hard to see. Give me a red and white GR sign any day.

After about fifteen minutes my compass showed we were going in the wrong direction. We retraced our steps about half a kilometre to where I had taken the wrong turning. I remembered looking at this path earlier and dismissing it with the thought "it can't be that way" but it was.

We were no longer on a track but more a wild boar trail. Fallen trees blocked our way at several points and it was uphill walking with no breeze and high humidity.

But there was a surreal moment just before we escaped from the fuggy forest. We'd reached a point where I was reasonably sure where we were but the path had almost disappeared. I could see a grey circle painted on a tree but confusingly no number was painted in it. At this moment a llama walked into view and regarded us from a height of about two metres, looking disdainful down its nostrils at us. Had we suddenly been transported to the Andes? The animal turned around, discomforted by the site of a small dog going berserk on the end of its lead and trotted quickly off. We followed and soon the narrow path we were on joined the track I was expecting.

Charlie was hot, as we were, but he took the opportunity afforded by a trackside puddle to cool off. We have a mud coloured dog so he didn't look much different after his puddle bathing and it was easily washed off later using the hose at the campsite motorhome service point.

It would be no exaggeration to say we were on our uppers by the time we got back to the site. Walks 2 to 7 we will leave for others with a better sense of direction. The humidity and lack of breeze had been the killer.

The next day we drove less than ten kilometres to Gaiole in Chianti to have a look at the *sosta* but it was in an industrial section and looked far from attractive so we drove instead to Radda in Chianti.

The *sosta* here was much pleasanter, though nothing is perfect and the water pressure at the tap was unusably low. It cost €12 a day to park here, almost campsite rates, and the parking machine wouldn't work with my bank card (possibly finger trouble as the Italian instructions weren't clear) so I paid with coins from our precious hoard.

After leaving Charlie to keep guard we went exploring and it was soon clear this town was a popular tourist destination with English and American voices heard everywhere.

Tourists need feeding so there were plenty of restaurants. We chose the Bar Dante as it had a good terrace overlooking the road. It was graded 12 out of 30 in TripAdvisor with good reviews.

We both ordered a mixed antipasto. It was varied and filling.

We finished the meal with our first Italian ice cream, vanilla with espresso for me, plain vanilla for Mary.

The choice of ice cream was limited, vanilla or chocolate were the main options, but it was tasty. Afterwards I felt I should have chosen something less obvious, the panna cotta with wild berries sounded tempting. With a litre of water, half a litre of house white the total bill was under €40.

I can recommend the Bar Dante, not only for the excellent food, but also for its toilet, which is worth a detour as the Michelin guides say. The throne sits on a raised pedestal and the sink has a foot operated tap, unusual features worth experiencing but the photographs on the walls elevated the place onto a higher level. I'm not sure of their origin, photographs from waitress interviews from days past? This is one of them but there were others.

After lunch Mary visited a cash machine which she emptied and then went shopping for a handbag and cashmere wrap. The meal was cheap by comparison.

After a quiet night on the *sosta* at Radda we drove southeast to Pienza, another smallish hilltop town popular with tourists and deservedly so from what we could see. Our arrival in Pienza was a slight surprise to us because we weren't intending to go there. However, we made use of the opportunity by stopping at a small supermarket with an even smaller car park. To escape, shopping completed, we reversed back onto the busy road, a fraught experience given the temperament of Italian drivers and velocity of their vehicles.

The place we were trying to find was somewhere in the countryside but the otherwise usually reliable CamperContact gave the wrong coordinates for it. The coordinates shown took us instead to a *sosta* within a car park in Pienza. This wasn't a bad place but it wasn't what we were looking for. Eventually I found a website with the correct coordinates and away we headed. The route this time involving a drive on a gravel track for several kilometres before arriving at Podere il Casale.

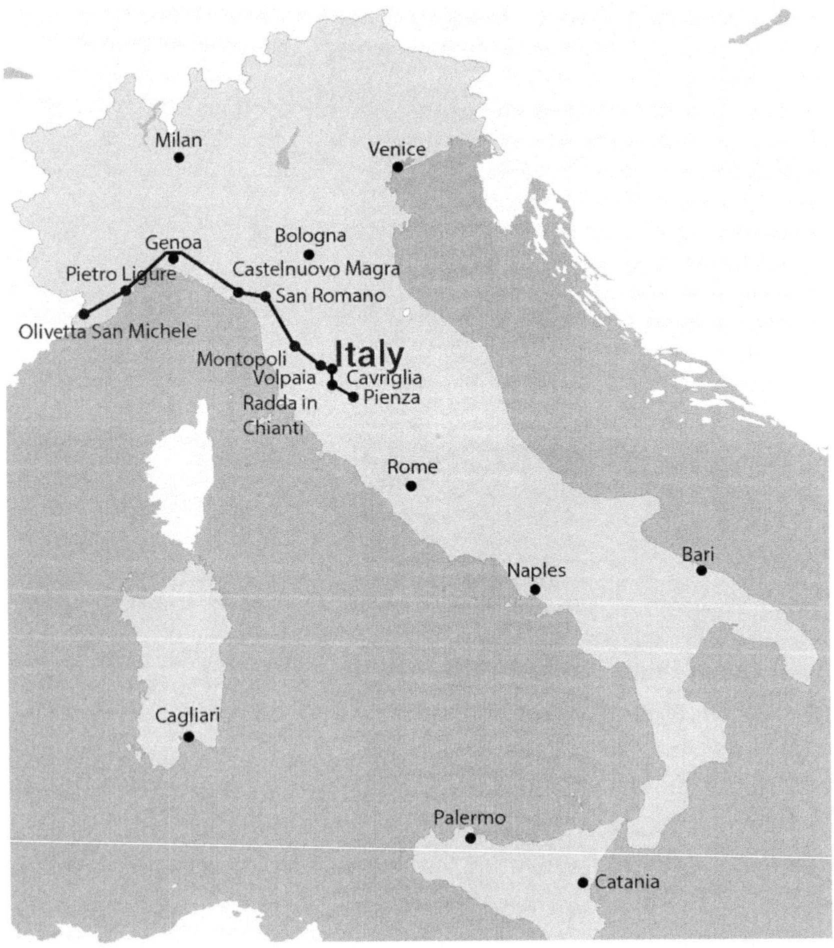

This was an organic farm on top of a hill with restaurant and accommodation. They ran courses on everything from bread making to truffle hunting and there were a handful of pitches for motorhomes and tents. The pitches were on gravel, useful as it rained heavily after we arrived but the water quickly drained away. Sadly the legions of flies returned even faster. The flies were attracted to the goats kept in a barn next to the camping area and so we moved pitch to get as far away from the goats and flies as it was possible to get.

We were on the northern edge of the Val d'Orcia, perhaps the "prettiest" part of Tuscany and the views from the restaurant terrace, reproduced in the image below, were exceptional. The mountain in the distance, above the low lying clouds, is Monte Amiata, described geologically as a larval dome, though reassuringly there has been no volcanic activity for about 300,000 years.

In the afternoon we experienced a further thunderstorm. It was brief but at its peak the flash from the lightning and the sound of the thunder was simultaneous. Between downpours we wandered around the farm and made a reservation for dinner in the restaurant for the evening. Thunder continued to sound all around us throughout the afternoon and into the night.

We entered the restaurant clutching umbrellas, it was in an old barn but not any old barn; there was a marble fireplace decorated with circus figures.

The figure on the left I thought was a wizard but a closer inspection revealed it to be a clown with an accordion. The wall lights in the restaurant are worth a mention. They struck me as an example of typical Italian design as we've had Italian lights at home in the past and they do have a certain look. These ones had a single horizontal light tube with chrome ends. They looked elegant until I noticed they looked like toilet roll holders. This detracted from their appeal though this wasn't the first restaurant we've been in with interesting toilet-themed fittings. Where we used to live in Kingsbridge in South Devon one restaurant had toilet seats made from clear resin containing a loop of barbed wire. It always gave you a jolt to see them in the gloom.

After ordering our starters they brought out a taster of ricotta and peas. It was delicately flavoured but helped build the anticipation.

Then we shared a plate of mixed cheeses from sheep, cow and goats and all different from each other. One for example was matured in crushed grape skins left over from winemaking, another with chilli in it. There was a set order for eating them, working clockwise from the youngest cheese. There were "dollops" of acacia and clover honey plus a chilli sauce. Honey with cheese was a new experience and it worked well. The menu offered another course of pasta between the starters and the main course, and we passed on it but this was a mistake as the portions weren't huge and on reflection I could have managed a plate of pasta. For the main course Mary chose the vegetarian option of deep fried courgette flowers with a courgette flan. It was tasty but the courgette flowers were so crisp they shattered when cut, sending edible shrapnel all over the table and surround bits of floor. I ate yummy grilled lamb served with chard or another sort of spring green as it was hard to identify.

For desserts we took the waitresses' recommendation; yoghurt mousse with berries. It too was good, the mousse was sweet but the berries had a sharp contrasting tang to them. However, before listening to the waitresses' sales pitch we'd set our hearts on the biscotti with a dessert wine. Given our regretted omission of the pasta course we had room for more. The solution to the Two Pudding Problem was easy, order a second pudding. When it arrived we were instructed on how to dunk the biscotti in the wine then eat it when it was softened. The wine was a fortified one and probably vile if drunk on its own but it did a good job of softening the biscuits.

When we got back to our motorhome at the end of the meal we found Charlie had elected himself to the role of travel critic and taken exception to one of our guide books. This was slightly annoying because though it was one I didn't use often it was the right thickness for putting under the coolbox to level it.

It might have been worse, no carpets or bedding were chewed and we could only have blamed ourselves if more damage had been done. Owners of vehicles leaving seven month old puppies in them unattended do so at their own risk.

It is worth mentioning we did not have much idea what the cost of our meal was as we were running up a tab. From what I could remember of the menu and including the litre of house red it would be around €80. We would settle everything on the morning we left and having witnessed Charlie's paper-shredding skills it seemed a good idea to bring him along when they presented us with the final reckoning.

Given the rain and thunder we had experienced yesterday it was with amazement we woke the following morning to find the sun shining when I took Charlie for his usual brief leg stretch at 06:45.

Unfortunately, dark clouds returned soon after breakfast but we decided a walk on the gravel roads surrounding us would be good. These roads deserve explanation. The roads between the villages and towns were normal metalled ones of the type you expect to find anywhere in Western Europe. But between these roads and linking the individual farms and estates was a network of gravelled roads. I have found similar networks in Brittany though the narrow roads amongst the fields in Germany are, with Germanic thoroughness often metalled.

We spent over an hour in high humidity walking from Podere il Casale to Monticchiello, another strikingly positioned hilltop village. It must have had a wall around it once but all that was left were square towers, several made into houses, and the original gateway.

It was a picture postcard place but without the tour buses of the nearby and much more famous Pirenza.

We could have eaten in Monticchiello but it looked like rain and though we were equipped for the wet walking back in a thunderstorm carrying metal framed umbrellas didn't appeal. So chucking the budget out of the window we went back for lunch in the Podere il Casale restaurant instead. It was a meal of two halves. The first course was a mixed salad, tasty after adding the farm's olive oil but not exciting; lettuce leaves with grated raw carrot and beetroot.

The game was saved by the second half of home-made *pici* (a thick spaghetti). Cooked more *al dente* than I do pasta at home but in fact was perfect. The *pici* was about the thickness of a decent sized lugworm tail if that helps imagine the size. But it was what the pasta was served with which clinched it, an intensely flavoured pork ragù. It was an exceptionally tasty dish. The meal was further enhanced by the entertainment provided by a dozen Americans on a pizza making course. This course costs €120 person if you are interested, lunch included but it is mean of me to poke fun at them as they were enjoying themselves and they in return must have thought we were a pair of miserable Brits, moaning over our salad and following it with a dish of worms.

We Decide to Go South

The weather forecast looked poor for the next few days and further north it looked even damper into the future foreseeable by long range weather forecasters. So we had a decision to make. Tuscany was as far south as we originally intended to go, the plan was then to turn around and head for Slovenia and Croatia but for perverse reasons we had lost our enthusiasm for Croatia. I know there is a lot to see there but did we want to drive so far to fight Germans over beach towels? There is much more to Croatia than beaches and I wanted to visit a town in Istria featured in a Jules Verne novel but Croatia would have to wait.

After discussing our options over and with a bottle of wine on our last evening we pushed on south and headed towards Puglia.

For completeness, the bill from Podere il Casale came to €205 for our two nights. This included one dinner, one lunch, the motorhome pitch and shopping (cheese and honey) on the morning we left. I gave them a generous rating of 7 on CamperContact but I suspect others might mark them a lot lower because of its poor facilities for waste disposal (the worst I've ever seen) and price. I couldn't speak with the owner before we left and didn't want to burden the young lady from Moldova in reception with too graphic a description of the waste disposal problem. They seem to do well teaching Americans how to make pizzas and the camping is a sideline.

On our last night there two young British cyclists turned up and pitched a tent. They started in the Netherlands and via Switzerland reached Italy and were on their way to Rome and then by ferry to Sardinia before returning through Corsica to Nice. A lovely adventure for them and it remains a regret I never managed a long ride in my cycling days. My travels in Europe are all motor-driven now.

From our current position we would aim for the Gargano peninsula, the spur sticking out above the heel of Italy. The peninsula is in the northern part of Puglia, the most southeasterly region of Italy. There is a lot to see in central Italy and Umbria is full of interest and less often visited compared to its more famous neighbour Tuscany but the weather trumps history so south we would go but in gentle stages as usual. We'd been away less than five weeks at this point with another six to go.

An earlier photograph showed Monte Amiata in the distance and our first halt after Podere il Casale was on the southern side of the mountain at a *sosta* in Santa Fiore, a town perched on the side of Monte Amiata. This mountain is the highest in southern Tuscany and it dominates the skyline all around the Val d'Orcia though the highest mountain in Tuscany is Monte Prado in the far north of the region. Eric Newby described crossing the Apennines as a prisoner of war on the run near Monte Prado in his book *Love and War in the Apennines*.

At first glance, as you walk in from the *sosta* at Santa Fiore it doesn't look much like a hilltop town. This is because the *sosta* is on what might be termed the uphill and new side of the town. The old town is built on a promontory reached by crossing a vertiginous bridge over a gorge.

The picture below is taken looking south into the valley of the river Firora. The walled pond beside the church is part of an

artificially constructed park called the *Peschiera* and the pond contains carp and other fish.

Inside the old town it was all the narrow streets I've shown photographs of before so for a change here is a shot of what I could see through someone's gate. Watering all those pots in the summer must be time consuming.

The following day our southward plunge continued with the use of a stretch of the A1 *autostrada* towards Rome and a good bit of tarmac it was, proving the Italian haven't forgotten their Roman ancestors' road building abilities. Before we joined the motorway we drove past Orvieto, a singularly spectacular town perched on a plateau with one of the finest cathedrals in Italy, the Duomo and a deep well reached by a double helix staircase. We could have stopped as there is a *sosta* near here but we were intent on going south, so couldn't stop. Which is nonsense, but the weather was too unreliable to linger.

Our target was the *sosta* near the Lago del Turano but when we got there it was uninspiring with no views of the lake and if this was France it would have been an *aire* with a neglected air.

So we chose instead the nearby lakeside parking at Colle di Tora on the other side of the Lago del Turano where we could park on the edge of the water and enjoy excellent views of Castel del Tora, a striking looking village.

I took Charlie to see the lake and he kept on walking into it and swam out and did a circle before returning to the shore. This was our first hint Charlie liked water and disliked heat. We were to be reminded of his heat allergy several times in the coming weeks and once in dramatic fashion.

The weather was dry when we started our little walk beside the lake but a flash of lightning and a crash of thunder suggested a hasty retreat to the motorhome. It was a wise decision as it was raining heavily by the time I got back with an already lake sodden dog.

The rain, with hail included for a time, lasted only briefly but it turned the track we were parked beside into the river you can see in the picture below. Our front wheels were probably under water but I was happy to take this on trust as venturing outside to get photographic evidence was not an attractive option during the cloudburst. The rain stopped and within ten minutes everything was just as before the onslaught. The river vanished but not before it caused damage to the start of the track which workman repaired the following day just in time for us to leave.

The Apennine Mountains lay in our path and to reach the east coast we needed to cross them. We did this using the modern motorway which took us close to the port of Pescara on the Adriatic coast. Though using a motorway is not the best way to get to know a country this was an interesting drive as we crossed over and through the Apennines. There were many tunnels, the longest five and a half kilometres and impressive bridges to rival anything I have seen say on the motorway along the north coast of Spain. What we didn't appreciate while crossing the Apennines is how geologically active this region is. Our lakeside spot at the tranquil Colle di Tora was only about fifty kilometres south of the village of Amatrice where over two hundred people were to lose their lives in an earthquake two months later. We had also been fifty kilometres northwest of Avezzano where over thirty thousand died in a magnitude 7.0 earthquake in 1915. But earthquakes in Italy are not confined to just this region. In 1908 an earthquake followed by a tsunami in

Sicily claimed over eighty thousand lives and in recent times nearly a thousand were killed in an earthquake in the extreme northeast of Italy in the Friuli Venezia region in 1976.

On reaching the coast near Pescara we turned southeast stopping for lunch at Marina Di Chieuti. This looked run down and with the beach choked with plastic litter we decided not to find a *sosta* here, the original plan, but continue on to Gargano.

The next bit of road was interesting. It was an old main road superseded by an *autostrada* but still used by trucks. The haulage traffic may be why all along the side of the road young ladies were standing every kilometre. They may have been waiting for a bus but somehow I doubt it. A few of the more enterprising or experienced had plastic chairs and shade but most were standing under the full glare of the sun. It was difficult to tell their nationalities but I would be surprised if any of them were Italian though those controlling the trade would have been Italian. The nearest mafia to Gargano are a very violent group in Foggia but Naples was not far away and the Neapolitan mafia of Naples are the well-known Camorra. Then again we were near the toe of Italy where the fearsome 'Ndrangheta hold sway. This was of academic interest only as I was much more focussed on drinking a cold beer so we left these ladies to their lonely sad vigils and drove directly east onto the Gargano peninsula.

I drank my cold beer in the evening at a campsite in an old olive grove near the village of Peschici. The village was draped attractively over the hillside above us, looking like one of the white villages of Andalusia. Peschici has at least one commercial *sosta* but it was cheaper in the campsite where we could sit under the welcome shade of the olives.

We woke the following morning to find genuine wall to wall blue sky we could celebrate only one way; by going for a walk. Due to minor necessities like running a load in the camp washing machine we didn't leave until late morning. Peschici is on top of a hill and there are many sets of steps to choose from to take you to the top. When we reached it we found the place highly commercialised.

We've visited several Italian towns and villages perched on hills but this was the first where every house was converted into a retail outlet or a restaurant. It wasn't too tacky but it was hard to see the original town underneath the merchandising.

The climb up rewarded us with wide view of the bay and the busy beach.

After walking up to the top in the sun Charlie was feeling hot. His coat is thick and it must have been like wearing a duvet. We gave him water but he kept stopping and trying to lie in the shadows. By gently coaxing we almost got him to the beach but suddenly two dogs ran towards him, a little yappy one but the second, a much bigger animal promptly attacked Charlie. No damage was done and the owner ran up and dragged them away. Charlie walked on a few paces then promptly keeled over, kicking his legs with his jaw opening and shutting. I thought he was having a fit so I picked him up and he recovered almost immediately in my arms. I carried him to the water's edge where he walked in and sat soaking and cooling until he seemed fully recovered. We'd just confirmed, and in the most alarming way, Charlie did not cope well with heat. Thankfully we learned this without a fatality but from now on it looked like gentle walks only for him and no excitement like getting into fights with other dogs.

On a happier note we subsequently left Charlie in charge of the motorhome during the evening and everything remained intact. We'd taken steps to tidy everything away so there were no books or maps left lying around to tempt him to adopt his critical personae. We left him so we could visit the camp restaurant where we had been assured there was a pizza chef from Naples. Our expectations were raised as soon as we arrived at the restaurant when we saw a proper pizza oven glowing like a wood-burning blast furnace. The pizzas did not disappoint when they arrived. They were unlike anything I've eaten in the UK. The toppings were thinly applied, in the Neapolitan way, but they were delicious despite having no obvious herbs such as the shaken on dried oregano we use at home. With a half-litre of house wine and a coffee our meal came to under €20. This exposure to Neapolitan pizzas subsequently changed the way I make them at home. We had traditionally made Sicilian pizzas with thick crusts, lots of toppings and baked on a metal tray. A Neapolitan pizza is much thinner and with sparser toppings and ideally needs to be cooked in a few moments in a very hot pizza oven. Lacking one of these I have improvised and the technique I arrived at by trial, error and reading was to turn the oven on to its highest temperature setting using the elements at the bottom of the oven only. I then roll out the pizza dough onto a non-stick "Teflon" cooking mat after sparingly adding the toppings then place it the lowest shelf of the oven. The pizza cooks from below, as it would in a pizza oven and the subsequent pizzas are readily consumed by the family so I assume others find them as delicious as I do. I have more recently upped my game further and bought a pizza stone and make the dough with only a little yeast, one or to grams for 500g of flour and allow the dough to develop in the refrigerator for 3 of 4 days. The long proving adds considerably to the flavour and texture of the finished pizza base.

On our last morning at Peschici I wandered around the campsite photographing the old olives. Their bark was highly figured in places.

My first guess of their age was something around two hundred years but they could be considerably older and were planted far apart and sometimes in pairs or threes. Grouping olive trees like this I'd seen in Spain with young trees so it must be deliberate. Olives can grow to immense age. In Crete there is a tree believed to be at least two thousand years old and possibly twice that. Accurate dating of the tree is impossible as the heartwood has rotted away although the tree continues to bear fruit.

But apart from the old trees there wasn't a lot to keep us at Peschici so we moved on to near the tip of the Gargano peninsula to a campsite ideally placed right above a pleasant beach. To reach it we drove through Vieste, the main town of Gargano. Sadly we didn't see it at its best as a strong wind was blowing and dust filled the air as we passed through it.

Gargano may be unknown to many current day visitors to Italy but this was not the case in the past. On the southern flanks of the peninsula lies Monte Sant'Angelo where, to give it its full name is the Sanctuary of Monte Sant'Angelo sul Gargano. Around 490 the Archangel Michael appeared here several times in a cave before the Bishop of Siponto, a coastal town to the south. The angel said the cave should become a place of Christian worship and he would protect Siponto (or Sipontum as it was known then) from pagan invaders. A few years later the reigning pope caused a basilica to be erected around the cave and over the years the Sanctuary and Monte Sant'Angelo has built up around it. The site was a popular pilgrimage site for pilgrims heading for Jerusalem and it has been visited by many popes including recently John Paul II and numerous kings, queens and saints before him. Francis of Assisi considered himself unworthy to enter the grotto and stayed outside to pray. Ownership of the area changed several times throughout its history. For example, less than a hundred years after the angel appeared the Lombards conquered most of Italy. The Lombards sound Italian as their name is given to a region in northern Italy and the Lombardy poplar is to be found almost everywhere, but they originated from Scandinavia and came to Italy by way of modern day Germany and Austria where they first settled. The Lombards were eventually conquered by the Normans, yet another tribe originating from Scandinavia.

The Norman conquest of Italy was a long drawn out affair, unlike their invasion of the British Isles where the matter was settled with a sharp arrow and one decisive battle.

The site had a large bar but we visited it only once as our waistlines couldn't have coped with a second visit. Sitting at a table on the terrace I ordered two glasses of wine. When the waitress came with them she brought three huge bowls of nibbles, think breakfast cereal sized bowls; nuts, cheese biscuits and at least fifty olives. It seemed disrespectful to send them back uneaten, so the crisps and cheese biscuits were dispatched but there were just too many olives. I like olives but you would have to be a serious fan of them to eat fifty at a sitting.

Directly below our pitch was a broad shingle beach which Charlie enjoyed immensely.

While walking along the beach on another afternoon I saw number of gulls on the water. They looked dark and I wondered if they were an exotic and rare gull. After peering at them through binoculars I decided they were immature herring gulls. Had they been this would have been a sighting of a rarity because herring gulls are not found this far south. They were later identified by my brother as yellow legged gulls, similar to herring gulls except for the eponymous legs and in my defence these can't be seen if the bird is floating on the sea.

Charlie was oblivious to all this.

What you can't see in the photograph was the fan was set on a high speed and all his fur and uppermost ear were waving in the breeze. The fan is an Endless Breeze model and though expensive it is the best 12 volt fan you can buy.

The Gargano peninsula where we stayed on this long weekend is a great area to visit if you can find a good campsite, as we were lucky enough to do. The peninsula protrudes a hundred kilometres into the Adriatic and is surrounded by sea on three sides. This gives it clean water and makes it cooler here in summer than the rest of the coast. A welcome characteristic of the location is litter on the coast was virtually non-existent. Sadly this can't be said for much of the rest of the Italian coast.

Trulli Delightful

Leaving the Gargano peninsula we followed the coast to a point almost halfway along the stiletto heel of Italy.

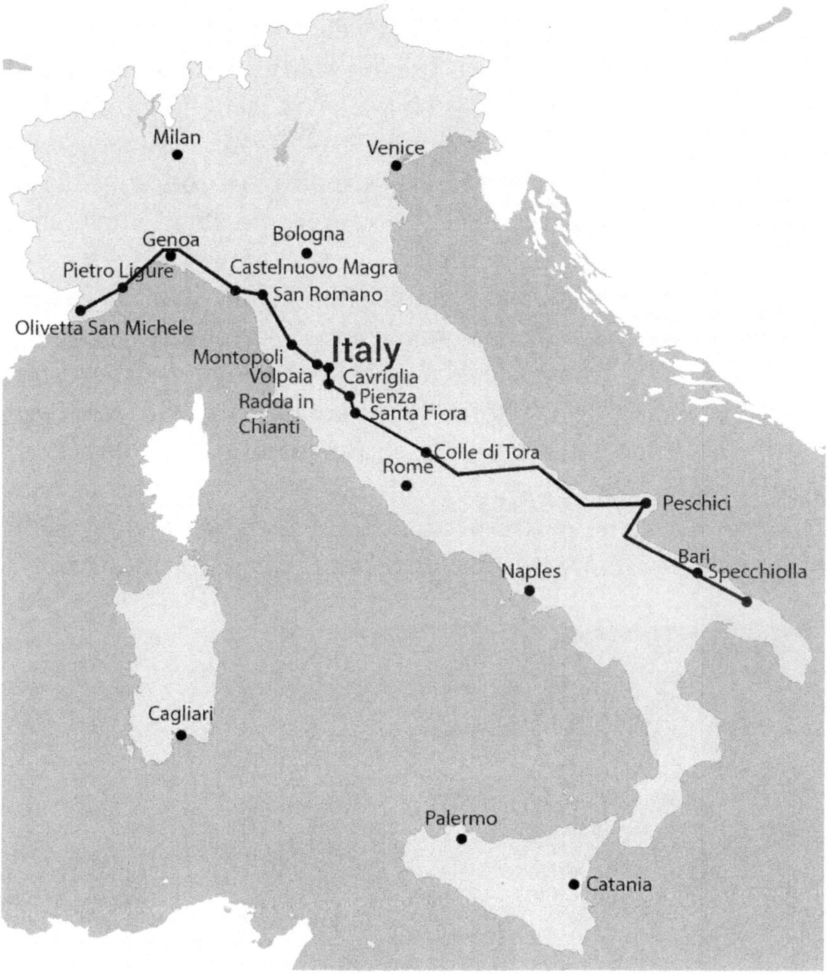

We were at the southernmost point we would reach this year and for no good reason we were staying at an uninspiring campsite near an uninspiring coast. All the signs were there on the map to suggest this was a boring bit. A long straight coastline with no hills inland and no wiggly roads on the map should have been sufficient warning.

There are things to see further south including Greek ruins but we had passed the psychological halfway point in terms of time so we turned around and started back. Sicily and the other interesting bits beyond would have to wait for another day. We resolved to return and the following year we did.

Our reason for going even this far south is explained by the painful pun in the title of this chapter. We were here to see the trulli houses. The trulli (singular: trullo) are curious round houses with conical roofs and are at their most concentrated in the small town of Alberobello. However, we slightly overshot the trulli so after one night on the coast we moved again for two nights at the aptly named Camping dei Trulli. This was a site with a clientele of German motorhomes, several Swiss and a lone Dutchman. Unusually, given what we found elsewhere, not a single Italian motorhome was here. Only the northern Europeans it seemed wanted to see the quaint trulli houses.

We arrived by a scenic route avoiding the coastal dual carriageway, going past Ostuni, a white town perched on a hill surrounded by impressively old and well cultivated olive groves.

Trulli houses are found throughout this region and we saw several on the way to the campsite. Many looked as if they had only been recently and no doubt expensively converted into private houses or holiday homes.

The campsite was about a kilometre and a half from Alberobello on a busy road but with the help of Google maps on my 'phone I found a quiet route on back roads. Which I explored alone soon after we arrived as far as the outskirts of Alberobello. The campsite runs a shuttle bus but if it was not too hot the following morning we decided we would walk in.

On my exploratory walk I found some abandoned trulli houses in the lanes.

The external roof photograph below shows how they were constructed. First an inner layer of blocks are placed which are self-supporting like the roof of an igloo. Then a layer of rubble is added topped by the flat stones to keep the rain off and give these houses their distinctive appearance.

Here's another abandoned hobbit house ready for renovation.

The houses above were in the countryside but in Alberobello there are something like fifteen hundred trulli.

This rooftop shot of part of Alberobello shows how closely packed they are, sticking up above the more modern buildings.

Parts of Alberobello were quiet. These are holiday or second homes I think.

But other bits were much more touristy with shops selling the usual stuff they think tourists want.

Charlie survived the walk despite temperatures approaching 30°C. We gave him lots of drinks and regularly poured water over him, he enjoyed this and it worked best for cooling him

In the picture above he's standing beside one of several public water taps dotted around the town. And then it was our turn to cool off. Lemon and pistachio and yummy.

The origin of the trulli houses is not known for certain. The popular explanation is they were built without mortar so they could be dismantled quickly when the tax inspector showed up. This sounds convincing until you realise many of the houses are not old. A photograph from the late 19th century shows much fewer trulli houses in Alberobello than there are today. An unexplained building explosion of trulli occurred in the early 20th century before they were later abandoned as folk moved to larger houses or drifted away from the area. It is possible trulli houses are just a useful way of using the local limestone cluttering the fields and are cool in summer.

Heading North

After leaving Alberobello we drove to the *autostrada* and put a few miles in before stopping around mid-afternoon at a *sosta* west of the Gargano Peninsula. We chose Agriturismo Padre Pio Girvane near Chieuti, inland from the coast and above the coastal plain.

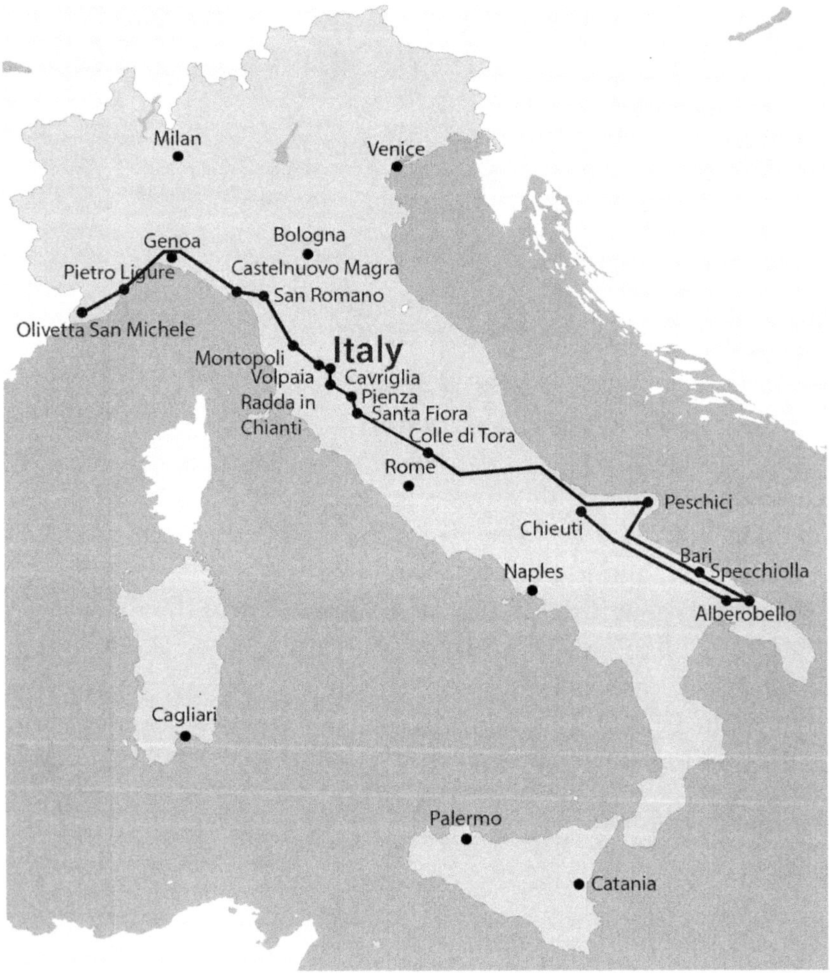

My Italian being non-existent beyond ordering a limited range of food and drinks I never found out the reason for the name of the place. Padre Pio was a Twentieth Century saint and one of the most popular saints in the world. He died in 1968 and canonised soon afterwards in 2002. You will see images of him all over Italy including Sicily.

CamperContact described this place as having all the usual waste dumping facilities but it didn't. I spoke to two people including someone who I think was the manager and both agreed this was "a problem".

However, it is smart with a long tree-lined drive and about half a dozen gravel pitches with electricity, or not electricity as I thought when we first plugged in as the usual lights didn't light up. On investigation I discovered our main circuit breaker had tripped. When checking all this I found our solar panels weren't charging either. All this I hasten to add in high heat and humidity convinced me I would look at the solar panel problem in the cool of the next morning.

While waiting until supper time I heard a melodious warbling in a tree, so with a long lens fitted I searched for the culprit. The bird remained deep in the canopy of a walnut but the briefest flash of yellow confirmed my suspicion based on its skulking habit; a Golden Oriole.

We ate in the restaurant and it was a different experience to our previous meal out. It was nothing elaborate, just good tasty cooking and large portions. The Italian phrase *cucina casalinga* means "home cooking" and describes our meal perfectly. The word *nostrano* could also be applied. It means "local" and this food was. These words can all be found in Eric Newby's books about Italy and do not reflect a sudden increase in my knowledge of the language.

The starters were a delicate ham and sweet melon dish. Not original but the ham wasn't like the renowned Parma variety you sometimes need sharpened teeth to eat, this was much softer. I then had dish of pasta, tomato and basil, Mary declined on the basis of stomach capacity but they brought her an empty plate so she could steal from mine. It was good pasta and another reminder how *al dente* they serve it in Italy. The dish would have been sent back to the kitchen in the UK as uncooked.

For our main course I chose grilled chicken and Mary fillet of beef sliced thinly and served cold with parmesan shavings and balsamic vinegar. I think she made the best choice though my chicken was equally tasty. Both dishes were served on a bed of rocket.

We finished with ice cream and coffee. Total bill €40 with a bottle of wine made on the estate. Even the pasta was made using grain from their fields.

When we returned from our meal I dusted off the TV, which we hadn't used since leaving the UK, to see if we could find anything on BBC World about the EU Referendum vote which was held today. But the TV was silent so something was wrong and another matter to be investigated in the morning.

We were woken at five thirty by the dog being sick (the joy of puppies) so after cleaning up we made a pot of tea and checked online for the Referendum results.

We showered in the motorhome but before it was my turn I rummaged in the back of the wardrobe, getting hot and sweaty even this early in the morning, to check the fuses. I'd already studied the wiring diagram in the Murvi manual and one fuse fed both the TV (defunct) and solar panel (not charging) and as I hoped this fuse was blown. I changed it from the stock I carry (I have been in this position before) and by magic both the solar panel and the TV, if we wanted to watch it, sprang into life. I never found out what blew the fuse or tripped the circuit breakers but everything was working.

We made another long drive of nearly three hundred kilometres stopping at an excellent Dutch owned campsite near Monteciccardo.

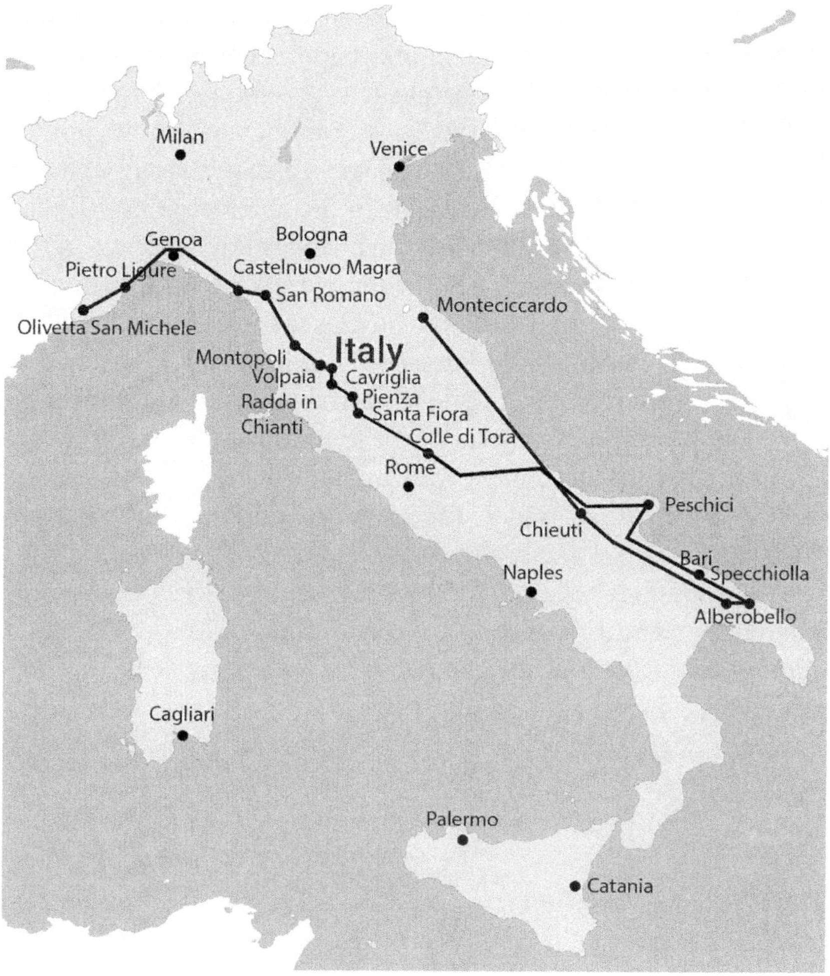

This was the furthest north we would go on the Italian east coast. After here we would turn inland and head north for the Dolomites.

Being Dutch owned the site was full of visiting Dutch with a few Germans and us as the loan UK representatives. The first conversation with the owners was about a Referendum result they found incomprehensible.

The site was excellent but the heat and humidity was uncomfortable. Luckily we were on a fully serviced pitch with water and waste point within easy reach, reducing the need for me to walk far. The toilet blocks were small but there were a lot of them dotted all around the site so again it wasn't far to walk for a shower. This site had masses more character than the nearby and not so nearby coastal sites.

Friday and most of Saturday were uncomfortably hot. It wasn't the actual temperature, though it peaked at about 32°C but the humidity was high. We sat in the shade reading all day. Even going on a short walk with the dog was hot work.

In the early evening of Saturday clouds built up, thunder rumbled distantly then as I was having my evening shower the rain arrived. It only lasted twenty minutes and I watched it from my shower cubicle, the door of which opened onto the site.

When it stopped I returned to the motorhome to find Mary coped well with the deluge and hadn't got too wet while she shovelled furniture under the awning, closing windows and skylights.

It was much pleasanter the next day, hot but the air was clear and the humidity back to comfortable levels. I tried photographing one of the many lizards scurrying around. They were wary blighters and easily spooked.

Lakes and Dolomites

The lure of moving to somewhere cooler was strong so the next day we drove to Lake Corlo in the foothills of the Dolomites and a place described as "the most peaceful campsite in the world".

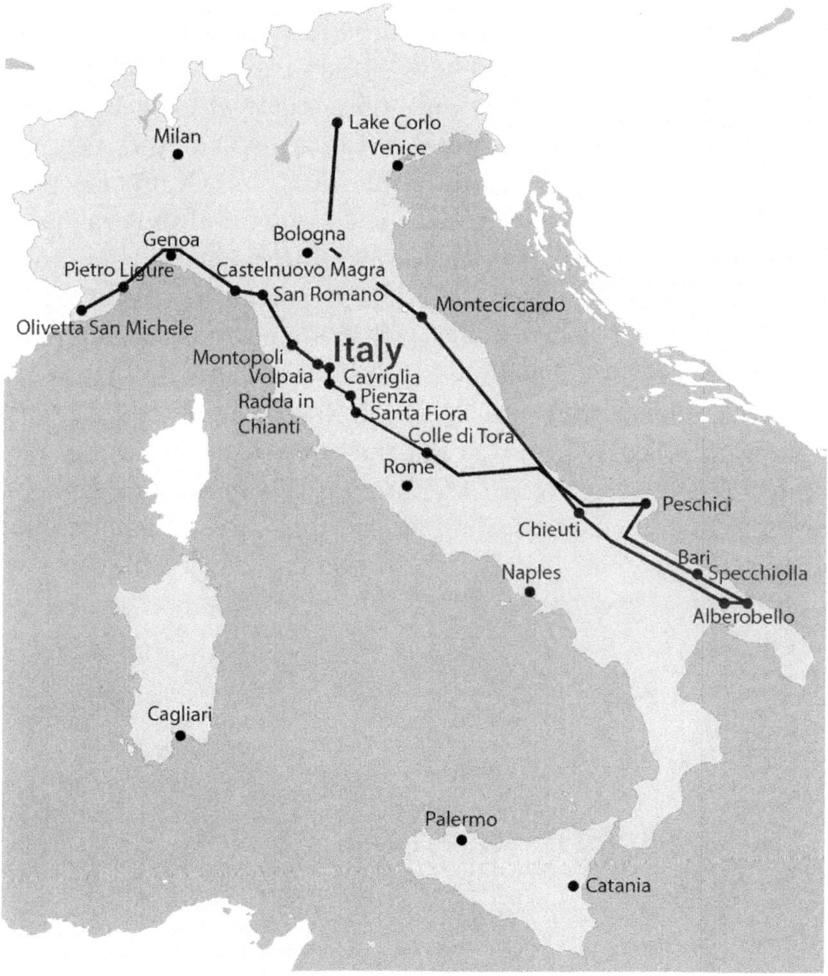

We used *autostrada* almost all the way and found them safe by Italian standards and with a better surface than the rest of the Italian road network. It wasn't too expensive, about €20 on tolls but if we'd normal roads it would have taken two days. We planned to reach the Dolomites in two stages but the *sosta* around Parma, where we would have stopped, sounded unexciting. They were car parks and the thought of arriving at one in the heat of the day wasn't attractive. There are lots of campsites south of Venice but driving through the afternoon in our air conditioned cab was a more attractive option than sitting still in the heat so we pressed on for the mountains.

I would have liked to explore around Parma, if only for the cheese and ham. It would have been instructive to see if in Parma their famed ham is any more easily chewed than the stuff they export but I think a visit to Parma will need a cooler time of the year for us wilting wallflowers. In fact my question was answered the following year when we stayed in Soragna, a town close to Parma on our way to Sicily. Parma ham from Parma and ideally when served with a glass of red wine is excellent and not chewy. If you have the opportunity seek it out.

Camping Gaiole was directly beside lake Corlo and we soon explored along a path running beside the shore of the lake. For a path on a lake side it was not flat with steep bits where the path climbed up and over rock outcrops. There were good views of the lake in places and where the surface was smooth and not disturbed by birds, fish or swimming dogs there were picturesque reflections.

We enjoyed a pleasant walk with lots of butterflies flying about and flowers flowering and a brief moment of excitement when we caught a fleeting glimpse of a snake. Greenish and without obvious markings it might have been an Aesculapian snake, but probably wasn't as my knowledge of European snakes is non-existent. The habitat was about right, mountainous, but a five second glimpse is hardly definitive. The Aesculapian snake is named after Asclepius, the Greek (and later Roman) god of healing. Classical depictions of the god show a snake entwined around his staff and this symbol of snake and staff is widely linked to medicine today, for example in the cap badge of the Royal Army Medical Corps.

The following day we explored further along the path to the curiously named village of Arsié. We left at half nine to avoid the worst of the heat which had followed us from the south.

Arsié wasn't the most exciting of destinations but we sat at an outside table in the centre of the village at a bar and enjoyed a cold drink and an ice-cream.

Charlie found the walk back hot work. He repeatedly flattened himself against the ground in any shady spot. When we returned to the lake he knew what he wanted to do. Why walk to boring villages when there are sticks to fetch from the water? Later, in the early evening I saw another snake. Though again visible only for a fraction of a second I could see it was distinctive because it was black. A Western Whip Snake I thought. These are usually green and yellow (I've seen them in France) but there is a larger black variant in Italy and Malta. Regarded as non-venomous they can bite and have a reputation for being aggressive. The pair I saw in France crouched under a bush and hissed loudly at me.

We didn't move far from Lake Corlo to our next halt, forty kilometres as the crow flies but it was to take us over two hours climbing past spectacular Dolomite scenery.

The road went over the Passo di Rolle but I couldn't found much about it in English on Google but it is well known to German, Swiss and Italian bikers because there were dozens of them going over it. The road has a smooth surface and numerous hairpin bends and with light traffic, apart from the motorbikes, it was fun driving even in our motorhome.

We stopped for the weekend at a campsite near the village of Predazzo. There were lots of walks from the site into the surrounding forest, so we resolved, weather permitting to enjoy some exercise over the weekend. The weather was finally cooler and Charlie would enjoy the walks.

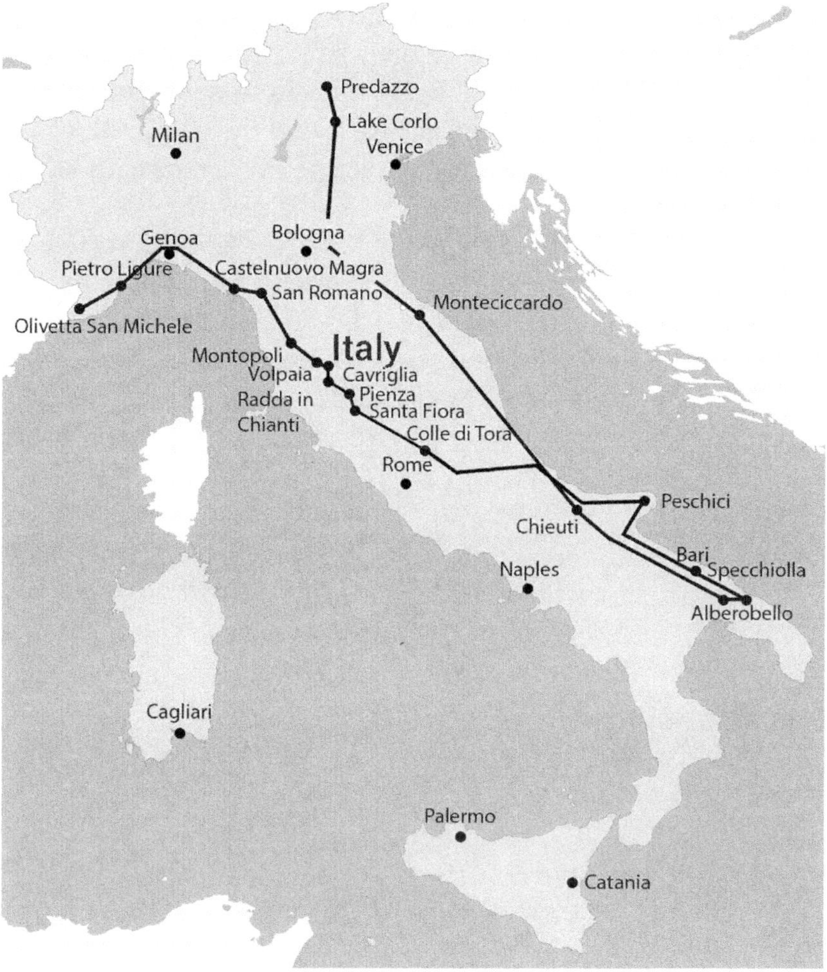

It rained overnight but we woke the next morning to blue sky though with clumps of low cloud down to treetop level in places. These quickly burned off and at ten we started on a circular walk of seven and a half kilometres.

We should have learned to distrust free campsite maps, even the one we were given by reception here. It resembled a copy of the Italian version of the Ordnance Survey and looked authoritative but the first part of the walk wasn't drawn well and we were forced to backtrack several hundred yards and lose height to get on the right path. Once we realised we were following a GR route it was much easier to navigate following the red and white marks. The problem was the map showed the path as a straight line going directly south and a track, marked correctly for the start of the walk, went in this direction but it was a dead end and coming back we found the GR sneaking off into the trees. This climbed in a zigzag up the mountain not shown on the map.

But it was a pleasant walk; humid at first, becoming cooler as we ascended. At the top of the zigzag path was a font with cold water and a wooden refuge hut. There was a wide variety of flowers, including lilies and a profusion of common spotted orchids. The walk was level for a while then gradually descending for about two kilometres until we were above the local town of Predazzo.

The descent from here was steep and a repeat of the ascent with a zigzag path through the trees. The path at the beginning had been recently strimmed but the bottom half was heavily overgrown so we not only got wet from the grass but it was hard to see where to put your feet amongst the rocks and tree roots. Our walking poles were useful at this point.

We joined a road before entering the town and found wild strawberries growing on the verge. Seeing us eat a few Charlie got the idea he should try them. With much lip smacking he decided they were good for dogs and foraged for them himself.

From Predazzo we returned to the campsite along a path by the stream. Although only seven and a half kilometres long and with four hundred metres of ascent it was a demanding but satisfying walk.

The next day we took a gentle stroll back into Predazzo, using a forest track beside the stream. Predazzo was a pleasant little town with good shops catering for the many tourists who visit. Compared to most of southern Italy this was a prosperous area. We woke on Sunday to the prospect of more rain so my idea of a long walk on my own was shelved. This was disappointing but when it rained the clouds covered the mountain tops and made route finding tricky and when I got to the top I was aiming for there would have been zero view.

So we drove to one of the less popular Italian lakes, Lago d'Idro, west of the much larger and considerably more popular and well known Lake Garda. Camping Venus was directly on the lake shore and with an altitude of about three hundred and fifty metres it was noticeably warmer in the evenings compared to our last stop in the mountains.

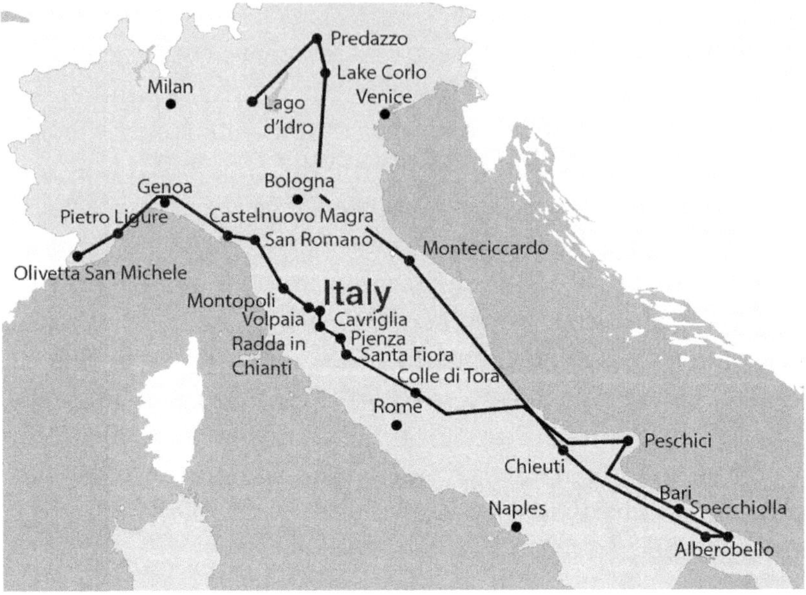

The following morning after yet more overnight rain there were clouds hanging about but the weather prospects looked good. This is the view looking up the lake from the shore at the campsite.

Yet another path along the shore took us around the bottom of the lake and over a bridge into Lemprato, a village well stocked with bars and cafes for its size. We ate pizzas at the Bar Pizzeria Cinzia sitting at a nicely shaded outside table as the sun was shining strongly. The pizzas were huge and bigger than the plates they were served on. Two pizzas, half a litre of house red and a big bottle of water came to €19.50. I didn't realise until later there was a face on my pizza made using anchovies.

After lunch I tried to take photographs of the bird life on the lake. A pair of juvenile great crested grebes remained tantalisingly too far away but the coots were more trusting.

Return to France

From the Italian Lakes we headed directly west using the *autostrada* for most of the way. The road was busy with trucks outnumbering cars at least five to one. Our route skirted the busy cities of Milan and Turin and was a main artery for trucks reaching southwest Europe.

I identified a few potentially good *sosta* along the route and stopping at one would have shortened the day but with temperatures hovering over 30°C and high humidity we yet again stayed in our air conditioned vehicle and drove through the afternoon to somewhere cooler. This we found at an altitude of eighteen hundred and fifty metres inside France on the Col du Montgenèvre. This is a well-known historical route and was used by Julius Caesar on his march to Gaul and possibly, though there are other contenders, by Hannibal going in the other direction on his ultimately unsuccessful mission to return to the Romans what they had been giving to the rest of Europe. It is an important crossing point between France and Italy and unusually the French customs post was manned and vehicles were being stopped as they entered France. A consequence I suspect of the movement of refugees entering Europe.

The *aire* had electric points and the water taps were all inside a building where they wouldn't freeze. Both hints this was a place largely used in the skiing season.

We wouldn't have needed the electricity for a single overnight stop but our refrigerator was still proving reluctant to stay lit when turned to gas so I didn't hesitate plugging in.

The next morning Charlie, who hadn't been 100% yesterday woke us early and was keen to get outside. I won't describe the subsequent events but they were messy. I think the problem stemmed from the Italian lake at the last stop. He loves to play with sticks and stones and when paddling in the lake on our last afternoon he took it upon himself to dredge a large pebble up and he kept putting his head under the water to pick it up in his mouth. The clear water was soon cloudy and I suspect he swallowed a lot of it together with sundry single-celled organisms now passing through him.

From the Col du Montgenèvre we drove the first part of the next day down the Durance valley. We first met the Durance earlier near Les Mées of the penitent rocks and the source of the river is at Montgenèvre where we spent the previous night.

We soon passed through Briançon, the highest town in Europe they claim at 1,320m and an interesting looking place. There are major fortifications either side of the valley reflecting the importance of the Col de Montgenèvre as a border crossing. Briançon may be the highest town in Europe but it is lower than the highest village in Europe. This honour is claimed by Ushguli in Georgia at 2,100m. It is a debatable point whether Georgia, on the eastern shores of the Black Sea is a European country. They have competed in the Eurovision song contest a few times with mixed results and not without political controversy. In 2009 they withdrew their entry when the organisers asked for changes to the song mentioning Vladimir Putin. Taking part in Eurovision doesn't give geographical credence to their being part of Europe as opposed to Asia but I wouldn't reject any claim from Georgia to be part of Europe. They need friends. Georgia is an isolated country, cut off from the rest of us by a large chunk of Russia and with a breakaway western region, Abkhazia, aligned with their northern neighbour and creating a situation unlikely to be resolved for a long time.

The colour of the upper Durance was the unique milky blue you see from rivers fed from high mountains and melting snow. We left it at the Lac de Serre Ponçon, a large reservoir of an intensely blue colour. Soon afterwards we passed through Gap, the chief town of the Haute Alps where a busy open air market was being held. Gap is another town with a colourful history. The origin of the name is obscure, tempting though it is to think of the "gap of Gap" as being a mountain pass. Neolithic evidence has been found in the area but Gap didn't come into existence until the Romans built a fort here. Occupied by the Saracens for a while it almost ceased to exist in 1692 when troops of the Duke of Savoy started a fire destroying all but a few houses. Rebuilding didn't start until nearly thirty years later. Gap was then honoured, at least by those living there by a brief visit from Napoleon after he escaped from Elba. He returned to France by the Alps, avoiding the Rhone valley, a Royalist stronghold and local tradition holds he tried unblocking the chimney in his room on the night of 5 March, 1815 by firing a pistol up it. The resulting noise and clouds of smoke and soot made those in the street outside believe Napoleon had been murdered until he put his head out of the window to explain what happened. It was only a reprieve, Napoleon's career did not last much longer, ending on the 18th June the same year in what is now Belgium, south of Brussels at Waterloo.

The last part of the day's journey was through the Gorge de Sainte May. This is a gorge for those unhappy with steep drops as the road is only twenty feet above the river and the cliffs above the road, though vertical, are not high.

It had been a picturesque day of travel and I can strongly recommend this region of France. There is wonderful scenery and it isn't too hot in summer due to the altitude.

From the Haute Alps we stopped for the night in a different region at the Ferme de la Condamine near Bresignan. This was another great *aire*. It was free with a proper motorhome service point and it was on a lavender farm as we had reached the lavender fields of Provence.

The only charge was an optional €3 for electricity and we readily paid due to Mr Dicky Fridge. There was also a moral obligation to buy something from their little shop stocking all things lavender.

Besides being in CamperContact the farm was part of the France Passion network. This is a grouping of farms, small holdings and vineyards offering parking for motorhomes around France. Unfortunately, many of the entries in the large (and expensive) France Passion book do not offer waste disposal points or even a water tap but this place did and we made use of the service point as soon as we arrived. When we stopped for lunch earlier in the day Charlie found something exceptionally smelly to roll in so we drove all afternoon with the ventilation on full to keep the smells at the rear of the motorhome. Shampoo followed by a rinse with cold water at the service point restored him to a more acceptable condition to share the same space as us overnight.

The lavender in the fields surrounding us wasn't fully in bloom and we could hardly smell anything when we first arrived but the next morning we could readily detect the distinctive scent in the air and when I looked more closely at the flowers they were covered in honey bees.

These came from over sixty hives in a nearby copse and inevitably we bought a pot of lavender honey from the shop on the farm before we left, together with several other lavender-themed items. One purchase was a lavender oil Mary uses to make room freshener spray, mixing a few drops of the oil with water. Economical and with a genuine as opposed to chemical smell of lavender.

Leaving the lavender farm we drove through the Gorge de l'Ardèche which is nearly thirty kilometres long by road and well used to tourists. There are several viewing platforms or *balcons* dotted the length of the valley where you can stop and look into the gorge. With my brother I cycled this route a few years earlier. Driving it made me realise how many steep hills there were. I couldn't do it now. I have lost my cycling legs, such as I ever had.

The sides of the gorge are steep in places. The *balcon* I was standing on to take this picture was on the edge of a cliff like the one on the left.

The river is popular with canoeists. They start from Vallon Pont d'Arc at the head of the gorge where there are numerous companies renting out canoes. The idea is you float down the river and are picked up at the bottom and brought back to the start. From a board I saw trips varied in length from eight to thirty kilometres.

The drive through the gorge is best started from Vallon because the *balcons* will then be on your right so you won't, unlike us, have to cross the traffic to park. Fortunately, there wasn't much traffic coming the other way and intriguingly half of what we saw seemed to have come from Belgium. The journey is easy except the bit near Vallon where there are narrow unlit tunnels (one with a 3.5m height limit) and fearsome looking rock overhangs where the road has been cut into the cliff. But once passed these the driving is easier with no sense of vertigo as the road doesn't follow the gorge edge but is set back and the view is often obscured by bushes. To see into the gorge you have to stop and get out at a viewing point.

There are numerous campsites at Vallon and we chose one intending to stay for two nights to catch up with the laundry. It was only after we arrived did I discover we were in the wrong one. I had chosen the ACSI listed Camping de L'Ardèch but we turned too early into another site just before it as I had forgotten the name of the place we were aiming for. This was a double mistake as we soon found the site was soulless and lacked interesting dog walks for Charlie. The dog might not speak but he casts his proxy vote through me and he voted for a move. So the next day we did.

It wasn't far in distance but it took nearly three hours, dodging the endless stream of Belgian cars coming towards us. Our route took us first through Saint Jean du Gard, where we stayed on the *aire* with the disappearing steam train on our outward journey but today we didn't stop, taking the road along the Corniche des Cèvennes. From the map this looks as if it must follow a gorge as it has so many twists and turns but it crosses over several small passes amongst low hills, reaching a maximum altitude of only around 700m. It is an attractive region and the road climbs at first through a forest of sweet chestnut and pine. The driving was easy on the wide road though there were many sharp bends. We saw little evidence of cultivation other than in a few places where the top of the hills were flat.

At the end of our journey we stopped outside Florac on an excellent site beside the river Tarn. The lady in reception had an American father so naturally her English was good.

We found a spot tucked away in a quiet corner. There were about five other British couples on the site though they were nearer the river where the site was busier. The water in the Tarn running beside the site was clear and not too cold. We resolved to have a swim in it the following day after walking the four kilometres into Florac along the Stevenson Trail because we had stumbled across the footsteps of the great author yet again. The campsite is a regular stopping place for folk doing the walk offering both cabins for the humans and a field for any accompanying donkeys.

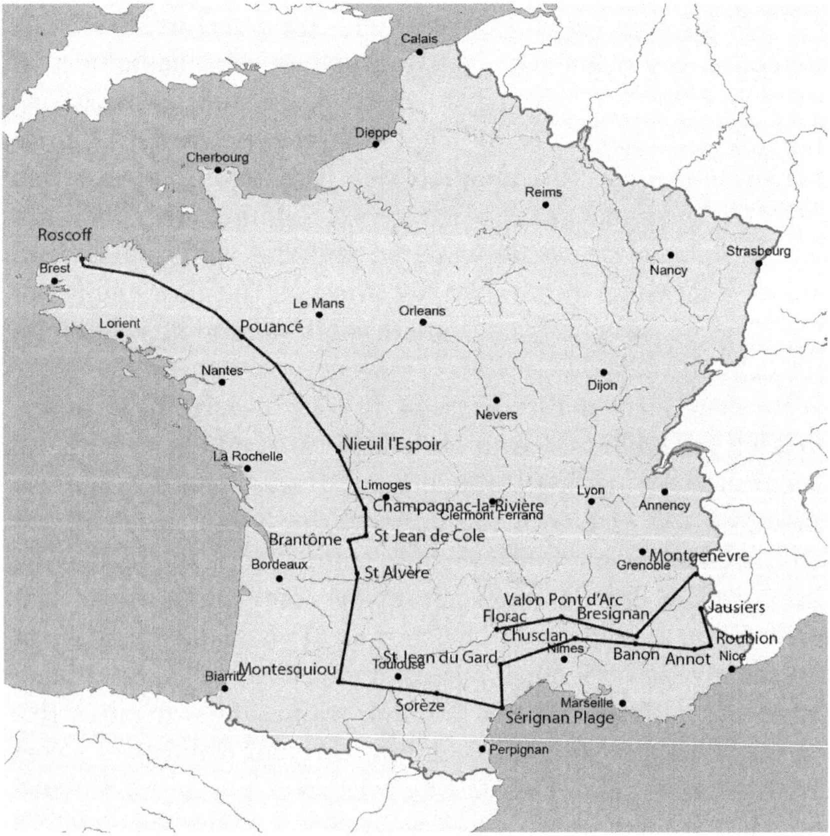

The path into Florac left directly from the campsite and as we expected Charlie struggled with heat towards the end especially after we left the shade of the trees. We found a conveniently placed font on the outskirts of the town where I baptised him by immersion, generating a quick recovery, spiritually and physically.

Florac is an attractive place and has a well-reviewed *aire* I am sure Charlie would have preferred us to have used instead of the campsite as it would have shortened the journey to the village by several kilometres.

The window in the top left in the following photograph isn't what it seems. A clever bit of *trompe-l'oeil*.

As we promised ourselves we subsequently swam in the river and very pleasant it was. I can strongly recommend the Tarn at this spot for gentle wild swimming.

While we were at this site Mary made a meal so good here is the recipe.

Baked Stuffed Peppers (Serves two)

Ingredients

Two red peppers

Packet of couscous with dried Mediterranean vegetables

Blue cheese, for example Roquefort or Gorgonzola

Lardons or mushrooms or even both

Cut the peppers in half lengthways and clean out the seeds and white bits. Par boil for 15 minutes to reduce cooking time in the oven. Strain and dry off.

While the peppers are boiling take a sachet of dried couscous and Mediterranean vegetables and cook according to the packet instructions. We brought ours with us from the UK but they can be found in supermarkets elsewhere in Europe.

You can now add what you like, fried mushrooms or in our case fried smoked lardons.

Mix the mushrooms or lardons with the couscous, adding the oil from the fried lardons if used.

Oil a baking tray and lay the peppers on it stuffed with the couscous mixture and top with slices of the cheese. Bake for about 20 to 30 minutes until the cheese has melted and the peppers are soft.

Not all motorhomes have an oven but there are alternatives, such as the Remoska pan or the double skillet pan.

Our idyll by the river had to end as time was catching up on us so we left the site, but not the river, and spent the best part of six hours driving through the Gorges du Tarn. This is another famous tourist magnet but we found the traffic delightfully light with even the Belgians in reduced numbers.

The satnav tried hard to keep us away from the gorge as it was slow going in there and a detour by way of Paris would have been quicker. The result of the device's concern for our welfare was I missed the turnoff for the start of the road through the gorge and we had to swing round and join it later. This was a fortuitous accident as it meant we drove over a *causse* region. The *causse* are dry uplands intersected by numerous gorges at the southern end of the Massif Central. The one we crossed was the Causse de Sauveterre and the calcareous soils are excellent for flowers, including orchids.

Finding the *causse* was pure happenstance, a word I use for no other reason than opportunities to deploy it are seldom, but this is an area worth returning to and especially earlier in the year for the orchids.

Ignoring the pleas of the satnav to take any route but this one we dropped down from the *causse* and entered the gorge. The road starts at river level and then climbs above the river towards the middle of the gorge for a while before dropping back again at the end. This is a another good gorge for those who don't like heights as there are no poorly guarded edges although you learn to duck as the road is cut into the rock face in places and large overhangs result. There are also many unlit tunnels with height restrictions.

The road has extensive narrow sections where they have painted a white line down the middle of it but this doesn't mean there is room for even two cars to pass. For most of the time I was straddling the line and going round corners gingerly.

There are attractive villages you pass through, Sainte Enimie and La Malène but there are cute smaller villages on the opposite bank.

The photograph on the next page is Castelbouc and the remains of the twelfth century castle can just be seen above the village on a rock spire.

And scoring even higher points for cuteness, Saint Chély du Tarn.

The road over the bridge into the village is a dead end with only a rough track beyond it.

Next we came to Hauterives, a village on the left bank of the Tarn with no road and only accessed on foot or by boat. A cableway crosses the river for the transportation of light goods and mail. The houses all looked in good repair so I guess they were holiday, retirement or second homes.

The final stretch of the road was much wider and busier so if coming from the west you could be fooled into thinking the road is like this all the way. It isn't.

Reflecting afterwards on our day in the Gorges du Tarn we should have found a place to stop overnight and explored the villages. There is a lot to see here and having found it free of visitors we should have taken advantage.

The Cathars

My plan was to visit the historic homeland of the Cathars in the part of southwest France inland from the Mediterranean coast. On our way to reach this area after leaving the Gorges du Tarn we stopped overnight at an *aire* beside the Lac de Pareloup. Operating the automated ticket barrier to gain entry to the *aire* was an initiative test but we were ultimately successful. There is always the risk French machinery of the sort dispensing drinking water or operating a barrier will not accept a UK bank card, but this one did. The Lac is a reservoir and Charlie enjoyed a swim in it. There were little waves breaking on the shore and he spent a few frantic moments trying to catch them in his jaws.

We woke the next morning to rain and the forecast said it wouldn't stop soon so instead of the leisurely scenic drive I planned we spent most of the day driving, ending at Lagrasse, southeast of Carcassonne.

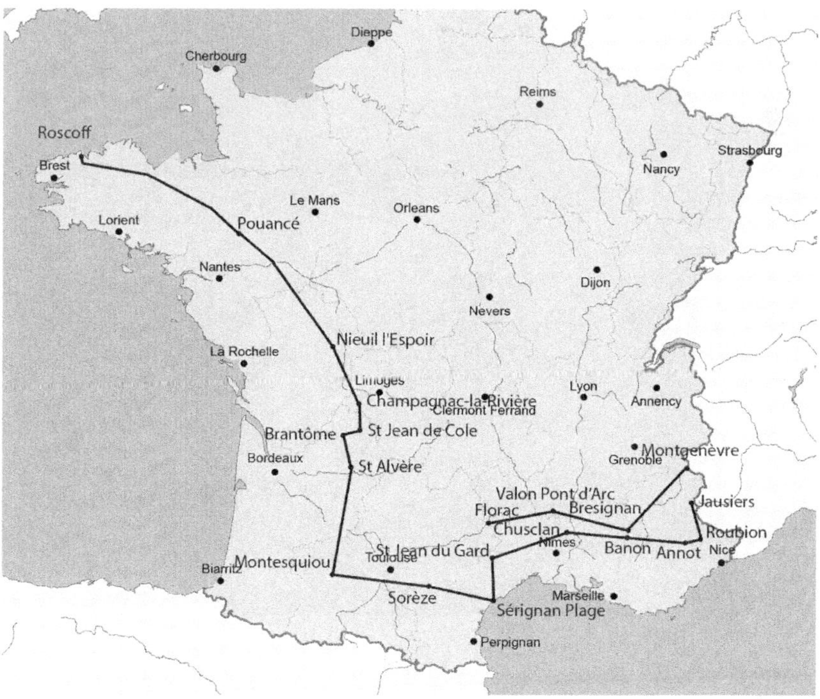

This is a town with a large abbey.

And an interesting bridge amongst other diversions.

We stayed on the municipal *aire*, cost €6. This wasn't very attractive to look at but it was at least quiet. Later three French motorhomes pulled up alongside us and they literally circled them, forming an inner space. Here they cooked and talked LOUDLY but after several glasses of red I mellowed and slept well.

There was brown grass on the *aire* so little rain had fallen before we arrived but yet again we brought the showers with us. It makes me wonder if clouds follow our travels, especially after our experiences on our first visit to Spain. There must be drought afflicted regions of the world we should visit to relieve the suffering.

Geographically we were in the northeast corner of the Corbières wine making region. There were small vineyards dotted around but the total production must be small compared to places like Bordeaux as there isn't the same acreage of vineyards.

The Cathars were a 12th to 14th century religious sect who rebelled against the perceived corruption of the Catholic Church. As expected for such brutal times they came to a sticky and unpleasant end but it took time and the odd crusade to bring about as they had a habit of building castles in remote spots. It was to see the Cathar castles we came here so we lost no time going on a castle hunt.

We started with a drive south to visit the Chateaux Villerouge Termenes (previous page) originally a Cathar Castle but unlike others it was not destroyed and stayed in private hands until the 1980s when the municipality took it over and restored it.

It was €6 to get in but Charlie was allowed in for free. An audio guide with earphones was available in English but they didn't have one in Dog so we decided not to take them so Charlie wouldn't feel left out.

There are old frescoes on the walls and a few dummy figures in places, showing how life in the castle might have been.

Charlie, under close supervision, behaved himself the whole of the time we were inside the castle but as soon as we reached the battlements he had a sneaky pee when I wasn't looking.

The descent from the battlements was by way of a narrow staircase running between the outer and inner walls of the tower, like a Scottish broch.

The gap was very narrow and I was forced to walk sideways. How the larger visitors coped remains a mystery.

In the village we found a shop selling local produce or *products de garrigue* as they called it. The *garrigue* is the name for the scrubby, dry, limestone countryside to be found both here and elsewhere in southern France. We bought 3 bottles of a local wine at €7.50 a bottle. These were not the most expensive but after tasting the others on offer we think we chose a good one. I planned to give a bottle to my cousin when we called in again to see her before we caught the ferry home. She had recently fallen from her horse and broke and bent various bits so was in need of cheering up.

After the restored castle of Villerouge Termenes we visited two of the more ruinous and remote ones. These were more typical Cathar castles and gave a better impression of what life must have been like back then. You don't go to the trouble of building a castle on a remote pinnacle unless you are expecting trouble.

Our second castle was the Château de Quéribus, one of the last Cathar strongholds. The castle overlooks the village of Cucugnan and is built on a natural rock jutting up from the skyline.

The road up to the car park below the castle was steep, first gear most of the way and the footpath from the car park to the castle is also steep. I estimated a visit would take us two hours so we contented ourselves with a few photographs.

Though the sky was at first blue dark clouds swept in and it became cloudy with spots of rain when we came to the Château de Peyrepertuse, built along a thin and lofty ridge above the village of Duilhac Peyrepertuse.

There is an *aire* in the village although we saw no signs for it. You can barely see the castle from the village as only a few towers are visible sticking up above the line of the ridge. The scattered towers give no hint of the large structure behind them. It is not until you drive around the back of the castle, as we did, you see how big it is, with a massive wall overlooking the valley.

We stopped for the night at a pleasant free *aire* (always welcome) on the banks of the river Aude in Espéraza, due south of Carcassonne.

The Corbières region had been a revelation. It is an area you need to set aside a week or more to explore and have the time to give the remote castles full justice by visiting them. The local wine is good too.

Briefly into Spain

Leaving the *aire* by the river Aude but not the river, we followed it upstream and through the obscure Gorges de Saint Georges. The road is the D118 and marked as a yellow road in the Michelin atlas but I've been on wider white roads. There was a disturbing amount of small and not so small rocks on it, especially at the bottom end.

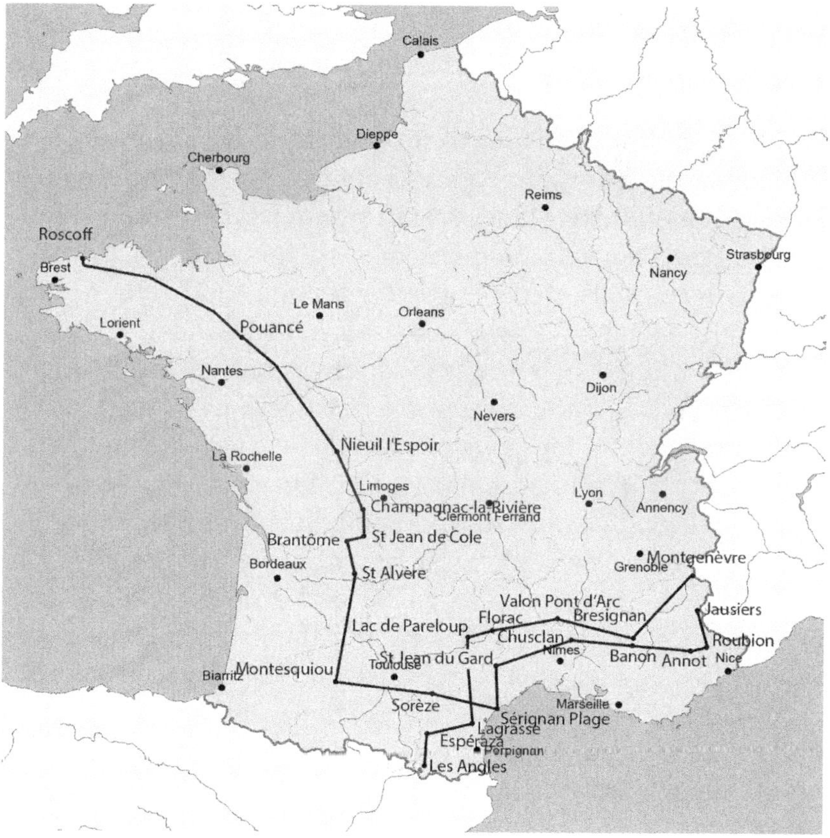

The road is another which looks straight in the atlas but this is deceiving. It is extremely twisty but as in a few other places twists were so close together the scale of the atlas couldn't represent them. I found it one of the more challenging and enjoyable roads yet encountered.

We overnighted, still in France, at the free *aire* above the ski resort of Les Angles at an altitude of about 1600m.

It was warm in the sun during the afternoon but became chilly as the sun set. This made us turn the heating on for the first time in many weeks.

The *aire* is a large car park below the ski lifts and from it we followed a marked trail towards the Lac d'Aude. We didn't reach the lake as it was a twelve kilometre circular walk, or possibly twelve kilometres to the lake. The single board at the start of the walk was unclear on this critical fact. My skiing days were short lived after dislocating my shoulder in Bavaria and were a long time ago so I didn't at first recognise the tall pole-like things beside the *piste* as we walked past the bottom of the ski lift. Then I realised they were artificial snow machines. A Mr Whippy of the *pistes*. These are becoming much more common in Europe as climate change makes snow less predictable.

The path skirted the perimeter of an outdoor zoo with Pyrenean animals. There were mouflon and other large mammals including a wolf and sadly, somewhere, a bear. I suspect the latter does not take kindly to captivity but the few remaining bears of the Pyrenees face extinction so I guess it can at least be grateful for being alive. If it was a local bear and not as more likely, one imported from East Europe.

We had good views of distant mountains from the path to the lake and the flowers were interesting. One tall foxglove-like plant with blue flowers was a puzzle as the only book I had with me was of Mediterranean flowers but the internet came to my rescue; it was monkshood or wolfsbane, *Aconitum napellus*. A poisonous plant though deaths from it are rare as it tastes bitter. The active ingredient is aconitine which causes amongst other unpleasant symptoms slowing of the heart leading to death. An American doctor practising in the UK in the Nineteenth Century with financial woes created by morphine addiction was convicted in 1882 of murdering a young relative with it to profit from an inheritance. Doctor George Lamson made a Dundee cake containing Wolfsbane and as a backup filled one of the newly invented soluble capsules with a mixture containing aconitine. These he gave to the eighteen year old

Percy John with fatal results. He was subsequently hanged at Wandsworth after an unsuccessful attempt by his family in America to persuade the court he was insane.

The Lac d'Aude as the name suggests is the source of the river Aude. We didn't reach it but we walked on the track leading to it so I can claim to have *almost* reached it.

The *aire* was quiet and peaceful during the night but not everywhere in France was the same. This was the night a truck was driven into crowds celebrating Bastille Day in Nice killing 86 and injuring 458.

We arrived in Spain the next day before we realised it. We entered the Túnel del Cadí, a five kilometre long tunnel costing us the precise sum of €11.57 to traverse. In my mind, not having looked at the map well, I assumed the tunnel would be the border. It wasn't and we crossed into Spain without knowing it about ten kilometres before reaching the tunnel. I guess we should have realised this when the lady in the toll booth at the entrance to what I assumed was the French side greeted us with a cheery "Hola". I might also have twigged earlier when we saw a group of French customs officers stopping cars going the other way in what appeared to be the middle of nowhere. It is extraordinary how borders have vanished within Europe. Their presence on the road may have been linked to the dreadful events in Nice but we saw no obvious border point with "Welcome to Spain" written on it.

It was only a quick drive after the tunnel to our chosen campsite but most of the route was steeply descending. The road must drop a thousand metres and the temperature on the dashboard gauge soon read a reassuring figure in the low twenties. When I gave Charlie his first walk at the *aire* by the ski lifts at Les Angles there was frost on the grass in the shade.

But we were now somewhere much warmer. Though Camping El Berguedà was in the foothills of the Pyrenees, southeast of Andorra, we were barely above ankle height in terms of typical altitudes for the Pyrenees and well below the chilly heights. We were in a region rich in wildlife, the Parc Natural de Cadí Moixero and a pleasant place to sit enjoying the warmth.

The reception gave us a map showing two or three local walks and this time we hoped we wouldn't get too lost. Our experience with campsite walking maps was not good but we were now in an area where my GPS had a map card showing the local area at 1:25K scale. This was to prove invaluable as events unfolded.

Soon after we arrived I took Charlie for a walk along a local road where he met a Pyrenean Mountain Dog. The dog was guarding a herd of goats in a field beside the road. A wire fence separated the road from the field but the big dog came bounding over and seemed friendly enough. Coincidently the goatherd at this point came by in his car. He wasn't what I imagined a Spanish goatherd would look like as he had dreadlocks but he strongly advised me to be careful because if the dog thought Charlie was a threat to the goats he would get chomped. Even Charlie understood enough of what was said to be on his best behaviour. You don't mess with a Pyrenean Mountain Dog.

The next day was meant to be a short walk for us but the Curse of the Campsite Map struck again and we completed a slightly longer walk than planned.

A path from the back gate of the campsite took us after about ten minutes to the start of the walk. The path, protected at first by a concrete wall climbs up the side of a canyon then crosses the canyon on a concrete footbridge with iron railings. Thereafter, no concrete or railings are involved on the route.

After the bridge the path climbed up further for a while and then remained level for the next six kilometres. You can't see the path in this shot but it runs amongst the trees along the edge of the cliff.

This is the view looking back once we gained height.

You can see a long ridge above the road stretching into the distance. We were on a similar ridge running in the opposite direction.

We could soon look down onto the campsite. The path was a safe distance away from the edge except in a few places, such as here, where it was nearer.

The campsite map showed a ten kilometre route with an option to reduce this to five kilometres but we found both routes impossible. The first option, for the shortcut, was barred with rope and plastic tape and the ten kilometre route seemed to go right over the edge of the cliff. We had been following the white and yellow local footpath markers (as opposed to red and white GR markers) and these were visible for most of the walk but towards the end they became faint and hard to see and were not visible near the critical point where we should have descended. My GPS showed if we carried on for another kilometre there was a track at a remote farmhouse and this would take us to the lower ground. Which is what we did but without the GPS we would have been forced to go back all the way to the start as the break in the ridge we eventually used to descend was not visible at the point where the ten kilometre route vanished.

By the time we got back to the campsite we had completed almost twelve kilometres. It took us four hours and Charlie did well but it wasn't too hot, just pleasantly warm so he didn't overheat.

The next day I went for a walk on my own, retracing the start of our first walk but turning right instead of left and following the ridge in the opposite direction for a while. Looking back I could see the scene of our unexpectedly extended hike.

I brought my tripod with me intending to take shots of flowers but this part of the ridge was arid and there weren't the flowers we saw yesterday on the other section of the ridge. On the way back Charlie enjoyed a drink from a cold spring beside the road but I'm not sure he enjoyed the excursion. It was a lot hotter than yesterday and when we got back he did his abused dog impression.

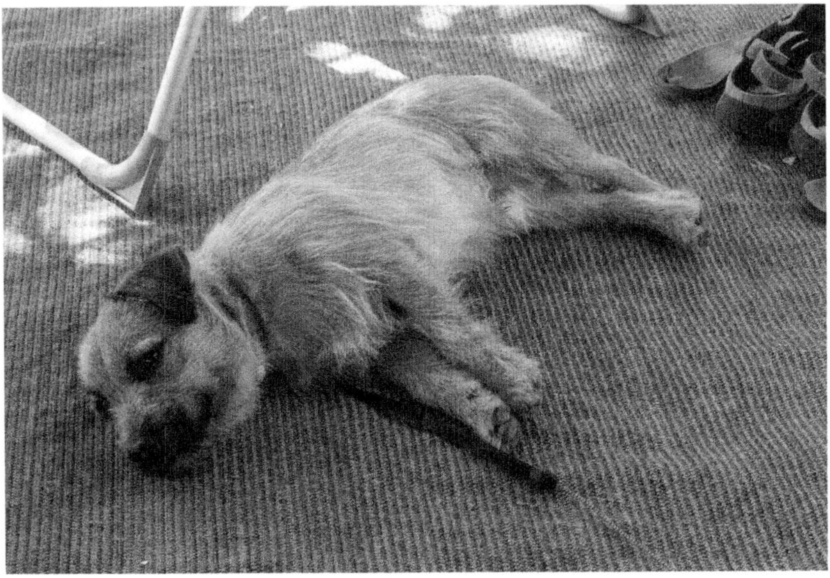

Our time in Spain was limited because we needed to hop over to France to meet up with my cousin before coming back to Spain to catch the ferry home. It might seem odd we didn't visit her before entering Spain but she was already booked with other visitors so we waited for them to depart before there was room for us.

So we moved again and left behind the Parc Natural de Cadí Moixero and after shopping in Berga where we bought fino sherry (I will miss Spain) we headed back north through the Cadí tunnel paying another €11.57 as unlike say the Severn bridge you pay in both directions. After the tunnel we turned directly west on the N260. This is marked as a major road but it becomes a minor road as it goes over the Coll del Canto. We were still on the Spanish side of the Pyrenees as we had one more place to visit here before crossing into France.

Stopping for lunch on the way up to the Coll del Canto (picture below) the thermometer read 31°C and this was at about 1500m but there was a gentle breeze and the humidity was low so it was pleasant in the shade of the motorhome.

From the curiously named town of Sort we drove north up the valley of the river Pallaresa, a fair sized river and one popular with canoeists. Sort and all the villages north were busy and I wondered if our chosen campsite would have room for us, not having made a booking. We needed have worried, Camping Voraparc had some pitches left although the remaining few with electric points were all gone by the end of the afternoon. The site is about a kilometre past Espot on the road leading to the Parc National d'Aigüestortes, a name meaning twisted waters. This is an area of striking Pyrenean scenery. Sadly, I didn't think we would see much of it due to limitations on time, temperature and legs but if the following day wasn't too hot we would have a gentle stroll up the valley to see what we could see.

In my keenness to explore the area I bought the 1:25k map at the campsite office. It came with a booklet containing amongst other things the park rules.

No wild camping

Do not deviate from the paths

No swimming in the rivers or lakes

I already knew the Spanish took their national parks seriously and they were trying to keep this remarkable area in pristine condition.

From the campsite we walked up a footpath to the entrance of the park. The path was a GR and well-marked and even we couldn't get lost. The image below was taken looking back the way we had come after an hour of walking. The campsite is in the valley in the distance.

As we went higher we could see the peaks of big mountains appearing and these spurred us "onwards and upwards" as they say. The path became much wider as we entered the park and we had our first proper look at the peaks.

The pointy peak left of centre is Encantat Xie and is slightly lower at 2734m than Encantat Gran to the left of it. A path leads to the summit of this 2748m (9018 ft) peak. There were more distant peaks to the right with a few small patches of snow on them. And having only reached the entrance to the Parc we turned back, crossing the Riu Escrita river at a bridge where Charlie, probably in contravention of the rules, enjoyed a paddle in the cold water. Next to the bridge was an interesting sign in Catalán and Spanish (overleaf).

The trout and dipper I recognised, but what was the curious character on the right? It is a Pyrenean Desman, a nocturnal relative of shrews and moles.

From the bridge we walked on a wheelchair-friendly elevated path to a car park at the end of the road coming from the valley below. This was as far as private cars could be taken and it was busy. Only the Land Rover taxis can go on to the Sant Maurici lake otherwise you walk for about half an hour from the car park. It would have been rewarding to continue up to the lake but not in the middle of July. As it was we covered about seven kilometres in two and a half hours with 400m of gentle ascent. We returned by the road, it was easy walking downhill and we were encouraged in our step by lots of wild strawberries. They were as sweet as the ones we ate in Italy and we even shared them with Charlie.

The only disappointment of the walk, apart from not seeing more of the scenery, was the almost complete absence of bird life. Other than a jay and a blackbird that was it, even the usual twittering in the trees was virtually absent. I had carried my telephoto lens with me on the walk in case of a glimpse of something exotic like a Bearded Vulture but they must have all been snoozing. The only bird of interest seen was sharing a sign with a Pyrenean Desman.

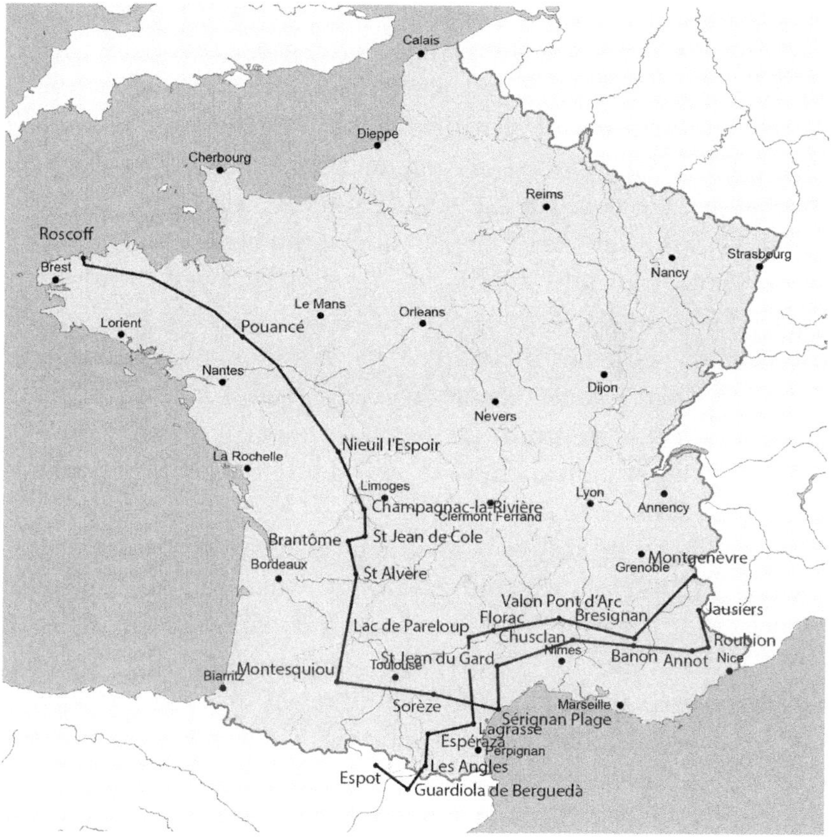

Briefly Back into France

West of Andorra there is a gap of about sixty kilometres before you find the first opportunity to cross over into France. To reach this we had to travel west inside Spain on a road taking us over the Port de la Bonaigua, another contender for the title of "most twisty road yet". It lacked the fallen rocks seen in the Gorges de St George but it does a good impression of a small intestine as we climbed up and over the pass then descend through big zigzags. The latter were unnerving. On the left hand turns, with the vehicle on the outside of the bend you could look straight into the airy depths as you slowly swept around the bend. Being the driver in a right hand drive vehicle gave me an even better view into the void. After this the actual crossing of the border was unspectacular. The entry into France is a "blink and you'll miss it" thing taking place on a level road over a bridge. The stream below the bridge being the boundary between the two countries.

We stopped in France in a rural area north of Montréjeau at Camping Baptistou, which the friendly owner was still finishing. However, there were hot showers and we were greeted on arrival with a free jar of paté. The only problem with Camping Baptistou is it was about a mile and a half to the local village and we were surrounded by farmland. There were one or two permanent residents but we were the only tourists and it was the middle of July. This may explain why we were given a free jar of paté.

The owners didn't speak a word of English and I can hardly blame them as my French is barely fit for purpose so I asked where the "poubelles" were and was shown the recycling bins. I was looking for the grey bin for general rubbish but I couldn't find the right words. I eventually found the bins at the entrance to the site, where I should have looked first because this is where they usually are on campsites.

The next night we have stopped at a free *aire* at the small town of Miélan. We went for a walk after parking, going first to the nearby Lac de Miélan which was muddy and unattractive. I suspect it gets fertiliser run off from the fields and we could see metal pipes leading into it for the extraction of water for irrigation. From the lake we circled round and walked into the town. The main road misses the town centre so in a vehicle you wouldn't know about its timber-framed buildings and town hall of novel design.

The Mayor's office was on the first floor and underneath was a covered market - and a very French toilet with two footprints we made use of.

Some of the streets leading to the centre had interesting houses too, many with balconies with wooden railings. This restaurant looked fun, note the name and you may be able see two geese peeking out of the cauldron in the top right. It had curious opening hours; 07:10 to 14:30 Monday to Friday only. A "Marmite" is a cooking pot not the like it or loath it thing we British consume. Good reviews online too.

But not everything was traditional. We found a bread vending machine in the centre of the town. And not just baguettes, it did croissants too.

This is the *aire*. There were a few motorhomes using it but then the French love a free *aire*, as we do.

The discovery of Miélan's centre was another lesson learned. Even the most boring looking place is worth investigating, you never know what you will find.

We spent the weekend at a Dutch owned campsite south of Auch. The clientele were 99% Dutch, we made up the 1% who weren't. It was relaxing and with good dog walking. We could sit a few yards from the edge of a lake and watch dragonflies cruising, fish rising, and once a lone frog crossing the lake. We also watched the large numbers of Dutch children. They were well behaved and their parents didn't seem worried by health and safety. Despite having three lakes there wasn't a single life belt or throwing line in sight and the little blighters were out in canoes all day without an adult to be seen. At the end of the season they must dredge the lake to recover the bones of any unfortunates who have drowned. It was quiet in the evening too, no late night drinking parties or loud conversations.

We then made a quick call on my cousin, the one who fell off her horse after our last visit so I hoped nothing befell her after this second visitation. I know we bring rain wherever we go but accidents too? Life is so unfair. The plaster had just come off but her arm was still stiff so Mary cooked a supper of chorizo and chickpeas; a meal both tasty and suitable for the one-handed.

The Gers department may lack people but it has lots of sunflowers.

It was then a hop into Spain, using the main roads and we spent our last night at a fee *aire* south of San Sebastian at Errenteria beside a large picnic area in a park. This *aire* can get busy as it is a popular spot but on a Tuesday it was quiet with just a few families who all left in the late afternoon. The next morning we safely arrived in Santander where on driving into the port we were promptly waved to one side by a policeman. He demanded to see our V5 vehicle registration document whereupon he checked the VIN number at the bottom of the windscreen to confirm the document matched the vehicle. After boarding the *Pont Aven* we were requested to put a muzzle on Charlie before we got out of the vehicle. This wasn't something we've been asked before. The regulations say you should but almost everyone ignores it in our experience but this time they were sticking to the rules. Perhaps someone had been bitten recently? After settling Charlie in his on-board kennel, muzzle removed, and depositing our bags in our cabin we went to the Piano Bar for a glass of wine. We would sail in an hour. After our wine, more than one glass, we dined in the restaurant then after more wine turned in for a sound night's sleep on a calm crossing. The next day we arrived in Plymouth.

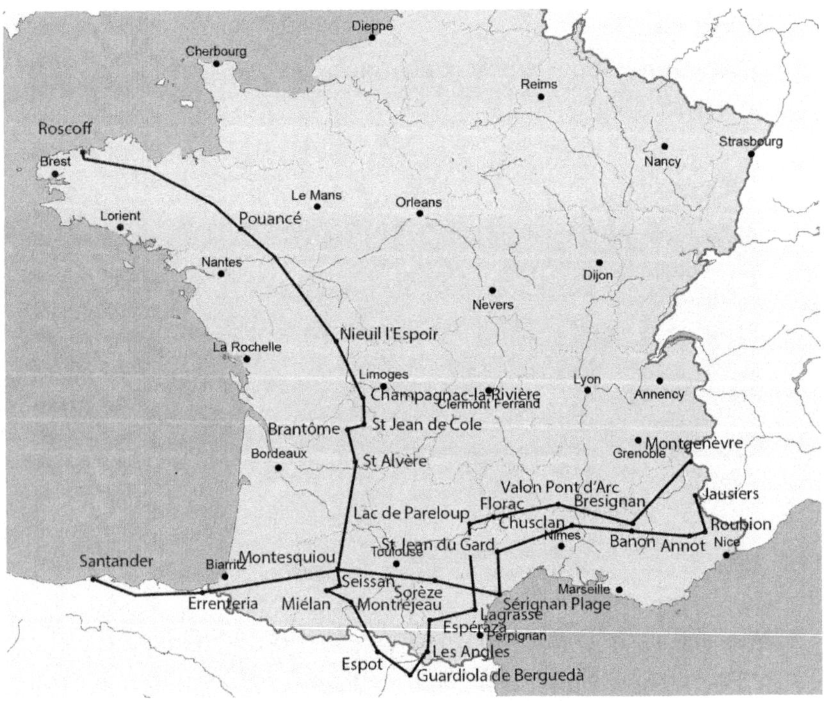

The Second Journey

We Go to Sicily

August to October, 2017

Through France

We had hoped to return to Italy in April but unforeseen circumstances meant we delayed our departure and it wasn't until the last week of August before we got away. Also due to unforeseen circumstances our previous trip started at Roscoff rather than Santander and the unplanned journey through France was enjoyable and we visited places we would otherwise never have seen. We like the ferry to Santander and especially the opportunity for whale watching but it is an expensive route so this year we didn't wait for the Spanish ferry to break down and change our plans but booked a ticket to take us directly to Roscoff and thus cut out the element of chance.

There are many routes to France. The cheapest are the shortest but it is nearly three hundred miles to Dover from where we live. In stark contrast the ferry port in Plymouth is just a fifteen minute drive from our house.

There are day and overnight sailings to Roscoff and both have advantages and disadvantages. For our outward journey we chose an overnight crossing and booked a four berth cabin. You can save money booking a twin berth cabin but the second berth is reached by something to be avoided; a ladder. Driving with a leg or foot in plaster is awkward.

I planned on taking ten to fourteen days to drive to Sicily, though it eventually took us longer. It *could* be done in a few days perhaps three or four if you were prepared to drive four hundred miles a day but this is not for us. The journey is always at least as important to us as the arrival. Sadly, this tends not to apply on the *return*. I've tried, but as you will discover once we turn and head home I find it hard to dawdle.

But at the moment we only looked forward to the going and the coming back was a problem to be addressed much later.

Southern Europe suffered during the summer of 2017. Extreme high temperatures led to many deaths. Forest fires, some deliberately started and water shortages were amongst the hazards we faced. I also loaded an app onto my phone called "Volcanoes and Earthquakes". This would alert me to any seismic or volcanic activity near us. We were looking forward to seeing Mount Etna and after being quiet for several months it recently started rumbling again. The volcano must have been getting as excited as we were at meeting each other.

Compared to previous journeys our Murvi motorhome was loaded with luxuries; a hairdryer for Mary and an espresso machine for me. Knowing my luck the cheap electrical inverter I installed to power these gadgets would fail on us, depriving us of the joys of dry hair and hot coffee but we could at least set out in hope.

Charlie the heat-hating terrier had been clipped to within an inch of his hide. We'd taken him to someone who was supposed to hand strip him but when I returned to collect him they said they hadn't been able to so used the clippers on him instead. He looked a different dog, more whippet than terrier but it would give him the best chance of staying cool. Charlie suffered in Italy the previous year so we bought a cooling coat for him. This was a waistcoat made from a thick absorbent material soaked with water before being put on. The theory was as the water evaporated, the dog within the waistcoat was cooled. Like a wine cooler but lacking the alcohol. I also bought for him a cooling mat to lie on and a folding dog paddling pool. He might find me sharing this with him if it was hot. Finally, we replaced the folding metal dog cage with a dog harness attached to an anchor point I fitted.

The Plymouth to Roscoff overnight ferry docks early in France so we didn't expect much of a lie-in but what occurred exceeded the bounds of civilised behaviour I think. Having boarded at Plymouth we immediately made for a quiet spot near the bar but were mildly horrified to hear an announcement saying the ship was arriving at six o'clock instead of the seven o'clock shown on our ticket.

Sneakily, they didn't make this announcement until after we left Plymouth. You wouldn't usually complain about a ferry arriving early but when it means setting the alarm clock to five o'clock I think these are reasonable grounds for complaint.

The next morning was a repeat of our arrival at Roscoff the previous year. Charlie, having spent the night asleep in the motorhome our first action on disembarking was to pull over in the car park at the docks. I took him for a walk while Mary prepared breakfast. Afterwards, refreshed and replete and in Charlie's case relieved, we started for Italy.

We spent the first night next to a cemetery in a municipal *aire* at Beignon, southwest of Rennes. This is a village with bars and a restaurant closed for the owner's summer holidays. Many businesses close in France during August. Charlie enjoyed people watching (but secretly I think he prefers other dogs) while we drank wine at a bar by the church.

Our direction of travel to Italy was southeast from Brittany and skirting around Rennes the next day we crossed the Loire at Angers and stopped at Brissac Quincé.

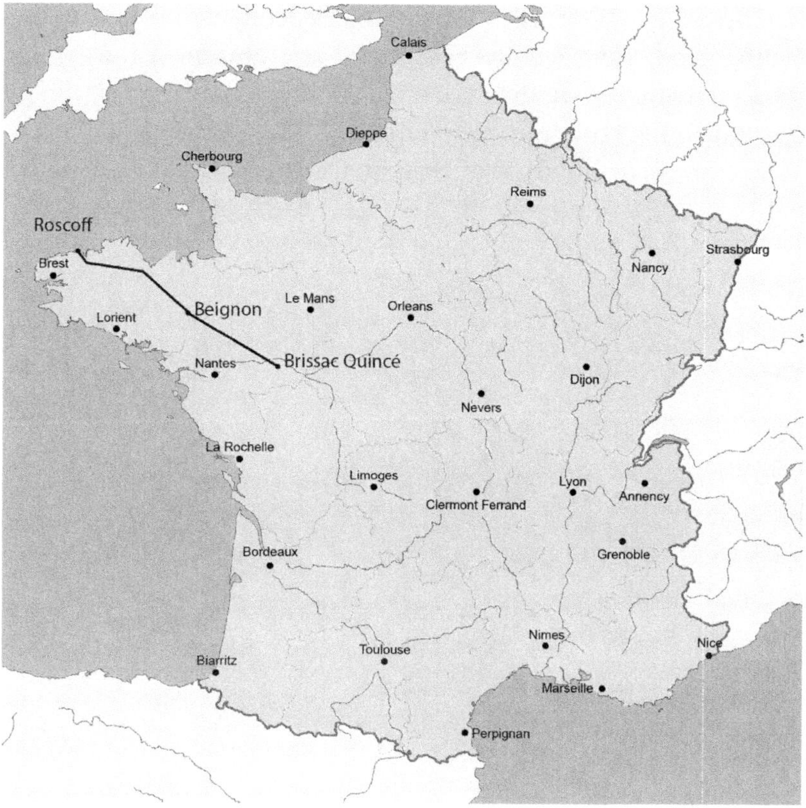

This is a place worth visiting especially if you have a dirty motorhome as the LeClerc supermarket has a motorhome washing point. It is like other vehicle washing points but with a gantry to access the roof.

The *aire* in the town is a reserved area to one side of the main car park and was supposed to cost €4 but we couldn't see how this was to be paid. A temporary notice said the *aire* was closed although in contradiction to this edict the *aire* was almost full with motorhomes. These municipal *aires* often use someone to collect the monies and there must be a French website where the times the money is collected are published. I suspect this because if they come around in the evening then after they have made their circuit the French motorhomes are likely to arrive. If they collect the money in the morning then the French will leave early to avoid meeting the revenue collector. The cleverer municipalities collect both in the morning and the evening or even at random times. The response from the dedicated cheapskates is to boycott such *aires* and choose the free ones only.

The *aire* (possibly free) at Brissac Quincé is beside a disused canal.

Brissac Quincé has an impressive château, the eponymous Château Brissac but we did nothing other than admire it from the outside when we went for our afternoon walk with Charlie.

This was because a balloon festival was being held and the château was to be open to the public in the evening for various ballooning and non-ballooning activities.

When we returned to the *aire* I asked one of our neighbours about the notice saying the *aire* was closed during the balloon festival. They told me to ignore it. I love the French attitude to authority. It is unsurprising the same nation invented the guillotine to deal with the old order.

The evening's balloon festival, once it got going, was spectacular. It was held in the grounds of the château and entrance was a reasonable €5. There were no signs of any balloons when we arrived so we made straight for the wine tasting. The wine was €2 but a €2 deposit had to be paid for the glass. We paid the deposit but were then charged the same again when we came to refill them. Despite the support of a French lady the crooked sommelier insisted I pay another deposit. I did but we subsequently walked off with the glasses and used them daily for the rest of our trip. The wines, both red and white from the Loire region, were excellent and worth €2 for a decent glassful and tasted even better after we planned our nefarious thievery.

Before the ballooning began a weird procession appeared on the lawn in front of the château. It was led by members of the local post office with a horse and cart who were followed by more folk in traditional costumes. Behind these were a dozen figures in red cloaks who I think were the local council including the mayor though I wondered at first if they were representatives of an obscure society. perhaps the society of truffle snufflers or garlic garglers? The French love these sorts of groups especially if it allows them to dress up with sashes and funny hats.

The three groups all stopped in front of us. The post office folk didn't do much other than stand around but the traditionally dressed folk performed traditional dances. What was wonderful was it soon became clear they were all having a ball and were not in the least taking any of this seriously.

Afterwards, and after more wine tasting by us but no more glass thieving, about a dozen balloons were unrolled and inflated. Three started from the château lawn and the rest from further away behind us in the grounds.

These two were the stars, one carrying the town name and the other a replica of an original Montgolfière with a wide skirt at the bottom.

When all the balloons were launched we realised there were a lot more in the sky than left from the château. Many more balloons ascended from other sites further upwind. joining those rising from the château. Someone cleverly calculated distance and wind speed accurately to bring them together and get several dozen simultaneously in the air above us. The following morning, while we were having breakfast yet more balloons went overhead.

The pilots must have been up early or our breakfast was late but whatever the merits of early balloons or delayed breakfasts we left them to their festival and drove towards Limoges, stopping at another free *aire* at Lathus St Rémy.

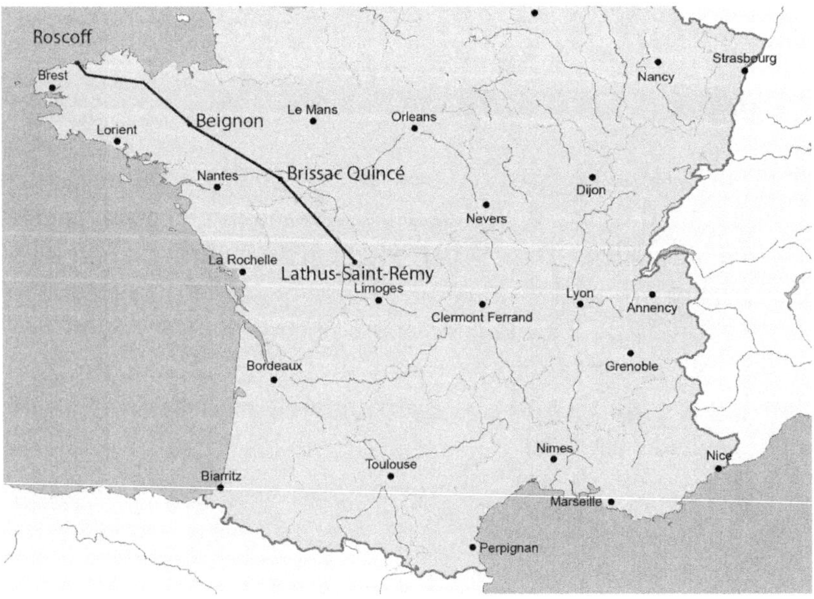

The road network in France doesn't lend itself to driving from the northwest to the southeast unless you want to detour via Paris, and we didn't. There is the large lump of the Massif Central to get around too. So there is no obvious route to take. We could have saved time using the *autoroutes* but many are *péage* or toll roads and in France these can be expensive compared to Italy. I planned to use the *autoroutes* later but in this part of France there were good options for avoiding them.

The *aire* at Lathus St Rémy was a former municipal campsite. This is not uncommon in France and reflects the change in camping habits of the French and the explosion in the number of motorhomes or camping-cars as they call them. Or at least some of the French call them camping-cars because this term is not universally recognised in the country. On another visit to France we saw a notice stuck to the service point at an *aire*. The notice read:

"Faites-le savoir! Le mot CAMPING-CAR est un faux anglicisme.

Le terme Français est AUTOCARAVANE"

The accusation is camping-car is an Anglicization and the French term autocaravane should be used instead. My French contact tells me the same people who worry about this type thing have no problem going to the supermarket and following the signs for "Parking" which isn't a French word either. Her perspective is our languages are all derived from the same Greek and Latin origins so there is no need to get worked up. In case you are wondering the first phrase "Faites-le savoir" doesn't seem to have a literal translation but means "spread the word" or "be aware".

Most of the former campsite was fenced off and only eight pitches remained in a row along the front, separated by hornbeam hedges.

Opposite these bays was a car park with a motorhome service point. This dispensed the essential requirements of motorhome owners for free and had a single electric point a local motorist used in the afternoon to recharge his electric car. After a few hours he returned and drove the car away and the Frenchman from the motorhome next to us promptly shot out and unrolling a long extension lead from a drum ran it back to *his* motorhome after connecting to the electric charging point. Sadly, though the antics in the *aire* were amusing to watch this was about all that seemed to happen around here. Lathus St Rémy is neat and clean but many houses were for sale and the only bar we could find was closed and also for sale. But they were trying hard with lots of flowers everywhere. The octagonal church tower in the photograph on the next page below is twelfth century according to a notice we found.

On the other side of the road from the *aire* there was access to an old railway track and Charlie and I walked along it but not for long as Charlie lay down after ten minutes complaining of the heat. I feared he would not like Sicily when we got there although he would have the sea to swim in and he swam frequently once we arrived but swimming in inland water in France was something I couldn't encourage. There had been reports during the summer of dogs dying after swimming in the

Loire and other places. The low water levels and high temperatures created the conditions for toxic algae to rise to the surface. Much of France was suffering from the lack of water and a Briton living in France told me about 85% of France was under water restrictions while we were there. Things had not reached the position where they were turning off the water supplies to motorhome *aires* but this could happen.

From Lathus St Rémy our southeasterly movement came to a temporary end north of Limoges when we turned east. The idea was to keep north of the Massif Central then avoid Lyon by staying north of it as well. This route would take us past Guéret, Montluçon, Moulins, Mâcon then southeast from Bourg en Bresse to Lyon and Annecy and finally over the border and into Italy by the Col du Petite St Bernard.

We stayed overnight on the first leg of this route at yet another free *aire* on the outskirts of Theil sur Acolin. The town was within easy walking distance but it must have been twinned with Lathus St Rémy as it was another almost deserted place without a bar. The *aire* was smart with free services and we might have spent money if there had been any opportunities to. It is not surprising there are many cheap rural properties to buy in France. Most of the French seem to have decamped to the cities.

Charlie chose this moment to give us something else to worry about. He was hopping around on three legs and even refused to eat a piece of courgette created during lunch preparations. A treat he normally looked forward too. Things must be serious. In the picture below his impression suggests the rejected courgette should be replaced by a piece of steak.

We could find nothing obvious but he was protective of his "foot" and our hitherto very placid dog gave me a nip sharp enough to warn me off further investigation. We would have to find a vet on the Monday if things did not improve.

This incident highlighted deficiencies in our first aid kit. We had many potions for insect bites but nothing like a bottle of iodine or a spray antiseptic.

Later on I managed to wash his paw but we couldn't find anything wrong although the patient was difficult, making a detailed examination impractical.

However, on the positive side he was getting better at walking on three legs so could get around more easily.

The following night we stopped on a campsite at St Étienne du Bois. According to the ACSI book this was run by a gentleman who at 19 was the youngest campsite owner in France. My thoughts after our arrival were he needed to learn how to greet guests with a smile and hire someone to clean the showers if he wanted to stay in business.

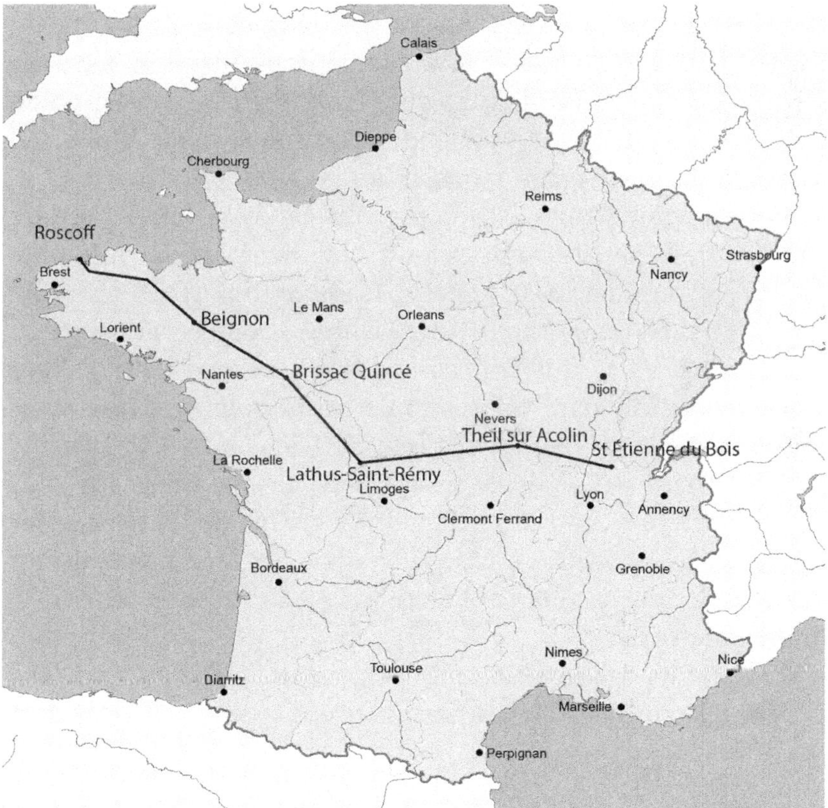

We came here to do our laundry but we soon realised they didn't have a washing machine. A better study of the ACSI guide would have told me this in advance if I had checked. The site was yet another former municipal campsite and this explained the lack of facilities. Municipal campsites don't normally have washing machines in my experience.

Just before our late lunch a battered looking purple emperor butterfly turned up. It seemed to be thirsty so I dipped a finger in my rosé wine and it drank it enthusiastically. Afterwards it spent a few moments sitting on my hand before flying away to sleep off the booze on the motorhome roof.

Not everything was gloomy, Charlie was getter better in the paw department so if his recovery continued we might yet escape a visit to the vet.

We spent most of the following day driving through the Haute Savoie region, stopping for the night close to the Italian border. The flag of the Haute Savoie department is virtually identical to the Swiss flag; a white cross on a red background. This was confusing at first and made me wonder if we had committed a grave error of navigation.

We had not planned to come this far east today because when we left the site without a washing machine our intention was to stop beside Lake Annecy. There are many sites around the lake but we soon found, after visiting a couple, they were all full. We had up to this point found nowhere busy so this came as a shock. How dare other people be on holiday at the same time as us? It was like driving into Keswick on an August Bank holiday, there were people everywhere. So we chose the only option open to us and carried on driving. This was August so we shouldn't have been surprised by what we found but all our previous journeys were in the off season so we were unused to finding crowds.

The site we found eventually with room for us was Camping de Montchavin at La Plaigne Tarantaise.

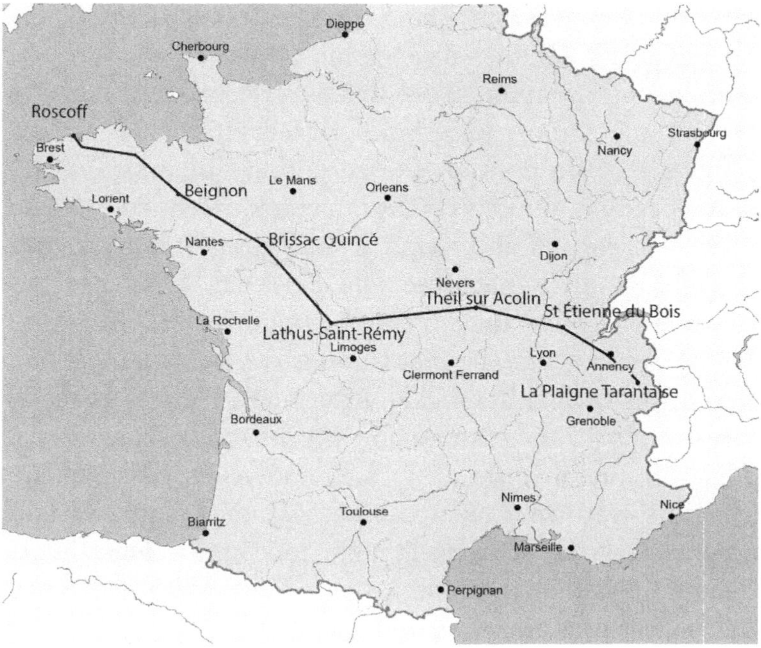

The views from the site were impressive. The display of matching underwear you can see on a washing line on the left in the image below was also impressive.

The white clouds on the far horizon in the middle of the picture conceal a big mountain. From the map it was probably Mont Blanc but if it wasn't it could have been a summit on the southwest side of the Mont Blanc *massif*, possibly part of the Aiguille des Glaciers. But it was a big hill anyway.

We would stay two nights here. It was a relaxed and relaxing place and uniquely in my experience for a campsite we found a notice pinned to the door of the reception office saying the office was closed on Mondays. This being a Monday no one was at home so we drove in and found a pitch after looking around to find their washing machine. The next day Mary did the laundry while I cleaned the solar panels and put the insulated cover on the windscreen. The motorhome was facing almost due south and it was getting hot inside. After these exertions I made myself two cups of espresso using my new coffee machine, running it off the inverter. The site had electricity but the electric points were in locked cabinets when we arrived and with no one around we weren't able to connect and things remained unplugged all the time we were there. With the strong sunshine we were experiencing and 190W of solar panels on the roof this wasn't a problem.

The lady who ran the office, who we met on the Tuesday when she came in to work was friendly and spoke good English. The site facilities were spotlessly clean too and in the communal room for campers was a free microwave. She confirmed the mountain was Mont Blanc and it must like to take Mondays off too as on the Tuesday the peak put in an appearance without clouds.

Though it was a relaxing day it was slightly frustrating. Soon after we arrived we caught a brief glimpse of a large bird before it suddenly flew away at great speed. The next day I heard what sounded like a buzzard, a common bird, so I ignored it for a few moments. But I eventually picked up my binoculars and realised it was no buzzard and was the same bird we saw yesterday. No sooner did I focus on it when it suddenly folded its wings dived into the valley just as it did before.

Booted Eagles, when I looked them up, make a noise like a buzzard but was it one? I don't know and I could only take comfort from the words in my book: "raptors can be hard to identify".

In the field below the campsite entrance were goats wearing bells. This was a first. I've seen them on cows, horses even and sheep too but not until now goats. How can you not enjoy staying at a place where they hang bells on their goats?

Italy

The following day we crossed into Italy by the Colle del Piccolo St Bernard as it is known in Italy. It was a drive with seemingly endless hairpin bends all the way up.

When we got to the top the col was bare and treeless and there was a long line of runners crossing it on a path.

I wasn't sure what the event was but the Ultra Marathon du Mont Blanc was being held to the north. This is a gruelling 105 mile race and competitors are only allowed to run in it by completing certain qualifying events. It is possible the runners we saw were on one of these and hoped to enter the Ultra Marathon the following year.

Unexpectedly, when we reached the col we found the road on the Italian side was excellent having been recently resurfaced. This wasn't how we remembered the roads of Italy. There may be no permanent border points but it is usually easy enough to know when you have crossed into Italy; your teeth rattle. However, though the road was smooth, as part of the refurbishment they lined the sides with large concrete blocks in places and on other stretches *very* substantial wood-faced barriers. The bends were sharp and I needed to check no one was coming up before swinging wide before the tight right-handers. With the concrete and timber barriers it was like driving through a channel. Once in Italy we didn't drive much further, stopping at Sarre in the Aosta valley.

A good *sosta* was supposed to be found further on but I was worried after our experience at Annecy it might be full because by all reports beyond it good *sosta* became thin on the ground as you approached Milan. So we stayed the night at a campsite where I successfully used my Vodafone sim card for the first time to connect to the internet. I hadn't been able to get it to work in France so I had reverted to using a Three sim card, which did work but the connection was often slow. Vodafone do not operate directly in France but they do in Italy so the MiFi connected directly to Vodafone and the connection was a fast 4G one too. I got the Vodafone card to work in France eventually by manually connecting it to Orange. Once this first connection was made it would reconnect automatically afterwards. The next morning we left Sarre, headed southeast and after a lot of driving on the *autostrada* to get past Milan we arrived in Soragna just short of Parma.

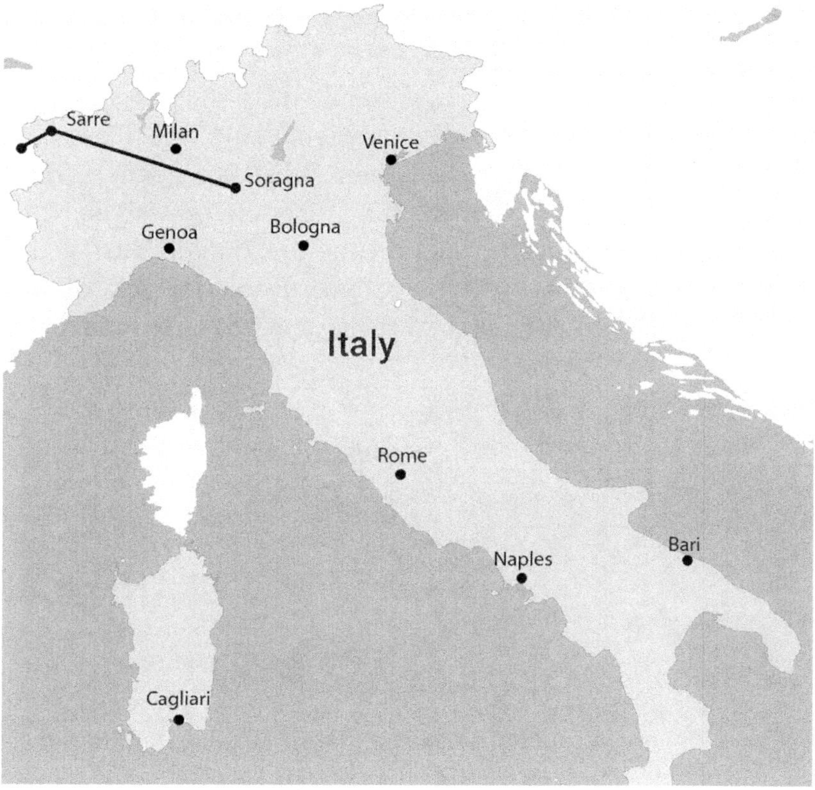

Our first experience of Italian motorways the previous year along the Mediterranean coast left me with an unfavourable impression of them but they are not all narrow and twisty. There are good motorways in Italy and these are an excellent way of travelling the long distances needed to get anywhere in a reasonable time. They *are* treated like a race track by the locals and they have short slip roads, making joining them fraught. It doesn't help the Italians don't know how to use the slip roads but like the rest of the driving experience in Italy once you know how they drive you can keep out of their way. In France the cost of the *péage* roads is high and many drivers don't use them. However, the French non-motorway roads are good but the same does not apply in Italy. You can often drive on a road parallel to a motorway but it will take much longer and the potholes in the road will make everything in your vehicle shake. So we have no hesitation in using the *autostrada*, even when we have to pay. They are not all toll roads but where they are the charges are less than those of France.

The *sosta* in Soragna was a normal car park in a built up area. There were no dedicated motorhome bays but this didn't seem to matter. People parked their vehicles anywhere they found room. This was after all Italy and having watched the total disregard for speed limits on the *autostrada* during the day I doubt the owners of the Concorde on the left of the photograph below, taking up several bays would be troubled.

It was hot and little rain had fallen here recently. We had seen brown grass on the sides of the motorway and the leaves on the tree behind our parking spot, a *Ginkgo biloba*, were wilting. Despite or because of the drought the tree bore curious white fruit hanging in pairs I don't recall seeing before.

I checked if water was available from the tap at the service point as I was worried they might have turned it off, but they hadn't and I gave Charlie a quick shower to cool him off. The temperature was 34°C when we arrived.

We started this day in Sarre, a town surrounded by mountains and the rivers there were full. Even the river Po, when we crossed it at Piacenza seemed to have a reasonable amount of water in it. However, things might be different the further south we went. Here in the north the drinking water comes from the many springs emerging along the northern edge of the Po Valley along the *fontanili* or spring zone. The major centres of economic and industrial activity in Italy; Turin and Milan are sited below the *fontanili* where they are able to enjoy a reliable supply of water.

Soragna is worth visiting and the centre was a few minutes' walk from the *sosta*. The principal attraction of the town is the Fortress Meli Lupi (overleaf).

The appearance of the fortress today dates back to the seventeenth Century and is owned by the same family who built the first fortress here in 1385. It is open to the public but sadly was shut by the time we arrived. Either side of the main entrance are lions.

It seems to be saying; "it's my ball and you're not playing with it!"

As we returned to the Town Square we found a poignant memorial.

It marks an incident in March 1945 when Italy, though allied to Germany, was riven by conflict between fascists and partisans. Some of the latter attempted to capture several fascists to exchange them for partisan prisoners. The attempt failed and one of the Black Shirts as the fascists were known was killed. In retaliation five partisans prisoners were selected and executed by firing squad. The youngest was seventeen years old.

After our exploration of Soragna we sat at an outside table of a café and ordered two glasses of wine but they came with half a dozen slices of white crusty bread with Parma ham on them. A tourist special I thought with a price to match but I was wrong. The Parma ham was good being soft and easily chewed, the wine was good too and the total for the pair of us was €5. We also discovered Parma ham from Parma does not have to be chewy.

We stayed one night at Soragna but it is a pleasant place and had we not been in an unreasonable hurry to move south we might easily have stayed another night or two, if only to enjoy more of the ham.

From Soragna our route was southeast to Bologna where we turned directly south and headed towards Florence.

All this driving meant we needed to refuel and this came as a surprise. The price of diesel in Italy was almost the same as the price in the UK if not more.

After passing Modena, heading towards Bologna, we lost an hour stuck in heavy traffic. All four lanes of the *autostrada* were stationary. The traffic moved after a delay but was stop and start for a long way. We think the holdup was due to a nasty accident in the other carriageway. We glimpsed a car squashed between two trucks as we crept past.

While stuck in the traffic and stationary I checked Google maps on my mobile and was impressed by how good it was at reporting traffic problems. The road was marked in red, showing heavy traffic. I was less impressed with myself for not noticing this earlier as we might have usefully turned off.

The first time I visited Italy, as a child on a camping holiday to the then Yugoslavia, I vividly remember how hot the Po valley was. In the intervening years it has not grown cooler and our night in Soragna was uncomfortably warm. We were unable to sit outside in the evening as our door looked onto a footpath and we ran the Endless Breeze fan all night to cool us. Not wishing to experience another hot evening confined to the vehicle if we could avoid it we sought out a campsite near Arezzo where we enjoyed the shade under trees. A breeze started during the day and this kept the temperature down so we spent a much more pleasant night during which we heard an occasional clap of thunder in the distance.

Apart from traffic reports Google Maps is an effective tool for planning routes. Where we were heading for on the Italian mainland was Villa San Giovanni, the port where we would board the ferry to Sicily. Google Maps suggested we could reach this in eight hours of driving. The distance to go was nine hundred kilometres and based on our daily mileages so far, my estimate of the time needed wasn't eight hours but more like four days. In fact it was to take us a week as my restless urge to move each day was successfully overcome.

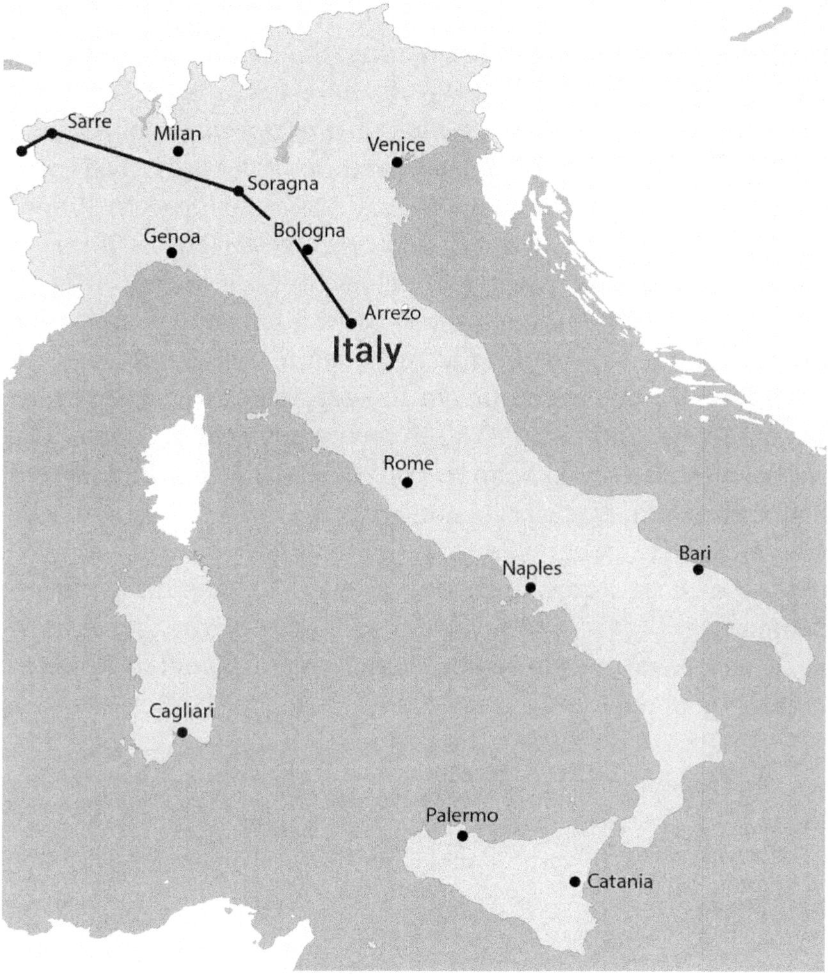

All Roads Lead to Rome

In 1391 Geoffrey Chaucer wrote in his treatise on the astrolabe "right as diverse pathes leden the folk the righte wey to Rome". This was the first English usage of a phrase written in Latin two hundred years earlier; "*mille viae ducunt homines per saecula Romam*". Which translates as "a thousand roads lead men forever to Rome". Nowadays we say "All roads lead to Rome" but the phrase isn't about roads or even getting to Rome it means there are many ways to achieve the same end. It is an example of an idiom, or a phrase whose meaning is not to be taken literally. We might say "it is raining cats and dogs" to describe a heavy downpour not to suggest puppies and kittens are falling out of the sky. The French equivalent is *Il pluet des cordes* meaning "it is raining cords" which I can understand better than our English version with the descending domestic pets. However, where we were in Italy nearly all the roads *did* go to Rome unless we wanted to take a significant detour.

Idioms aside, we paused overnight on our march to Rome at Montopoli di Sabina.

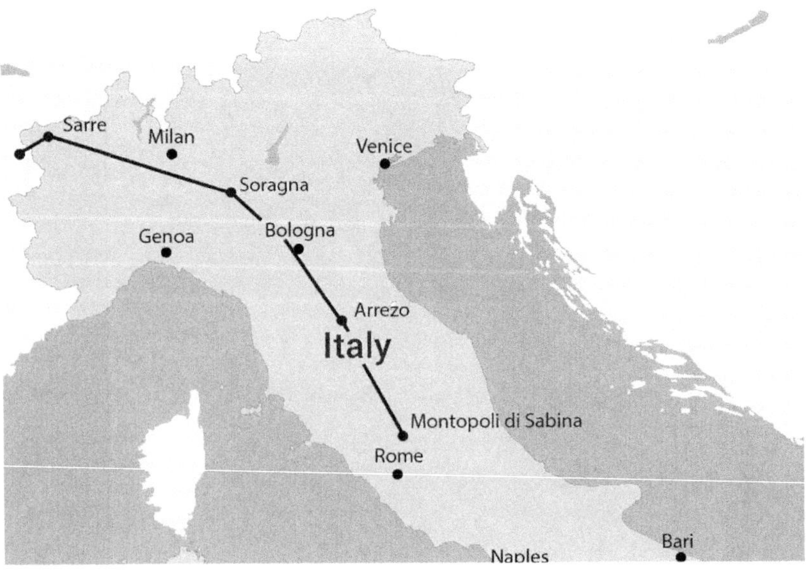

The road to Montopoli is one of the few in the area not going to Rome and it was bone-shakingly rough but the drive was worth it when we arrived. The *sosta* was a car park on the hillside below the town with far-reaching views towards the west. Free electricity was available if we wanted it, which we didn't for a single night halt. The only issue with the *sosta* is it is reached down a steep, tight bend. Several reviews reported wheel spin but none of them said no one was prevented by the slope from leaving. We would find out when it was our turn to depart.

It is worth mentioning why we didn't need electricity because the previous year our refrigerator misbehaved on gas. It would light but go out immediately so we ran it on mains electricity. Although the problem was not cured we learned how to tame the beast. When we are driving the refrigerator uses 12 volt power and if we left it for half an hour to cool after stopping it would light and remain lit reliably.

There is another Montopoli in Italy with a good sosta and we stayed there in 2016. This year's Montopoli is a classic village on a hill and impossible to photograph unless you have a drone. So I took a photograph of a mural under an arch instead showing the view from outside.

The views *from* the hill onto the surrounding countryside are impressive.

From another viewpoint we saw evidence of a recent fire which had singed a few olive trees.

The village is worth a walk around. It was virtually deserted when we explored its streets in the afternoon but in the evening the few bars in the centre of the town were busy, too busy in fact for us to even get a seat.

Bee-eaters were flying around below the *sosta* although I heard them first. A distinctive "wheet, wheet" to my ear although my bird book says it should be "prrut". It must be a local dialect.

As the *sosta* faces west we were rewarded with a sunset but I think the view looked even better the next morning.

Our departure from the sosta was accomplished with the wheel spin the reports warned about and I wouldn't have liked to have done it in rain. To return to the *autostrada* we didn't have to retrace our bumpy arrival route as there was a shorter road joining the *autostrada* further south. Today was Sunday when heavy trucks are banned from moving on the *autostrada*, making the roads quieter but there were still plenty of cars about. The trucks don't leave the motorway but gather in the service stations where they park up in solid blocks.

While looking at the road atlas during lunch I noticed we were about halfway through Italy. We had driven about fourteen hundred miles since Roscoff and the dashboard trip data revealed it had taken us thirty six hours behind the wheel.

We saw more evidence of fires throughout the day. Most were small affairs of just a few acres, but these were the ones near villages where presumably everyone turned out to tackle them. One fire in a more remote location covered half a mountainside.

We drove past Mount Vesuvius and it is an impressively large mountain I failed to photograph as I missed stopping at the only service area with a view of the dormant volcano.

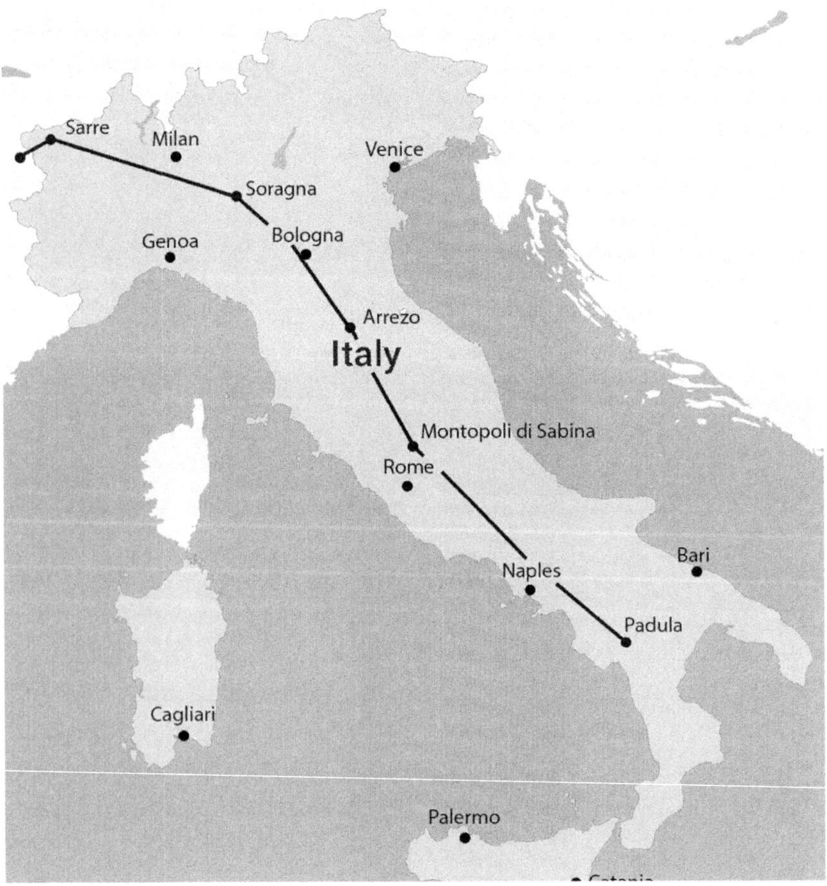

The night was spent at a privately owned *sosta* near Padula. The owner Mario was a great character who grew figs, tomatoes and other vegetables on his smallholding. He gave us a handful of figs as soon as we arrived and they were a revelation. I have never tasted such sweet ones and compared to the tasteless things available in the UK they were almost a different fruit. The site was very secure and when we first arrived we wondered how we would get in as the substantial gate was firmly closed. Closer inspection revealed a button and an intercom system and despite my almost complete lack of Italian and Mario's similar lack of English we gained admittance and subsequently got along with each other well.

In the early evening Mary reminded me today was her birthday. I had forgotten and not even noticed the birthday cards she hung up in the motorhome while I was walking the dog. After being reminded of the day, in a voice with a hint of sarcasm I quickly found the birthday card I had pre-packed. I think I was forgiven as I was fed later.

We couldn't leave the next day without buying a kilogramme of small tomatoes and in hindsight we should have bought more and some of Mario's other vegetables as the tomatoes were as delicious as the figs. Mary used Parma ham (non-chewy), figs, tomatoes, goats' cheese and lettuce all dressed with oil and balsamic vinegar to make a splendid lunch.

I have a video camera mounted on the windscreen behind the rear view mirror in our motorhome and before we left I noticed it was saying the memory card was full. This struck me as odd as it is supposed to overwrite the oldest files. When I investigated I found the card was full of write-protected files. These are created if the camera senses the vehicle has been in a collision so any evidence of the accident isn't lost.

There had been no accidents but we *had* been driving on the Italian roads. Even the generally smooth *autostrada*s may have been partly to blame. The Italian motorways generally have a good surface but they seem as a race to be incapable of forming a smooth joint between the road and any bridges. To allow for expansion all bridges have joints where the bridge and the road meet and often there are further joints between every span of the bridge. Perhaps the Italians haven't discovered the spirit level? If so this may explain the well-known tower in Pisa but hitting these joints at motorway speeds can be a noisy experience. The misalignment is often so great the crash and bang going over them tricks the sensor in the camera into thinking we had crashed. Off the *autostrada* there were the numerous potholes and the combined total of potholes and wonky bridge joints in Italy had comfortably exceeded the storage capacity of a 32GB SD card.

The Sea

We had come a long way over the last two weeks so we stopped for two nights by the sea to take a break from driving. Up to this point we only saw a few distant glimpses of the Mediterranean but from here on and for the next several weeks we would seldom be far from it.

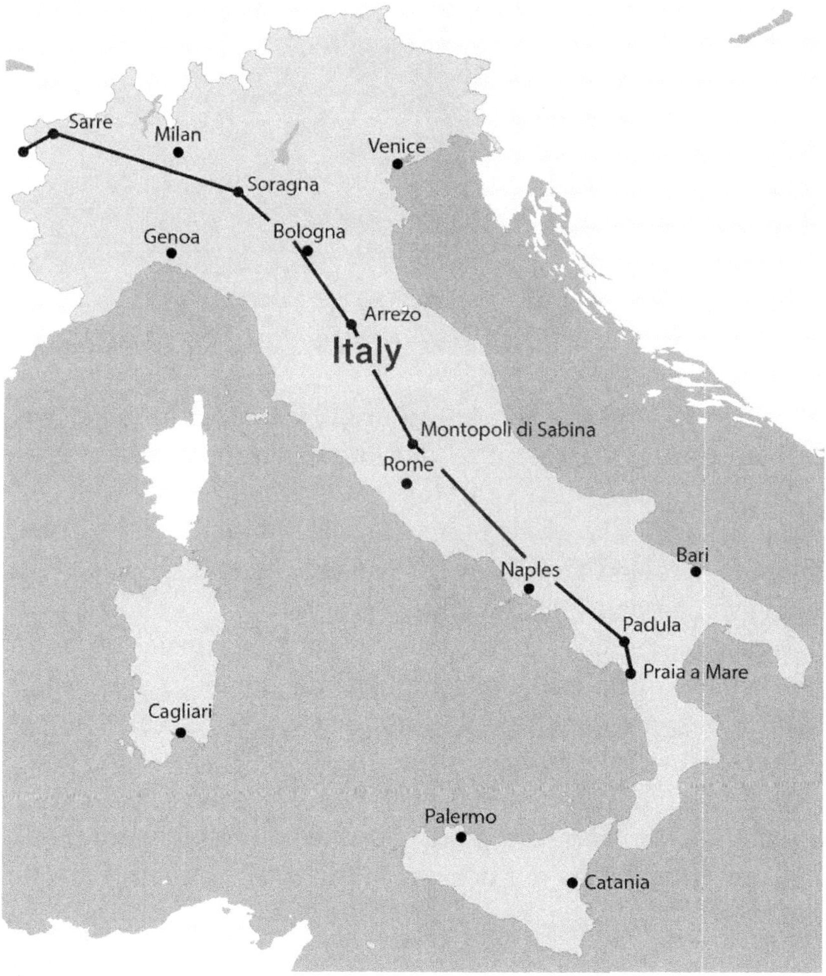

The campsite we chose at Praia a Mare was near a curious looking island, the Isola di Dino. The origin of the name is uncertain although it might come from the Greek *dino* meaning a storm or vortex, something hopefully we wouldn't see while we were there. My theory is it is named after someone's pet dog as the island looks like the head of a swimming Labrador.

The campsite had a restaurant where I took Mary for a delayed birthday meal. This was only a day late so not too bad for me.

We both chose pizza and Mary's was a "*Buffalina*" with real buffalo mozzarella while mine was a "*Romana*" with lots of olives, capers and anchovies. They were filling and we had no room even for an ice-cream afterwards.

When we got back to the motorhome loud music started in the distance. I opened the roof light for some air but it was facing the source of the noise and acting like an ear trumpet redirected the sound down inside to us. As it wasn't too hot I closed it and this made things quiet enough to fall asleep. There was an official quiet period but it started at half past midnight and a few hours after our normal bedtime. The Italians must be night owls.

We swam in the sea the next day but found the water cold. A website I looked at said the sea temperature should have been 26°C and I'm sure it was but the contrast between the much warmer air and the sea made it feel chilly.

Later the sky was filled with ominously dark clouds but the threat of rain was not fulfilled. This suited us but the local farmers would have preferred rain after the dry summer.

From Praia a Mare we moved to what mountaineers might call the final camp before the summit push. In our case this was our last stop on mainland Italy before we crossed the Straits of Messina. Avoiding, I hoped, the attentions of *Scylla* and *Charybdis*, the mythical sea monsters noted by Homer and living on opposite sides of the Straits.

In reaching this point, driving virtually the full length of Italy, we ignored millennia of human history. Naples, Pompeii, Herculaneum, Sorrento, Capri and the Amalfi coast we drove disdainfully past. These are places we should have visited but we would never have reached Sicily if we turned off every time we saw an inviting signpost.

I reminded myself we weren't in a race to reach Sicily so we stayed a few days in Tropea. Praia a Mare was winding down for the end of the season but Tropea was busy with holidaymakers.

Tropea is on a lump of land sticking up from the toe of Italy like a bunion. It was an easy place to reach from the north by the coast road. When we left we should have returned by the same route instead of cutting south across the bunion. But that lesson was for later.

From the site we couldn't yet see Sicily as the coast faced northwest but we could see Stromboli, the northernmost of the Aeolian Islands and near the northeast coast of Sicily. The Aeolians are a group of eight islands formed by volcanic action. The name is derived from the mythological God of the Winds, *Aeolus*, who was supposed to have lived there. In Homer's Odyssey, Ulysses landed on one of the islands, Vulcano, where the God of Fire also lived and met the cyclops Polyphemus who threatened to eat them all.

Stromboli is a new island and is thought to have been formed only about forty thousand years ago. It has been in continual eruption for the last two thousand years. Stromboli's eruptions can be violent and are characterised by bombs of hot larva being thrown into the air. The term "Strombolian eruption" is applied to other volcanoes around the world erupting in the same way. In the distant shot of Stromboli below you can see a cloud of steam or fumes at the summit. I was hoping when it was dark I might see a glow but the volcano must have been having a quiet day as sadly nothing was visible even through binoculars.

You can go on organised tours to Stromboli, sailing around the coast and even ascending the mountain, now clear of man-eating cyclopes although the Gods of Wind and Fire are probably still around.

At the end of Jules Verne's Journey to the Centre of Earth the survivors escape by being ejected from Stromboli and JRR Tolkien may even have used Stromboli as his inspiration for Mount Doom in The Lord of the Rings.

Tropea has a spectacular setting, perched above the sea and busy beaches on a cliff. Steps lead up into the town opposite the Monastery of Santa Mari dell'Isola.

There has been a religious building on this site since at least medieval times but what you see today was rebuilt after the 1905 magnitude 7.2 earthquake which hit southern Italy on Ash Wednesday, killing many attending church services.

The town is well prepared for tourists and there were many restaurants.

One displayed a prominent sign saying "*Gelati*" so as it was a warm day we tried it but sadly the ice cream was too sweet for us. We have tasted better in Italy so more fieldwork was required to find the best.

If the ice cream was a disappointment the shops were colourful and interesting.

The photograph below of a shop front shows a lot of chillies and in the bottom right onions. The region around Tropea is famous for its red onions *cipolla di Tropea* and there are some in the bottom right of the display to the right of the door. They are shaped a little like banana shallots, long and thin.

After walking around and getting lost for a few minutes before we found the steps back down to beach level we ascended another set to the monastery. It cost €2 to get in but the fee was worth it for the views. The shot of Tropea on its clifftop was taken from the monastery.

The beach at Tropea, it would be fair to say, is fully exploited. We saw one sign saying the cost for two sun loungers and an umbrella was €15 a day with a hot shower afterwards a chargeable extra.

Tropea is worth visiting but don't come if you don't like steps. Leaving Tropea is also taxing. The road under the cliff is one way so on leaving the campsite we turned right. The road climbed around the western edge of the town until we encountered a sign warning of a height restriction ahead. We turned around and headed back into Tropea, this time at the level of the top of the cliff. We had managed to get mildly lost on foot here and the satnav was of little help but with dead reckoning and luck we eventually found a road away from Tropea going in the right direction. A glance at a map will show you there is no main coast road going all the way round the blunt peninsula of Tropea. We could only cut across country, heading south and southeast. This made for *extremely* slow going and we would have done much better returning the way we arrived by heading back east and joined the *autostrada* where we left it two days earlier.

But we escaped from Tropea's bunion eventually and headed quickly southwest once we joined the main coast road. We were close to Sicily and I hadn't thought about what to expect. Would it be like crossing the Channel with your destination virtually out of sight until you approach the far coast? It isn't and when we first saw Sicily it came as a shock. The sea was on our right but as we neared our destination what at first glance looked like a major headland appeared and soon occupied virtually the whole of the horizon. This was Sicily and it was big, it was close and it was mountainous.

At their closest point mainland Italy and Sicily are only about two kilometres apart although the ferry crossing from Villa San Giovanni to Messina is about four kilometres.

I hadn't done much research on the ferries other than establishing you didn't need to book one but could just turn up. So we followed the signs to the port and after a while I saw a sign saying "Caronte & Tourist" and although I didn't know what a Caronte was I knew we were tourists so I followed these signs which took us to a long car park with an office on the right hand side. A man showed me where to park and then took charge of my ticket buying. I have come across this arrangement before and I am happy with it but others might object to having to pay €5 to achieve something you can easily do yourself - buy a ticket from a window. I view it as encouraging entrepreneurship and the local economy. I suspect part of my €5 found its way to the local mafia boss as I can't imagine this going on so close to Sicily and the mafia *not* being involved. The cost of the open return ticket we bought was €93 and what I expected. I had done *some* research.

The ticket office is not near the port but Five Euro Man had a solution to this. "Follow that car" he told me after I paying him his fee. So I followed the car as it shot through the centre of

Villa di Giovanni and subsequently joined a line of vehicles on the quayside. As it took us so long to escape from the clutches of Tropea we didn't arrive at the port until the afternoon and this being a Friday it was busy. Had we arrived about fifteen minutes earlier we would have been able to board this ferry.

The name on the vessel was the name of the shipping company and it was their signs I followed as we entered the town! The service is frequent and we only waited another quarter of an hour before we could board the next ferry, which was painted a cheerful bright yellow. We left Charlie in the motorhome after boarding though I think we could have taken him with us. The crossing takes about half an hour and though it was overcast the sea was calm. There was a lounge with seating but we made our way to the front deck to watch the approach to Sicily. About halfway across it rained gently but we stayed on deck, excited at reaching our goal. Disappointingly no whirlpools or sea monsters were visible during the crossing but we saw waves breaking over a reef or shoal and evidence of strong currents. The moon was nearly full at the time of our crossing so the tides would be at their highest. The forecast tidal range at Tropea when I checked was a shade over one metre. This surprised me as I always thought Mediterranean tides were much smaller. Perhaps the disturbances in the water gave rise to the myths of sea monsters?

This was the view from the ferry from near Messina. Somewhere in the distance and lost in clouds is Mount Etna. It would be another month before we were to see her summit.

Disembarking was fun. The crew dropped the ramp and stood back leaving the four lanes of vehicles on the ship to drive off and merge into two lanes on the ramp. Welcome to Sicily, here is your first driving lesson.

Sicily

We landed in Sicily and I suggest if you do the same then as soon as possible after landing pull over and make a note of the coordinates of the port. This will save problems when you come to return as we were to discover many weeks later.

We had driven almost eighteen hundred miles from Roscoff and according to the trip recorder this took us forty six hours of driving and taken sixteen days. Longer than I expected but we made three stops of two nights each in campsites. You could do it in much less time, but even a full week would mean over eight hours at the wheel every day including halts. We hadn't come the quickest way. We avoided the toll roads in France until we got near Lyon and the diversion to Tropea must have added extra miles. Before we left home I estimated the distance would be sixteen hundred miles taking the fastest and most direct path.

Even coming from Calais it is a major journey. Calais to Milan in the north of Italy is about six hundred miles by the shortest route through Switzerland but Milan isn't even half way. It is another eight hundred miles from there to reach the ferry port at Villa San Giovanni.

Now we had arrived Sicily did not seem pleased to see us. It was raining heavily as we drove out of Messina and onto the north coast road. We would tour Sicily anti-clockwise for no better reason than going this way round meant we could end with a bang at Mount Etna. Not a real bang, I hoped, but it seemed appropriate to finish with Sicily's most famous site.

All this was for the future and our first two nights on Sicily were to be spent on a campsite at Oliveri, giving us an opportunity to wash Charlie's very dirty bedding.

We could allow ourselves a maximum of about four weeks on Sicily without changing the return ferry from Roscoff, but as things worked out four weeks was perfect for a slow circumnavigation of the island.

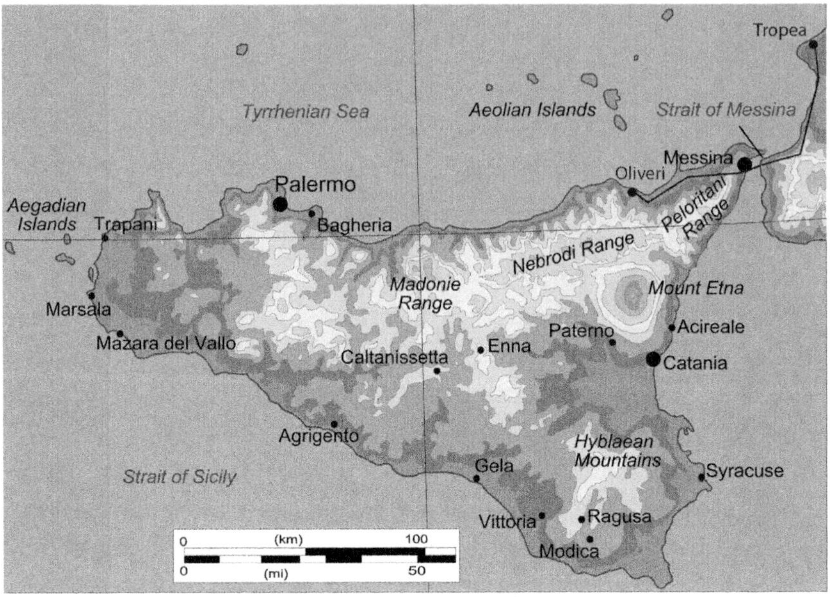

Charlie and I walked to the beach on the first evening. It stopped raining earlier and the sky was clear. There is a saying "what a difference a day makes" but here it should be "what a difference a ferry makes". Tropea was heaving with people, this place was empty. Charlie couldn't get a swim at Tropea, here he had the beach to himself.

After lunch the following day I went exploring. Immediately to the west of the campsite is the Tindari reserve and sand spit called the Laguna di Oliveri jutting out into the sea. There are several lagoons at the base of the sand spit.

The water is salt and small fish were swimming amongst what looked like eel grass, it was also warm and Charlie the water terrier had great fun running in and out of it.

The building above the lagoon is the Sanctuary of the Madonna di Tindari containing a Madonna Nera or Black Madonna. Once a year there is a pilgrimage to honour her and we just missed this because it was held yesterday, the same day we arrived on Sicily.

There are literally hundreds of Black Madonnas in Europe, both as statues and as paintings. The dark skin is thought not to represent any racial or ethnic aspect of the figure but may be linked to symbolic meanings and earlier goddesses. An alternative view is many of the figures are carved from woods which darkened as they aged though this explanation does not cover the paintings. The origin of the Black Madonna of Tindari is unknown. A legend suggests it was thrown overboard in a box to lighten the weight of a sinking ship. The box was subsequently washed up near Tindari and the figure taken up the hill to the Christian community living there. A subsequent legend even explains the sand spit. The story relates how a child fell from the cliff and the mother implored the Black Madonna to intervene by causing the sea to retreat. The child was later found playing on the beach.

On my walk I saw few children playing on the beach though none looked as though they recently fell from the cliff above. I also saw a peregrine falcon grab a bird out of the air above a lagoon. The falcon's prey was a swallow although it was too fleeting a glimpse to be sure but there were several swallows hawking over the water. One less now. After taking the bird the peregrine flew in a wide arc over the sand spit before landing momentarily low on the cliff then flying away again. It was too far away to see what happened but I suspect it either fed a juvenile or its mate was there and he gave her a bond-strengthening present of food. It *might* have been an Eleonora's falcon. Unusually these breed in the early autumn when they prey on migrant birds and larger insects like dragonflies. However, they breed communally and this was a single bird, or at least the only one I saw. It looked like a Peregrine but then so does an Eleonora's falcon but I'm convinced it was the former. The problem was I had left my binoculars behind. These being the small, light, easy to carry and less likely to be left behind and expensive binoculars recently purchased. The Eleonora's falcon is an interesting and rare bird and one of the last European birds of prey to be identified by science. It has the curious and macabre habit in the breeding season of catching small birds, removing their flight feathers then imprisoning them alive in a gully or crevice to be fed to their chicks later. Nature is cruel, inventive and diverse.

Excursion to Tindari

The last picture above showed part of the Sanctuary of the Black Madonna from the seaward side. Here it is from the landward side.

We left the campsite and after a sort drive found a spot in an overflow car park at the foot of the hill below the sanctuary. The road up to the sanctuary is closed to the public and there were officials and police on duty to enforce the rules. Parking was free but this was the hottest day so far and already over 34°C by mid-morning and we weren't looking forward to the walk up the hill. So it was with a twinge of concern for how hot it might get later we set off, only to discover after a few hundred yards a bus was available. After spending one euro each for a return ticket we were swept up to the church in air-conditioned coolness.

The annual pilgrimage mentioned earlier was held on the Friday we arrived on Sicily and this being the first Sunday afterwards the church was busy. The title of this chapter is taken from one of Andrea Camilleri's Montalbano stories. Excursion to Tindari describes the regular visits here by a group from the fictional Sicilian town of Vigàta. Despite a journey of several hours by bus to reach it the author describes how popular the trips were and from what we could see buses were still bringing visitors from all over Sicily. We could hear the sounds of a service so we didn't go in but went instead to the real reason we were here. Our first (of many) Sicilian ruins lay close by.

On the walk to the ruins we saw several forest fires in the distance. The wind was strong so bringing them under control must have been a struggle. Later on in the day we drove past a house in the country where a fire was lit by the edge of the road to burn rubbish. It was unattended, surrounded by parched vegetation and was probably about to be the origin of a new and bigger fire.

This site was Tyndaris, founded by the tyrant of Syracuse, Dionysius in 395 or 396 BC, after this thing get hectic. Tyndaris was one of the last Greek colonies on Sicily but it was taken by the Carthaginians in 264 BC. The troublesome Carthaginians, who came from what is now Tunisia , held it only for ten years before being thrown out by the Romans who had a serious downer on the Carthaginians and pursued them remorselessly in the Punic Wars, subsequently destroying their capital Carthage in 146 BC after a two year siege. The surviving population were sold into slavery and the victorious Romans utterly destroyed the city, leaving not a wall standing.

A considerable time later the Arabs came to Sicily and occupied Tyndaris only to be expelled in their turn by the Normans. Yes, the Normans, the same lot who may or may not have poked our Harry's eye out with an arrow.

The first image above is a temple and the second a small theatre, originally Greek but later altered by the Romans. The plastic seats at the front are of more recent origin.

We came upon proper Roman baths complete with mosaic floors. This is the *Tepidarium* where warm heat came from below the floor and through the walls in clay pipes. I would have preferred a *Frigidarium* given the outside temperature.

The attached museum to the site was small but worth visiting. There was a larger than life head of Augustus depicting him looking innocent and boy-like. In real life he emerged out of the chaos caused by the assassination of Caesar as a military dictator who overcame all rivals to eventually become the first Roman emperor.

The weather was unsettled as it was across virtually the whole of Europe so with no hope of escaping the rain we moved to Camping Rais Gerbi almost in the middle of the north coast of Sicily.

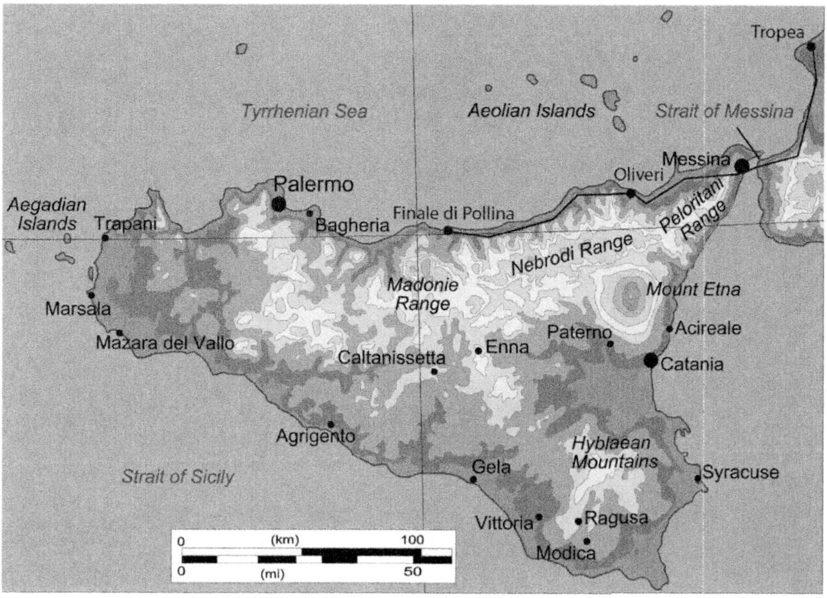

This was the perfect site when it rained as the pitches were made of concrete. The beach was uninviting boulders but they did have a swimming pool which we visited between showers. The first attempt ended in ignominy as the pool attendant threw us out for not wearing bathing caps. So we slunk away and returned with the correct headgear. We knew about the rule, it is widespread in Europe and there were bathing caps ready in the motorhome for this eventuality but we had never worn them before. The rule may be common but it isn't always enforced. Our bathing caps were unused and trying them on for was a surprise. They were painfully tight so our swim was quickly abandoned due to the loss of blood to our scalps.

The unsettled weather I blamed on butterflies in the Amazon. If they would stop flapping their wings or breaking wind or whatever it is they do to cause storms things would improve.

More Ruins

Glancing in the mirror the following morning I found inspiration for the day. It was time to find another ruin. So we headed west, where the views along the coast were almost as craggy as the view in the mirror. Our plan was to visit Cefalù, a striking town of Greek origin. The view below shows the impressive twin-towered cathedral dominating the town.

Cefalù is a popular destination. We tried twice to get in on different routes; both times I needed to perform three or four point turns to extract ourselves. There was a vehicle in every conceivable parking space and the streets became narrow as you approached the older part of the town.

Cefalù is worth visiting if you can get in but you should forget getting close in a motorhome or in any vehicle. We could have parked outside the town but it would have been a long walk and dark clouds were forming due to the errant behaviour of the Amazonian butterflies. Bikes or taxi would be best, or you could take the train, the line of which follows the coast.

So instead of visiting Cefalù we went inland to Caccamo, a hilltop town crowned by a Norman castle, or rather it was founded by the Normans but much of what can be seen today are seventeenth century extensions to the original Norman structure.

According to our guide book the castle is open every day except Monday. Today with our usual imperfect timing was a Monday but we wandered up to the castle anyway. We walked past several signs on the way up confirming the prediction it would be closed but when we arrived it was open. In our surprise (get the excuse in early) we somehow and unintentionally entered without paying. I'm not sure how we did it but behaving like two people walking their dog seemed to work. The castle is not huge but is worth a quick explore.

Signs pointed us towards dungeons. Some had drawings scratched into the remaining bits of plaster on the walls. They must have been luxurious dungeons to have plastered walls. There were a few metal chains fixed to walls but they didn't look original. Slightly more authentic was a small museum with a few artefacts.

It didn't take us long to see everything as much of the castle is not open to the public even when it isn't a Monday so after only half an hour of exploring we crept out quietly, trying not to catch the eye of the person at the ticket office.

The town below the castle was interesting in parts.

We parked the motorhome below the castle in what we assumed when we arrived was a normal car park. When we returned we noticed there were electrical and water points around the edge for motorhomes. Sadly they didn't work, as the reviews on CamperContact (it is number 15614) and our tap-twiddling confirmed.

After eating lunch in the late *sosta* we descended through the numerous hairpin bends to the coast and headed towards Palermo. The Satnav found a supermarket but too late to allow me to get off the main road in time. So I took the next junction instead and let the Satnav guide us back through the streets to the supermarket.

A lesson was learned here and one subsequently confirmed by others who have visited Palermo. The traffic of the capital of Sicily takes no prisoners. So if you come this way do your shopping beforehand in a smaller town. The four lanes into two ferry ramp was just a warm-up act for the traffic here.

There is a lot to see here but like Cefalu don't arrive in a motorhome. The city has a long history and is worth visiting if only to see one building, the extraordinary Palatine Chapel. Completed in 1140 it is filled with the most detailed mosaics and other decorative features but the frenzied traffic didn't encourage us to linger long enough to stay.

West of Palermo we found a campsite for the night near the village of Isola delle Femmine.

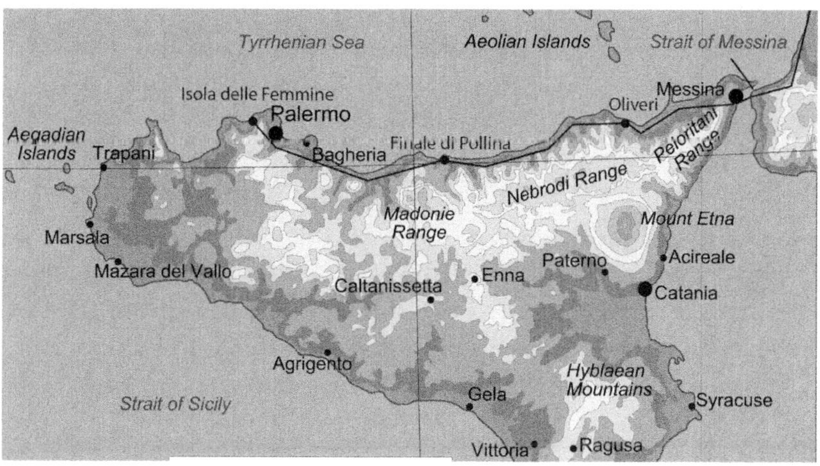

A gale was blowing and large waves breaking on the rocky shore so Charlie's evening walk wasn't too extended.

It is worth remembering this campsite as it is near a train station which would be the ideal way to visit Palermo. The site also introduced us to the Sicily Camping Tour group. With a free membership card and a map showing the dozen sites in the group we had access to a few more places than were shown in the ACSI book. Many of the sites are ACSI members already but a few are not, including one on the south coast we wouldn't otherwise have known about and it was one of the best sites we found on the island.

The aim for the next day was to see more ruins but when we saw them they didn't seem ruined. Apart from a missing roof it was intact.

And there *would* have been a roof, probably cedar with ceramic tiles. This "ruin" is the 5th Century BC Doric Greek temple at Segesta. It has done well to survive not having its stones pinched for two and a half thousand years.

Getting here was fun. Naturally we ignored the parking signs and drove directly towards the temple. Folk must do this a lot as they have a man stationed to tell drivers like me to turn around and drive back to the parking area and catch the shuttle bus. It was €7 for parking a "camper" but this included the bus fare.

The car park was noteworthy for being the only place on Sicily where we saw a UK registered car, though the occupants were absent so we couldn't hear their story.

At the site you queue for an entrance ticket. We were unlucky and arrived behind a large group of tourists but we were well chilled after three weeks and took the enforced wait in good humour.

The temple is built of limestone which has eroded over the millennia and is in need of support in a few places.

In my introduction to this site I said it would have had a roof, this is true but only if it was finished, because Segesta is an *unfinished* temple. The evidence for this can be seen in the photograph above. The columns are smooth. In a finished temple vertical fluting would have been cut into them as we were to see on the next temple we visited on Sicily.

On a hill above the temple is a more less complete (not another ruin) third century BC Greek theatre. It looked a steep walk on foot to reach it so we paid one and a half euros each for the shuttle bus.

The theatre is unusual in facing north although the orientation of Greek theatres varies enormously. Unlike Christian churches they are not all aligned in a particular direction other than never directly towards the setting or rising sun. One theory suggests they may be aligned towards a constellation linked to the god the specific theatre was dedicated to. However, topography is a factor and many face the sea as does the theatre at Segesta, which being near the north coast of Sicily means the theatre faces that way. Plays are performed from time to time in many old Greek theatres, as we witnessed with the blue chairs of Tindari and Segesta sees modern day action from time to time.

We missed the shuttle bus for the return so we walked back, which wasn't difficult as gravity aided us and the walk on the road rewarded us with the best views of the main temple.

After lunch of a focaccia sandwich bought from the on-site shop we drove to Castellammare del Golfo, a fishing port.

This is a place on the tour bus circuit and one full of British tourists pulled up behind us when we parked.

The port is attractive, Charlie swam in the harbour where traditional fishing boats were moored amongst the yachts. Unlike Cefalù finding a parking space wasn't difficult but getting out was tight. We parked in what I thought was a one way street so I kept going in the same direction and found the road getting progressively narrower. Yet again we escaped but when we returned a few days later I realised the street was only one way for cars. Larger vehicles could turn around and take the easy way out.

Castellammare del Golfo is on a wide bay with Palermo to the east and to the west a promontory projects northwards. At the end of the promontory and reached after a drive through parched and barren country is the small town of San Vito Lo Capo.

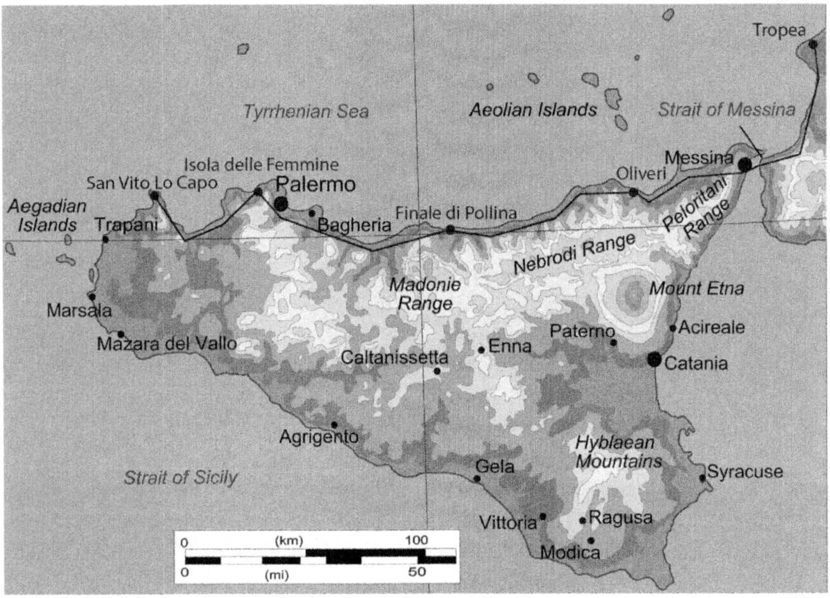

The sea here was cloudy from the rough weather but the forecast was much better with temperatures in the mid to upper twenties for the next ten days and light winds.

Mary was busy the next day with a big laundry wash, doing all the bedding but she didn't have to do everything on her own. I put up the washing line for her and I made a pudding for lunch out of prickly pear fruit. We cheated and bought them pre-packed although you can harvest them yourself and this seemed to be their season. Buying them pre-packed they were free of spines and could be handled with bare hands providing you were careful.

All you need to prepare them is a chopping board, sharp knife and a fork. Start by chopping the ends off then make a shallow cut the length of the fruit and with a fork remove the skin. The flesh inside tastes like watermelon and like watermelon is full of pips. Unlike watermelon the pips are much smaller than grape pips and are eaten with the flesh of the fruit.

There were big crags behind the campsite and I took Charlie for a walk along the road below them after the prickly pear lunch. Yet again I forgot my binoculars so the two birds I saw soaring over them will remain a mystery. On a balance of probabilities they were griffon vultures but they might have been golden eagles or (dare to dream) Bonelli's eagles, these are rare but they have been recorded at national reserve to the south of us.

Another mystery unresolved but the rocks are impressive. The cliff is nearly 400m high according to the map. The tooth shaped bit to the left of centre is a stand-alone pillar, separate from the rest of the cliff. Near the summit above the cliff there is a geocache for anyone feeling energetic. A three hour return walk I believe. While I enjoy geocaching I gave this one a miss.

Though impossible to see in the photograph on the extreme right of the picture where the cliff tapers away is one of the many limestone quarries this region has. There was not much sign of activity from it. You might think the mafia would knock down old buildings to generate trade in the same way they are reputed to start forest fires so they can get the replanting contract.

The beach at San Vito can't be easily accessed from the campsite so after two nights we moved on, returning to Castellammare del Golfo. This didn't take us much out of our way as the road to Capo San Vito is a dead-end so you have to retrace your steps to pick up the coast road again.

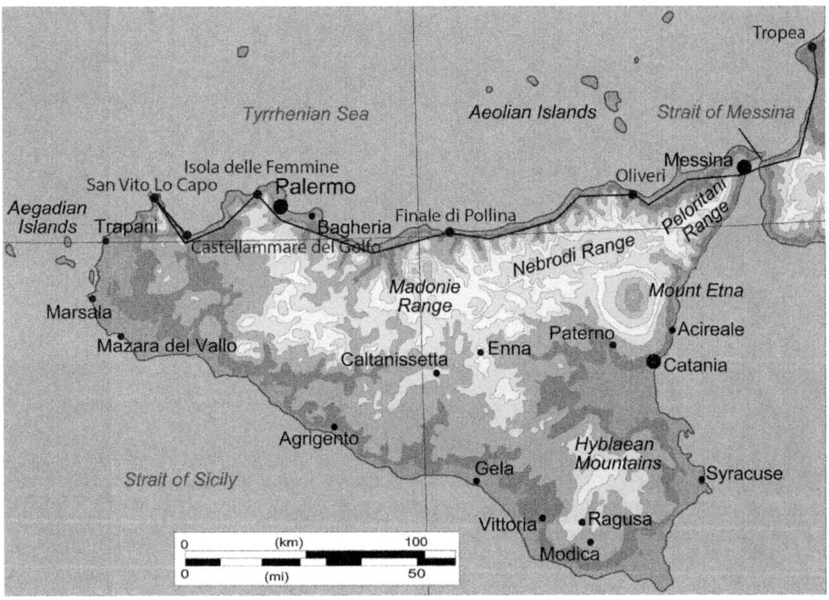

Our reason for returning was to have a fish lunch at one of the many restaurants beside the harbour. La Cambusa was graded number seven out of fifty on TripAdvisor and in an almost perfect location overlooking the harbour so this was our choice.

Starter for me was *calamaricci fritti* or fried baby squid. Mary ordered a prawn cocktail which she told me are becoming fashionable again. The menu had both a first and second fish course option to follow the starters but we opted for the second course only of grilled swordfish steaks with grilled vegetables. Swordfish (or *spada*) is a Sicilian favourite but we weren't over-impressed. They were overdone I think and dry. We have eaten much better tasting tuna steaks in Tarifa in the south of Spain and I fear it wasn't fresh but frozen.

For puddings Mary had seasonal fruit in syrup and for me it was a parfait with pistachios. The parfait, hiding under a green topping, was a squidgy meringue.

We staggered back to the motorhome after over an hour and half of steady chomping. The service was good, delightfully unhurried, as we like it, giving us time to digest and quietly ferment between courses. It was a pity the *spada* wasn't as tasty as we expected.

There are two options for staying in Castellammare del Golfo. A small campsite which looked busy with pitches close together or a commercial *sosta*. Both are within walking distance of the harbour. We chose the *sosta* even though our first impressions were not favourable. There was no drinking water but we could dispose of our grey waste and emptying the toilet cassette was an unusual experience. The owner took the cassette away and returned it empty and after washing the outside of it. It was best not to ask where they put the contents.

We spent one night at the *sosta* before heading inland to find Cyclopean walls. I try and research the places we visit but on this occasion my research failed because although I knew there were Cyclopean walls to be found I neglected to check what one looked like so we could recognise it when we found them.

Our aim was to visit Erice, a town named after the son of Venus and Neptune. The name is pronounced I think "ayreechay" but don't trust someone who can't recognise a Cyclopean wall.

Erice, oblivious to pronunciation is perched on a hill near the western end of Sicily. It is famous for its walls.

But before we get to the wretched walls the location of the town has not been unnoticed by the motorsport brigade.

As we climbed up the wiggly road to Erice it was obvious the road was being prepared for a race. The corners were protected by tyres and before every hairpin signs counted down the distance to the bend; 150, 100 and 50. A sign over the road identified the event as the 59th Erice hill climb and due to be held over the forthcoming weekend.

Near the top we came upon a bend with a road branching off to the left with signs pointing towards parking for buses and "autocaravanes". If you come this way take this and unlike us drive to the end where there is a gravel space to park and the opportunity to wild camp. Instead, we parked under trees well before the end of the road which for us was the right place as it gave shade as we planned to leave Charlie in the motorhome. We are well used to his dislike of hot dry streets.

The road we were parked on is called the Via delle Pinette and it ends at the Porta Spada.

So named (spada means sword, as in the fish) because numerous prisoners were put to death by the sword here in the thirteenth century during a revolt known as the Sicilian Vespers.

And the image above hints at my undoing. I formed the erroneous impression "Cyclopean walls" meant big stones with smaller stones on top, precisely what the photograph above shows.

I was wrong. Cyclopean walls are different. They are found all around the world but are named from Mycenaean (Greekish type) architecture from around sixteen hundred to eleven hundred BC. They are constructed using massive boulders fitted closely together without mortar. The walls in the image above are made without mortar but the stones have been heavily worked. Cyclopean stones show little signs of being worked other than with crude tools. Only one of my shots, by accident as I didn't recognise at the time what I was seeing, showed the Cyclopean walls.

And that's them nearest the camera. Rough boulders lying on the bed rock with the more finely worked stones of a later period on top of them. I'm not sure how old they are as accounts seem to vary but around 800 BC would be a reasonable guess. Old anyway and well hidden.

I should add websites describe the entire wall at Erice as being Cyclopean but I think this is the tourist board making the best of it. A Cyclopean wall doesn't have rectangular stones with neat corners.

The main church of Erice is the Chiesa Madre, and it lacks a homely feel, "austere" was the word in the guidebook.

There were the usual old doors throughout the town. Number 21 was an impressive one (overleaf).

The streets have remarkable patterns created in them which you can see below the door above. There is more to Erice than we saw, the remains of a Norman castle and a picturesque nineteenth century hunting lodge but they will have to wait for another visit.

The South Coast

We descended from Erice by a road which took us west and gave us a view looking down on Trapani and beyond it the Aegadian islands. Later we skirted Marsala, best known in the UK for the wine named after the town. This is made by a similar method to sherry and was created for the sherry-loving British market but to many Italians Marsala is more famous as the port where Giuseppe Garibaldi landed in 1860. With a modest force of a thousand he set about defeating the Bourbons who ruled Sicily at the time and with a much larger army at their command. Despite the odds Garibaldi succeeded and subsequently went on to unite the whole of Italy the following year.

Marsala is the most western point of the island of Sicily so after it we turned and began travelling along Sicily's south coast.

We stopped at Camping Helios. This isn't in the ACSI book but is part of the Sicily Camping Tour and well positioned for Selinunte. A site with temples they completed building.

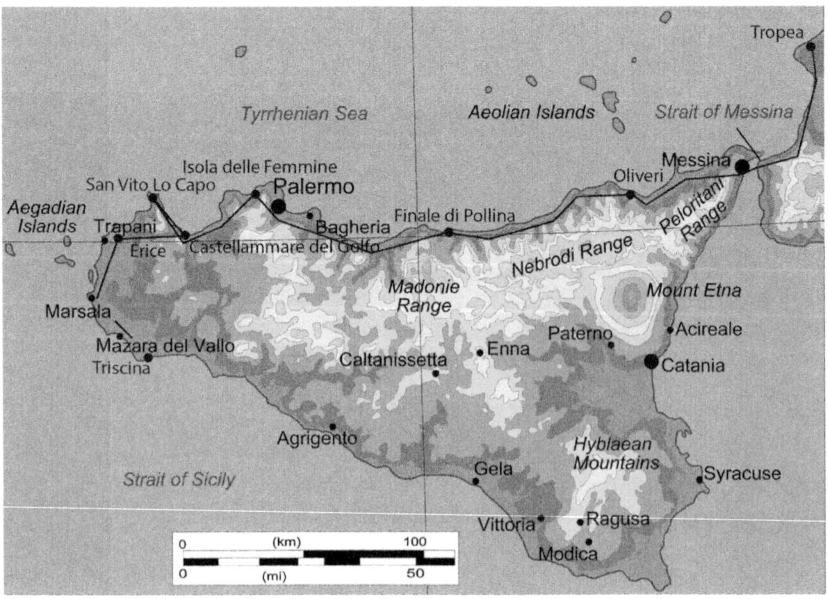

Selinunte was described in our guidebook as "amongst the most striking archaeological sites in the Mediterranean". A hint we might expect impressive ruins or a place with more tumbled down old stones than anywhere else. We would find out later.

Camping Helios, named after the Greek god of the sun who was hiding behind clouds when we arrived, is directly on a broad, clean sandy beach. Below is the view twenty paces from the motorhome. The couple on the beach are about our age and flying a kite. I suddenly felt old as we didn't have a kite.

The sea by the campsite was shallow and you couldn't get out of your depth unless you went a long way out. On one of our first dips with Charlie, as we waded in, he with his little legs got out of his depth quickly. He kept up with us by swimming for a while but decided returning to shore was a wiser move. He then stayed in the shallows and barked at us until we came back.

The site was full of Germans together with a lone Austrian, almost all in VW campervans ranging in age from the new and expensive to the much older but still expensive.

The humidity on our first evening was high, around 95% according to my little weather station but the temperature fell as it grew dark. The forecast threatened thunder but it didn't arrive which was a shame as we enjoy a thunderstorm and it would have lowered the humidity.

A few yards from our pitch was an unusual non-VW vehicle, a pop-up hearse conversion. The dark tube on the roof is a solar water heater, aerodynamic when the roof is lowered for travelling and a clever contrivance.

Selinunte, the main reason we came here was the most westerly Greek colony in Sicily. The historic records are contradictory on when the city was founded but the widely accepted date is 628 BC. The name of the city derives curiously from the Greek name for wild celery, *selinon*. This grew in profusion on the site and the celery leaf was the symbol of the city on their coinage.

The citizens soon came into contact with the non-Greek people of Segesta of the unfinished temple we visited a few days earlier. Relations between the two cities were not good (temple envy?) and intermittent hostilities lasted for well over a century until the Segestans played their joker and appealed to Carthage for help. In 409 BC the Carthaginians rocked up with a force of one hundred thousand. The siege didn't last long, partly because the city's defences were in disrepair and reinforcements promised by allies did not arrive in time. Most of the population of Selinunte were executed though the survivors reoccupied it after the walls were destroyed and they promised to pay Carthage tribute.

The site today is a shambles, to put it both politely and kindly. Before the Carthaginians were driven out of Sicily they evacuated the population then destroyed the city. A subsequent earthquake in medieval times would have toppled anything they missed. The result is what you see today, less the restored bits. Imagine buying a "Build your own model temple" kit, opening the box and tipping all the pieces of the model onto a table and then spreading them out with your hand. Restoration or to use a posh term "anastylosis" has been carried out on two of the temples at Selinunte, one less successfully than the other. Given all the temples when discovered were fallen down and only a fraction of them have been rebuilt there is scope for further anastylosis.

Selinunte is divided into two sections with separate eastern and western sites. Here is a general view of the eastern side.

And this is your intrepid correspondent standing before the rebuilt temple shown above. Please note any untoward bulges in my shorts you can see are due to a camera lens in my pocket.

And a close-up of the temple. Note the fluting on the columns of this *finished* temple.

The temple was reconstructed between 1956 and 1959 and to my inexpert eye seems well done though not all archaeologists agree. The reconstructed bits are not meant to fool the observer but they blend in well. They have used stone-coloured concrete and this I fear may be what the experts object to.

Behind this rebuilt temple are the remains of two further temples, one which when standing was one of the largest temples in the Greek Mediterranean. Some imagination is needed to picture what it might have looked like when upright.

If they ever find the assembly instructions they could put it all back together. The stones are massive. This is the upturned top of a column and it must be three metres square at least.

Luckily a Montalbano lookalike turned up in time to give scale to this bit of column.

The west site is built on top of a mound surrounded by walls, or rather the remains of the walls destroyed by the Carthaginians. This is called the Acropolis and was the centre of public life. There are traces of several streets once lined with shops and houses.

This has been less successfully restored.

The bits above, a capital I think and part of a column, have been staged or posed on other stones to display them.

The rebuilding work on this site started in the late Twenties so it would be wrong to criticise from this distance in time. I am sure they thought it was right when they did it. Only part of the temple has been rebuilt though no doubt most of the parts are there to complete it if they could find them.

After two hours under the sun we needed an ice-cream and at €3 a tub it was considerably cheaper than I feared.

Leaving Selinunte we visited a much smaller and less well known site, Cave di Cusa. This is the site of the quarry where the stones for Selinunte were extracted. Cave di Cusa was a thriving quarry until one day in 409 BC news reached them of the Carthaginians approaching Selinunte led by Hannibal Mago. This was not the Hannibal with the elephants who crossed the Alps, he was 200 years later, this was an earlier Hannibal but one to instil fear leading such a prodigiously large army.

The quarry workers' reaction to the news was to flee, wisely given what happened to the citizens of Selinunte. But their actions left the quarry as it was on that day, less two thousand years or more of weathering since.

The quarry was on a limestone escarpment overlooking what are now square kilometres of olive trees. This is a big olive oil producing area, in the sense they produce a lot of olive oil. The olives on the wild trees on the site were tiny - lack of water no doubt following the summer's drought and heat. We arrived at about one o'clock and found the ticket office closed. "You can go in" a lady having lunch told me. I don't think the entrance charge would have been much. It was only €6 at Selinunte although you could spend at least the same again there if you wanted to have a golf buggy tour or the audio guide.

The beginning of the quarry of Cave di Cusa looked unexceptional.

But as we went in further we came to the magical area where they cut the columns.

The above is a small one but you can see from this the technique they used. First they levelled the rock surface then cut two concentric grooves. The bit of rock in between the grooves was then broken out, probably with a rock before repeating the process. The finished channel is wide enough for a man to work in or for me to take a photograph (next page). The column is on the right in the picture.

When it was deep enough the rock on one side was removed to expose the column.

The column above was massive, around fifteen feet in diameter. How they released it must have been a significant challenge. One account says they used metal tools to undercut the rock then lever it free.

It is believed the rocks may then have been wrapped in timber and rolled to Selinunte with oxen power to assist. There were a few on the site still waiting for the oxen.

The quarry is worth visiting even if you have to pay to get in.

Intriguingly, as we left the quarry site we saw two tankers pull into an olive oil processing plant. This was mid-September and the oil harvest had not begun yet so the trucks weren't coming to take away this year's harvest. Charitably I will think they were here to take the last of the previous year’s oil harvest. Or they might have been over to Albania on a ferry from Bari to collect Albanian oil to be resold as Sicilian. Such things have happened and the heat and lack of rainfall this year would have hit the expected yield so the temptation to top up stocks must have been strong.

We returned to Camping Helios where I explored the little sand dunes behind the beach. There were beetle and lizard tracks to be spotted, the latter identified by the line left by the lizard’s tail. This is sea lily or sea daffodil, *Pancratium maritimum.*

If we ever return to Sicily it would be early in the year. The western part of the island is predominantly limestone so the flowers, especially orchids, should be impressive from about February onwards.

The Valley of the Temples

Egypt has many archaeological sites but one site stands above all others in terms of popularity, the pyramids at Giza. In Sicily there is a similar focus for tourists; the Valley of the Temples. We hadn't seen many people on the sites visited up to now but this was to change here.

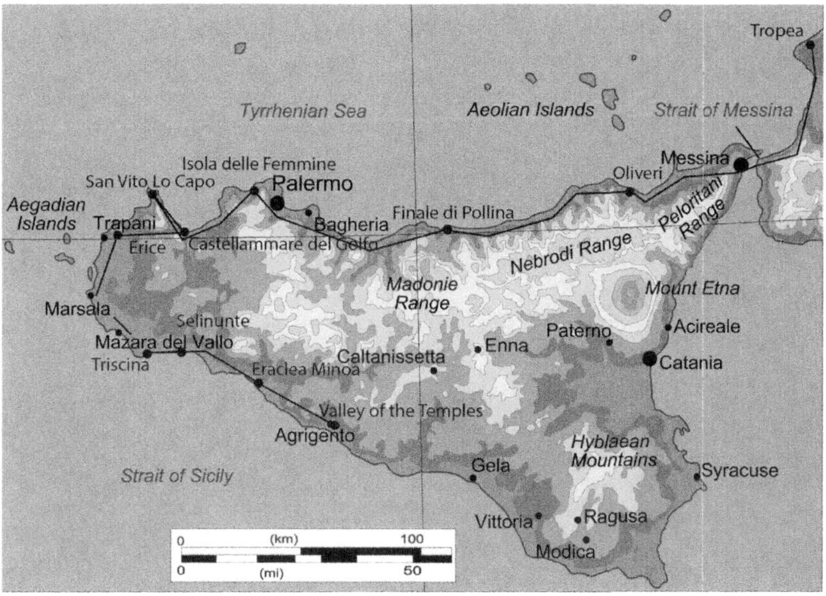

To reach the Valley of the Temples we continued along the south coast, doing a little ruin spotting on the way with a side excursion to Eraclea Minoa. This site was founded in the middle of the 6th Century BC and as all places like it here in Sicily subsequently fought over by sundry local factions plus Carthaginians, Arabs, Romans and Normans.

There wasn't a lot to see and what you could see were just low stumps of walls sticking out of the sand. A mud wall once stood on top of these stone walls but over time it was eroded away leaving only the lower stone part of the wall behind. However, in a small covered exhibit area some of the original walls were still visible because they had been covered by a protective layer of sand until the archaeologists excavated and revealed them.

Under another part of the site once also covered in sand they found the theatre. Sadly the stones were too fragile to leave exposed to the Sicilian weather so they built a low roof over it. This protects the remains but makes it hard to see the complete structure.

The little museum is worth visiting. Some of the pottery was finely crafted and decorated but I liked this head of Medusa the Gorgon. Character successfully prevailing over technique I thought.

After our brief tour of Eraclea Minoa we continued towards our real destination, the Valley of the Temples. We halted near Agrigento at the aptly named Valle dei Templi campsite a few kilometres from the temples. There is a highly rated *sosta* not far away but a report on CamperContact the previous week said it was closed while the owners went on holiday. It may now have been open but reviewers mentioned traffic noise so we chose the campsite instead. The cost difference was only a couple of euros so this wasn't a factor. It would have been a lot more expensive in the campsite but the magic "Sicily Camping Tour" card got us a useful discount at this non-ACSI site.

If the *sosta* was reputed to be noisy we found the same at the campsite during our first afternoon. For nearly two hours a seaplane flew around us though too low and behind trees for a decent photograph but when it briefly appeared I could see it was an interesting twin engine aircraft.

I had already wondered if it was for putting out fires and it turned out it was. On one pass I saw it dropping water about a kilometre away. Then I smelt burning! The smell was burning rubbish (or the related pastime of setting alight to the landscape) but it made me wonder what we would do if flames approached. The phrase "take steps, preferably large ones" came to mind. Happily we were surrounded by Germans so I was confident they would get organised if fire threatened. Alternatively, their huge motorhomes would shield us from the flames long enough for us to escape.

The Valley of the Temples lies south of Agrigento, a town fans of Montalbano might recognize as the inspiration for the fictional Montelusa.

The centre of population was originally where the temples are but it moved north later to the neighbouring hill (now Agrigento) in response to invasions from the inhospitable Barbarians.

The Valley of the Temples is a long narrow site and our visit to it occupied well over two hours and we didn't see it all. The park authorities claim it is the largest archaeological site in the world with an area of thirteen hundred hectares. A claim I think they are stretching by including the surrounding area outside the main part of the site.

A national monument of Italy and one of the greatest examples of the art of Greater Greece it is deservedly popular. "Greater Greece" was the term coined by the Romans to describe the part of southern Italy occupied by the Greeks. Why they occupied it is easily answered if you look at a map. The sole of the foot of Italy including Sicily faces towards Greece and is only a short scull away by *trireme*.

As with the other sites we visited, the Valley of the Temples has been the subject of reconstruction. Sicily is in an earthquake zone and this has meant over time almost any structure involving tall columns will eventually be flattened. But they have re-erected them tastefully here.

Excavations and reconstruction at the site started in the mid-Nineteenth Century and were led by the Duke of Serradifalco, who was a local in the sense he was born in Palermo.

Serradifalco also directed work at other sites in Sicily including Segesta.

I won't bore you with a description of all the various temples. There are plenty of websites covering these details so here are a few random images from our visit to give a feel for what there is to see.

One exhibit attracting attention from the passing crowd wasn't anything ancient. It was a bronze sculpture of recent origin though made to look old. After waiting patiently for a few minutes I managed to take a photograph when no one was posing next to it.

We stumbled across a temporary display of exhibits from the British Museum in the Villa Aurea. This is a modern building and the former residence of Sir Alexander Hardcastle who after service both in the Boer War and the First World War came to Sicily to retire in 1920. Here he financed excavations and reconstruction including the rebuilding of one of the temples on the site. He spent much of his time here searching for a theatre. Any ancient site on Sicily has to have a theatre but so far no one has found one at the Valley of the Temples although attempts to search for it again have recently restarted.

The British Museum exhibition was of artefacts found by Hardcastle and shipped back to London. I wondered if the park authorities would return them when the exhibition ended.

One of the exhibits, a silver *Decadrachm* coin believed to date from 409 BC shows the most extraordinarily fine workmanship.

This marble head was impressive until we read it was a reconstruction of the original dredged from the sea by a fisherman. On second thoughts it was impressive.

Our subsequent adventure after leaving the Valley of the Temples was less successful. I wanted to visit the *Vulcanetti di Macalube,* methane emitting mud volcanoes north of Agrigento. We failed because after the deaths of two young children in 2014 it was permanently closed and all signs to it removed, a fact not reflected in the description of the site in our guidebook. A minor inconvenience to us (lunch was delayed) but a tragedy for the family, especially for the father who saw his children swallowed up by the mud. The body of the seven year old girl was recovered but that of her elder brother was not.

Another site we didn't see in the area was the remarkable *Scala dei Turchi* which are brilliant white cliffs on the coast south of Agrigento. The name means the Turkish Staircase and stems from how these sloping, stratified cliffs have been eroded into a series of steps. They are worth seeing but we came across a smaller version of them near Eraclea Minoa so as it was getting warm again we gave them a miss. The cliffs are near Porto Empedocle, the home town of Andrea Camilleri, the Montalbano author and where he based the fictional town of Vigata. Though Porto Empedocle and Agricento (Montelusa) were the locations imagined by the author they were not where the TV series was filmed. These locations we were to visit later.

Montalbano Country

After the Valley of the Temples we drove to a campsite at Falconara, between Licata and Gela. There was a friendly and helpful German lady in reception and a clean sandy beach.

And broken and dirty showers with tepid water for us in the evening and cold water the next morning. We left...

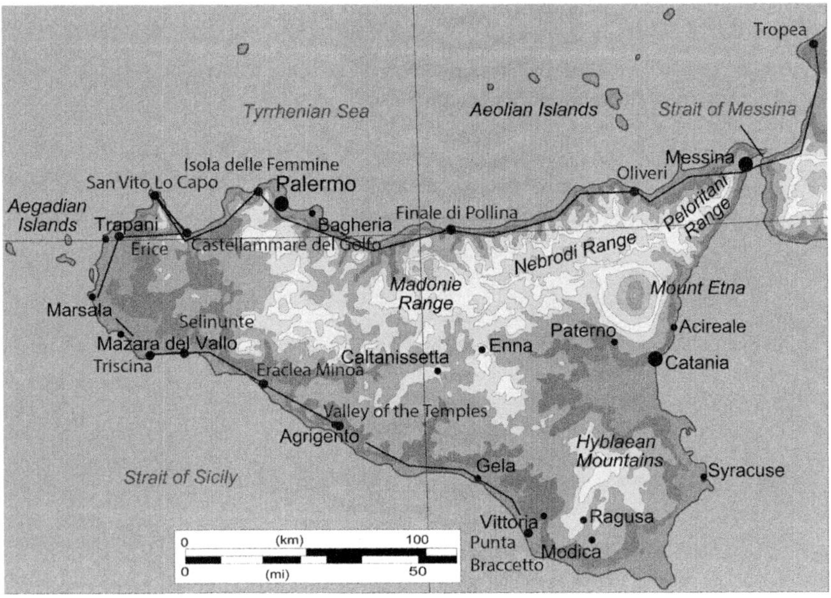

... to find a gem at Punta Braccetto. Camping Scarabeo was the same €17 ACSI rate a night as the place with the broken showers but it scored an impressive 9.2 on CamperContact and deservedly so. It was a small site and almost full with Germans, a lone Dutch motorhome next to us plus two huge Swiss motorhomes.

Everything was green in this part of Sicily and we saw large vineyards (Montalbano's father made wine) and acres of plastic greenhouses. These latter were like the ones you see in southern Spain but seemed to be in better repair.

The beach at the campsite was pleasant but we again found the water cold when we went for an afternoon dip but Charlie enjoyed a sunset swim later.

The day after we arrived was interesting weather-wise. While we sat in bed drinking our morning cups of tea we heard the distant sound of thunder. Rain was forecast but I was hoping it wouldn't arrive until a later and more civilised hour. This being Sunday I hadn't put the kettle on for the tea until nearly half seven.

While Mary prepared breakfast I took Charlie for a walk. Halfway through our excursion it started raining heavily. All experiences in life have the potential to be instructive and this experience was the one when I realised banana trees are useless for sheltering under from rain. The leaves funnel the water towards the trunk and onto the head of anyone standing below them.

I scuttled back to the motorhome during a brief lull in the rain but as soon as I arrived the rain returned with the serious intent of flooding us. I'd foolishly left the awning out, sheltering our table and chairs underneath it. As the wind increased in velocity I stripped off my shirt and secured the awning with a strap using a vertical metal post for the pitch shading conveniently in the right place to attach it to. Once this was done I returned to the motorhome to dry myself and watch the downpour. Our breakfast routine is to alternate between muesli one day then a fried breakfast with scrambled eggs the next. After my soaking I was glad this was a fry-up day. The bacon and eggs were what I needed. Sourcing bacon was always hit and miss in Italy but it can be found if you search the shelves of the supermarkets carefully and don't expect bacon like you are used to.

In the afternoon the sun briefly appeared long enough to dry things off, at which point I put everything away because our intention was to leave the pitch the following morning for a tour of Montalbano locations. The series was filmed here on the southern tip of Sicily and we planned to visit places used in the programs. Call us sad if you will but being fans of the Montalbano series and having driven halfway across Europe to get here we would not pass over the opportunity.

To get us in the mood I downloaded one of the new episodes using the BBC iPlayer app which now works in Europe. Previously, if you tried to use iPlayer outside the UK you were blocked. There were ways to get around this restriction but now they seem to be unnecessary.

In Scotland there are lists of notable peaks named after those who first compiled them, Munros and Corbetts for peaks over 3,000 and 2,500 feet respectively. I don't know if anyone has done the same for the "Montalbanos" but there should be such a list but even without one we found enough online to give us plenty of places to look for.

Our first stop and close to Camping Scarabeo was Punta Secca, the location used for Montalbano's house. Punta Secca is a small place and it wasn't hard to find the house. There were several signs pointing to it dotted around the little village.

It was white with olive green doors in the TV series. Now it's a pale green and is a bed and breakfast called "Casa del Commissario Montalbano". The bar next to it doesn't feature in the programs either.

This is Montalbano's beach where he often swam.

I couldn’t help putting words to the scene above. It is from an as yet unreleased episode called “Murder of the Microwave”.

"Livia! I wasn't expecting you!"

"Salvo! I'm checking on my iPhone and the meal Adelina has made for you, *Caponata*, has been cooked the wrong way."

(Montalbano stumbles in the water....he was looking forward to the aubergines.)

"So I threw it in the bin and microwaved fish fingers for you."

Postscript: At his trial Montalbano successfully defended his murder of Livia by claiming no Sicilian could be expected to eat fish fingers, especially microwaved ones. He was acquitted of all charges and promoted.

Around the corner from Montalbano's house, beside the marina, was a monument with the inscription:

10 July 1943
Honour to the Fallen
On the 60th Anniversary of
the Anglo/American landings.

This was slightly puzzling as I thought the Allied landings were southeast of here but they must have landed at other points.

From Punta Seca we drove to Scicli, which is unpronounceable but has a striking setting.

The town hall here was the Vigata police station but it is a place worth visiting for its own sake. Note the huge church on a rock on the left in the photograph above, looming over the town centre.

From Scicli we drove to Modica, which features in the opening sequences of the TV series. It has a high viaduct over a deep valley. Sadly I saw no obvious place to stop and take photographs which may explain why the shots in the program are taken from a helicopter.

The main part of our day was spent at Ragusa, a town used frequently in the series. There is a free *sosta* here recorded in CamperContact where we left the motorhome while we made our visit. Don't rely on your satnav to bring you to the *sosta*. Use the SS194 from Modica and approach from the southeast by the easy but wiggly and reasonably wide road.

Ragusa is in two parts. Following the disastrous earthquake of 1693, which killed 100,000 in southeast Sicily the survivors built a new town on the neighbouring peak above the old one. However, *Ragusa Ibla*, the original town was rebuilt eventually and viewed from the new town looks like this.

We explored *Ragusa Ibla* and saw several film locations, including the *Piazza Duomo* used in many episodes. I won't bore you with them but these towns are worth visiting without the TV hype.

After a rewarding day visiting the film sets we returned to Camping Scarabeo where I cooked buttery chilli prawns, under supervision. I bought the prawns from the "fish man" who visited the campsite earlier. From his little van he offered a selection of fish and both little and big prawns. We bought ten of the latter, weighing 600g and costing €12. This seemed steep but they were monsters.

I fried them for about five minutes on the gas BBQ, turning them regularly in lots of butter and olive oil plus two finely chopped garlic cloves and two dried bird's-eye chillies crumbled in. Eaten with crusty bread heated in the oven they were delicious. The buttery chilli oil left in the pan was wonderfully warming when eaten on the bread we used to wipe the pan clean afterwards. And at €6 a head I can recommend this restaurant.

We did more of the Montalbano trail the following day, visiting the castle at Donnafugata. This is a few miles inland from the coast in a region full of the low drystone walls often featured in the episodes.

In the TV series the castle Donnafugata is where Montalbano meets the mafia boss Balduccio Sinagra and when we arrived the entrance was full of studio trucks.

It seemed to be lighting people setting things up for filming later and sadly we weren't invited to appear as extras.

The castle is open to the public though no doubt the TV profile hasn't harmed the bottom line. It is full of exhibits from the 18th and early 19th Centuries. One cabinet contained what looked like a collection of Mary Poppins' memorabilia though I think the reality was more prosaic. The stuff found in old chests and the back of wardrobes I think. There were lots of hats too from the days of the flapper and earlier.

The gardens outside were interesting and included several huge trees.

There is a maze in the gardens with stone walls a shade too high to see over so I cheated and used Google maps. On the screen of my phone in satellite view the maze was visible and a blue dot represented our position in the maze. Modern technology defeats ancient puzzle. We found no dead bodies in the maze, unlike Montalbano in the episode "*Excursion to Tindari*" where the bodies of an elderly couple were found here. They should have used Google maps if they were looking for the way out.

After the castle we drove on around the coast, stopping at Camping Sabbiadoro at Avola.

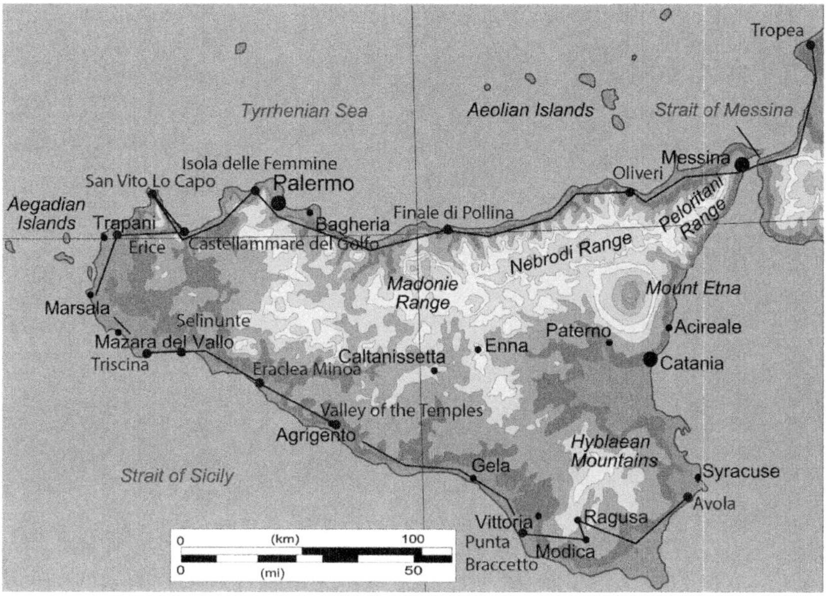

This was reached through narrow roads and sharp bends but it is worth the effort if your vehicle will fit. The site is so full of plants it was like staying in a dome at the Eden Project. Entertainment was laid on for us too in the form of a spectacular thunderstorm over the sea in the early evening, heralding a change in the weather for the next few days.

We woke the next morning to the sound of the same thunder and decided as sunshine wasn't playing today we would move on and see what we could find while on the hoof.

We stopped first in Syracuse, or Syracusa as it was known historically, using the free parking in the port as included in CamperContact.

Syracuse is a town with history and it was here Archimedes lived between around 287 and 212 BC. He of the bath and well known screw and an Archimedes screw would have been useful for pumping the floodwater which greeted us on our arrival in Syracuse. We must have missed a major rain storm. The streets were deep in water and broken down cars were everywhere.

From the port, once we reached it through the slow traffic, it wasn't a long walk to the oldest part of the town, the island of Ortygia, joined to the rest of the town by two bridges. Our aim was to visit the museum of Archimedes, which we eventually found in a narrow street.

It is called in full the Museum of Leonardo da Vinci and Archimedes of Siracusa. The museum is tiny but worth a visit. It is a display of models, a few of which you can play with, illustrating the various inventions of da Vinci and Archimedes.

Photographs are forbidden and we surrendered our bags too before we could enter so I have nothing to show for our visit. There is no evidence Leonardo da Vinci ever visited Sicily let alone Syracuse but the museum would be even smaller if they hadn't included him as the da Vinci exhibits outnumber the Archimedean.

Other than the museum Syracuse hasn't remembered Archimedes well which seems ungrateful as his last act was to organise the defence of the city from an attacking Roman fleet in the second Punic War. When the city eventually fell the Roman general in charge, Marcellus, commanded Archimedes to be brought to him alive as he considered him a valuable asset but something was lost in translation and Archimedes was killed. A tomb was built for his body but it was soon lost though it was rediscovered by Cicero a century later only to be subsequently lost for ever.

In the northwest of Syracuse is a compact archaeological site we visited after lunch and a visit to Lidl to restock the cupboards. The Roman amphitheatre was in need of weeding but it was interesting. The rectangular pit in the centre is thought to have been used to stage sea battles

A large Greek theatre stood nearby.

As at Selinunte the quarry where the stones were sourced was impressive. Sadly the flooding caused by the recent rains and closure of all but a few main paths prevented us from seeing as much as we hoped. The caves in the quarry were used as prisons in the past and one of the most famous is the Orecchio di Dioniso or Ear of Dionysius. We found if we waited long enough a moment arose when it was almost free of visitors.

The name, Ear of Dionysius, was coined by the painter Caravaggio. It refers to the myth the tyrant Dionysius (who founded our first Sicilian site at Tyndaris) used its supposed acoustic properties to listen to the conversations of prisoners or the screams of the tortured depending on what version you prefer.

We hoped to visit Pantalica afterwards but the weather inland looked dark and thundery. Pantalica is the largest necropolis in Sicily but is built in a gorge and when thunder, lightning and flash floods threaten gorges are places to avoid.

So we sped up the motorway to Catania where we would be within striking distance of Mount Etna except we found she had beaten us to it by several centuries if not millennia as the campsite where we stopped for a night was built on an old lava flow.

Our arrival in Catania coincided with another major cloudburst of rain, reminiscent of Syracuse except this time we *were* caught in it. The streets turned to rivers in a few minutes but as before we got through unscathed.

Etna

We stayed only one night on the Catania lava field before moving further north to a beachside campsite near Taormina.

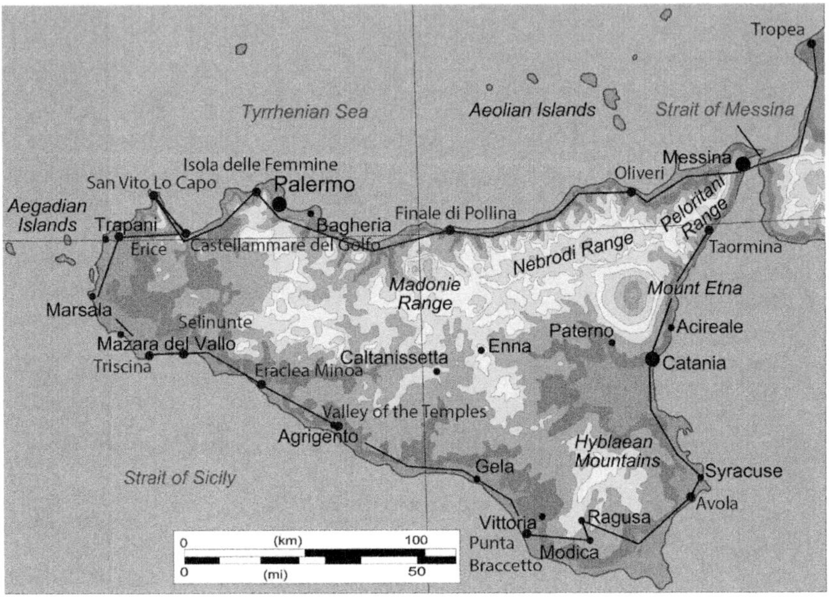

This would be our last stop in Sicily before we caught the ferry back to the mainland later in the week. The exact date of our leaving was uncertain because we wanted to visit Mount Etna and this needed good weather.

We knew Etna would be expensive but like the Montalbano excursions having come here we weren't going to miss the opportunity. The campsite we chose was Camping La Focetta Sicula which enjoyed the curious distinction of being the last site in the ACSI books. Looking north from the beach below the campsite we could see mainland Italy in the distance.

There are a few fishing boats on the beach, launched with the aid of a bulldozer.

And close by a fish shop sold the catch.

The swordfish didn't look fresh and at €28 a kilo they must only sell it to the well-heeled. The fish to the left of the swordfish with the large eye and pectoral fin is an albacore, a member of the tuna family. Passing on the swordfish we bought a whole bream instead for €7. The fishmonger descaled and gutted it with a cigarette in his mouth and threw in a free bunch of parsley. The bream was good and very fresh and we subsequently returned to the shop and bought more of the big prawns and fried them in garlic and chilli again. The dish was as tasty as the first time we tried it.

But the good news was the forecast for the following day was sunny. So having emptied my bank account at the ATM we were ready for Etna.

Responding to an 06:30 alarm call the next morning I checked the weather forecast and confirmed today would be perfect.

There is a car park at the *Rifugio Sapienza* where attempts at Etna's summit usually start and it is listed in CamperContact (#7800) so I set the coordinates in the satnav and off we drove. Given you start at sea level from the coast road and the *Rifugio* is at about 1900m it is a long climb to get there. On the lower slopes of the volcano we passed through a belt of sweet chestnuts where a dozen or more cars were parked and people were collecting large bags of the nuts. Soon afterwards all vegetation stopped and we drove through a predominantly brown landscape of old larva flows.

Parking charges when we arrived at the *Rifugio* were inflexible. With a "camper" as they called us we could only pay for a full 24 hours at a cost of €12. Not paying wasn't an option, a parking warden pointed out the ticket office before I even stopped the engine.

A short walk took us to the cable car station and here they painlessly removed from my wallet €63 per person for a ticket to the crater.

The cable cars were small six seater cabins but the route wasn't high off the ground and the cars didn't wobble *too* much as you passed a pylon.

At the top, at about 2,500m we boarded a red and white Unimog bus. Ours had a loud Canadian installed as an extra but I advise choosing a basic model without this enhancement if you have the option.

The buses drive up to about 2,900m (9,500 ft) through a black desert. At the terminus everyone milled around waiting for the guide to finish speaking to everyone in English and Italian. Our guide also spoke French so his briefings were conducted in all three languages.

From here we left on foot to the Barbagallo crater, created in the 2002 eruption and south of the main currently active craters.

The air temperature was 8°C according to a weather forecast for the summit and there were small pockets of snow on the ground in the shade but with virtually no wind it didn't feel cold and I was comfortable wearing a thin fleece under a windproof.

In the picture above you can see folk on the far side of the rim, which is where the walk led by the guide took us as we completed a circuit of the crater.

Off to one side and high above us was the main summit of Etna, nearly 3,400m high.

It was up there the April 2017 eruption which caught a BBC film crew occurred. From the television report I thought this was an isolated incident but it was the beginning of a major and prolonged eruption. Nearby Catania airport on the coast was subsequently closed for three months according to our guide. We learned eruptions of ash were still happening and the most recent was only this morning, though they might say the same to every group. There's nothing like "jeopardy" for maintaining interest.

The surface we were walking on was coarse grit but the recent larva flows were made of larger rocks.

The summit was frequently in cloud some of which came from steam generated far below condensing as it emerged into the cold air. The guide scraped a depression in the grit and you could feel the warmth with your hands as the hot water vapour rose out of the ground.

Seeing the summit of Etna was memorable. You can do it a lot more cheaply by walking but it's a long way and as you ascend you would be passed by cable cars and buses whipping by. This is because the path up largely coincides with the route these mechanical things take and without a guide it would be difficult to know what you were seeing once you got to the top. It is a thousand metres of ascent from the *Rifugio* to where our buses stopped and for the price of a tank of diesel I was happy to pay.

You can go further up Etna. We saw one group wearing hard hats walking towards the site of the 2017 eruption. An adventurous walk but you would need to be ready to run.

On the organised trips available for exploring Etna there may be good deals but we saw a company advertising what we did on our own for twice the price.

Farewell Sicily

We left Sicily but the good news is it is still there and we have vowed to return one day and in the spring when the flowers would be out. There is so much to see on the island and though we hardly touched the interior we did almost a thousand miles going around the coast over four weeks.

As I mentioned when we arrived on the island, record the coordinates of the port as soon as possible. Unlike the mainland side there are a *lot* of ports in Messina stretching over several kilometres. The port we wanted was right at the northern end of the waterfront and coming from the south we turned off too early. We got through the heavy traffic but we should have stayed on the motorway longer. From my subsequent studies of maps the junction we should have taken was the Messina-Boccetta one which has a sign for the "Traghetti" or ferries. The coordinates for the gate we wanted for the ferry to Villa San Giovanni are shown in Appendix 2 at the end of the Sicily section.

Once we arrived on the mainland I entered a new set of coordinates into the satnav and then we turned south to Reggio Calabria. The coordinates are also given in Appendix 2 and are for a car park which we found easily although it was almost full. The parking spaces were small and it was a tight squeeze for us. A short stroll and €8 per person entrance fee brought us into the company of this fellow (next page).

This is one of the two Riace Bronzes, about 2,500 years old and recovered from the sea in 1972 after a snorkeler saw an arm sticking out of the sand. The location was near Riace Marina sixty kilometres northeast of Reggio Calabria. The figures are each about two metres high and now mounted on marble slabs. The second figure isn't as impressive as the first I think but perhaps only be because he is missing an eye.

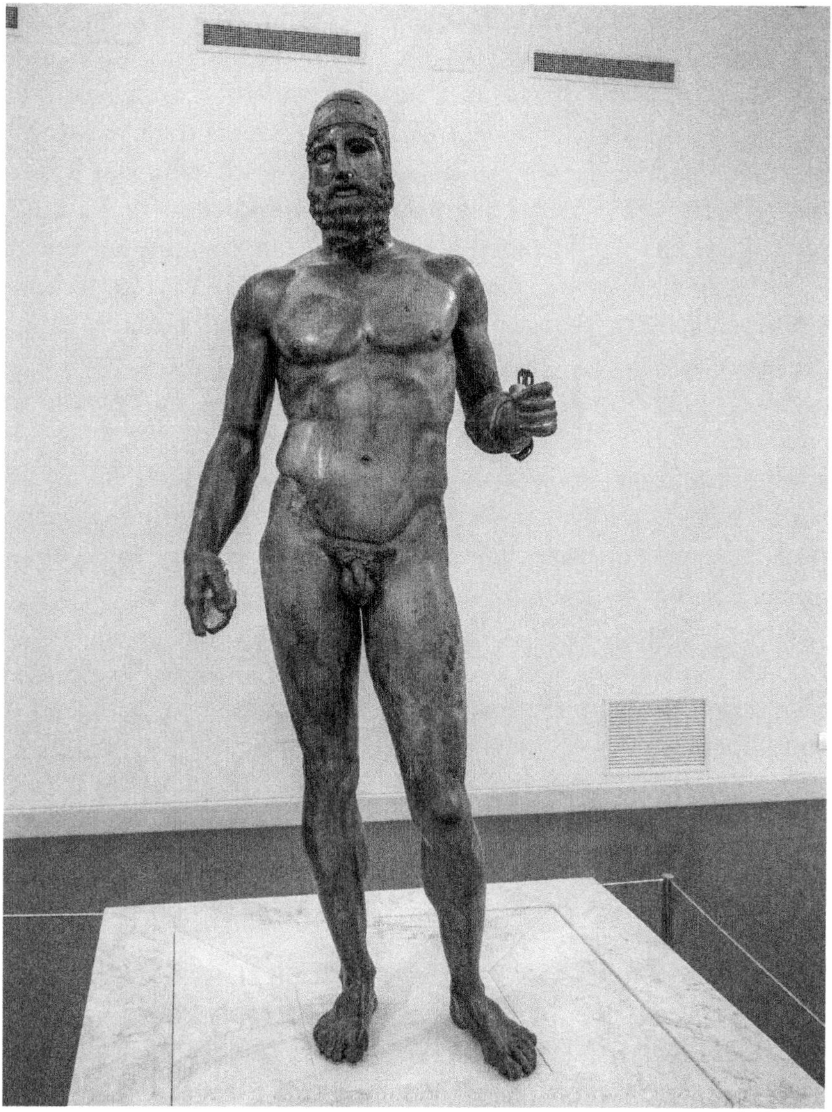

It is believed they once wore helmets and carried a wooden shield and spear. The bronze strap for the shield can be seen on both figures.

They are a sobering example of the skill of our ancestors. Made using the lost wax process the detail and above all the artistry is amazing. The poses of the figures are their most striking feature but even to get them to stand up on their feet was a tremendous accomplishment of design.

To enter the room with the bronzes you have to undergo a slightly curious purification ritual. We walked through sliding glass doors into an ante-chamber where we waited for several minutes. During this time the air is apparently changed in the room by fans blowing through vents. It would have been fun as we waited in the entrance airlock to hear an announcement warning us if anyone broke wind we would have to stay in there longer but sadly it was not to be. No sense of humour these museum directors. When we were deemed clean enough the opposite pair of glass doors slid open and we could enter the room with the bronzes. All sensible precautions to avoid contamination by pollutants from outside except there is no such arrangement on the exit. You walk out into the corridor near reception through a single door and while the door is open all manner of contamination could be drawn in.

After viewing the bronzes we bought street food at a cafe. One of us went for the interesting pizza with aubergines and courgettes. Someone else went for the one with chips and frankfurters but both were good and I helped finish the chips.

After Reggio Calabria we drove on the free *autostrada* to a site at Cropani Marina, close to the ball of the foot of Italy. We would have liked to have seen the 10th century Cattolica at Stilo by taking the coastal route but time was against us so we took the *autostrada* instead.

The campsite was a surprise with excellent facilities and free hot showers and no time limit or push buttons, a first for Italy. The doors to the toilet block even slid open automatically as you approached them. The beach was pleasant with no rubbish and lots of fine sand.

There is a lot to see in this part of Italy but after Sicily we were templed-out. The ancient city of Matera, where the population lived in caves until as recently as 1952 beckoned not far away but instead we put our heads down and drove north to Pompeii.

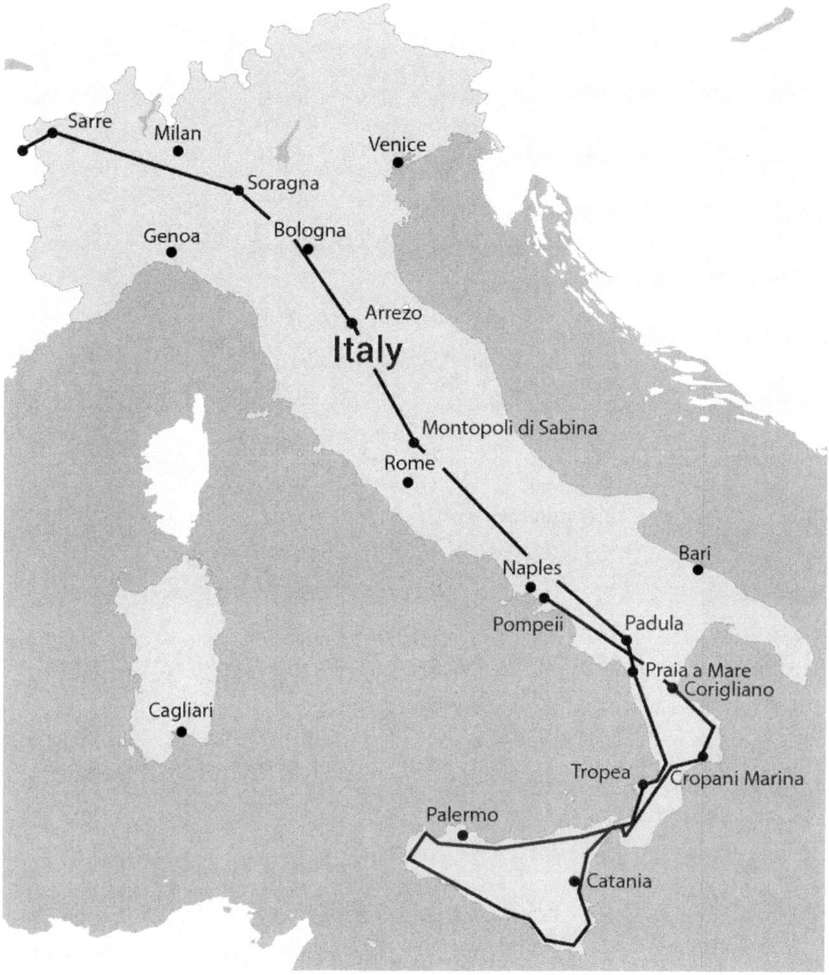

We were never going to come here, too much of a tourist trap I thought, the nearby Herculaneum sounded more our sort of place. But, with my new enthusiasm for volcanoes I wanted to see Vesuvius again, so to Pompeii we went. The urge to migrate north was strong and though millions of birds feel the pull of the south at this time of year our migration urges were in the other direction.

Here are a few images of Pompeii. First the inevitable theatre without which no city of the period could be without.

And here the gladiator barracks. There is a large amphitheatre nearby where no doubt they performed.

But what you see most of in Pompeii are the streets lined with shops and houses.

In the background of the shot above is the villain of the Pompeii story, Vesuvius. It's eruption at around one o'clock in the afternoon of the 24th of August, 79 AD buried the city in pumice and a pyroclastic flow of hot gas killed anyone still alive later in the day. The details are known because they were observed from a safe distance by Pliny the Younger. Pliny the Older may also have made notes but he went too close and was killed.

Vesuvius is a classic volcano in shape with a symmetrical cone and a single crater at the summit. It is different to Etna which has multiple craters spread over a wide area. Vesuvius also differs from Etna in being classed as dormant whereas Etna is active.

There are interesting details in the streets, including many holes made in the kerbstones to tether animals. In the main street a carving on the road can be found of what I might cautiously describe as a “male member” pointing stiffly towards a brothel. All the tour guides stop here so their group can photograph it. I looked at it myself during a lull between crowds and was unconvinced of its authenticity. It is carved on a flat stone on a busy street and looks to have suffered little wear. My guess is it less than a hundred years old and was carved as a joke. The brothel it points to is a popular attraction, so popular we couldn’t get near it so we gave it a miss. The carving would have been impossible to see on the road surface as the streets must have been so choked with mud and animal manure they built steeping stones to cross them.

The numerous small private houses didn't hold much interest for me but the villas have a few mosaics. The best have been removed to the main museum in Naples along with most of the rest of the good artefacts.

This though is the famous *Cave Canem* or beware of the dog mosaic at the entrance to a villa.

A longish walk from the main site took us to the Villa of Mysteries which had by far the best preserved wall paintings. Most of the tour groups don't seem to get this far but it is worth the walk.

The magic of Pompeii is not what you can see, if I'm truthful I found it drab and underwhelming. Visually, it lacks the impact of the massive temples of Sicily. The real interest of Pompeii is the glimpse it offers into how people lived their daily lives so long ago.

Going North

Leaving Pompeii we shot north and drove about four hundred kilometres on a quiet *autostrada* to a free *sosta* below the village of Monte San Savino.

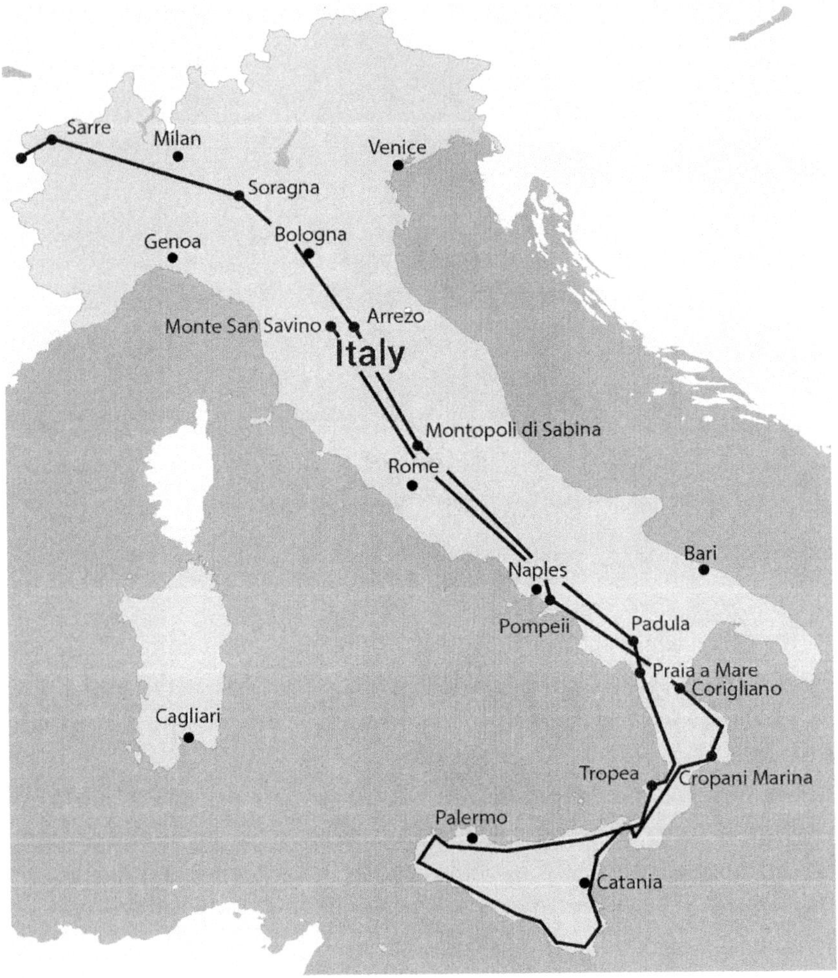

This long drive brought us to within striking distance of northern Italy and the next day we drove almost the same distance to reach the Italian Lakes region and the shores of the beautiful Lago d'Iseo.

We used *autostradas* virtually all the way, skirting around Florence, Bologna and Modena without encountering any of the heavy traffic we hit on our outward journey.

Many of the campsites in the Italian lakes were closed but Camping Covelo was open although it was winding down and would close for the winter soon after we left. Many of the staff would then move into the mountains to work in hotels catering for skiers. But while it was open we enjoyed meeting up with a couple I knew from the Motorhome Fun forum and we sat together on the first evening after we arrived watching the sun set over the lake.

We spent two pleasant and lazy days at Camping Covelo. It was an easy walk from the campsite to the village of Iseo, which was an upmarket place with expensive shops.

At a cafe in Iseo I ordered an espresso but Mary chose hot chocolate. The chocolate was so thick she ate most of it with a spoon. This is how chocolate is often served in Italy.

We spent the last evening sharing a table with our friends at the camp restaurant where we ate an enjoyable evening meal. Lago d'Iseo is full of fish (we saw big ones jumping in the evenings) which are caught commercially. Some end up in the local restaurants and as consequence I could enjoy a plate of perch. It was pleasant and reminded me of whiting. I know this is a sea fish but it possessed the same delicate flavour and looked similar, comprising thin fillets of white flesh.

We were led astray on drinks by being introduced to Frankiacorta. This is a local wine, coming from a triangular shaped area on the southern shore of Iseo and is made by the champagne method and tastes like it too with more body than prosecco. Even in the supermarkets it didn't come in at less than €10 a bottle so we tried not to develop a habit for it.

When we left the campsite the next morning we drove northeast along the lake and then up into the hills to the curiously named village of Zone. This is why we came.

These are the *Pyrimidi* and they can be best appreciated by looking at the two nearest to the camera in the shot above or in this close up (next page).

They were formed by boulders resting on a deep glacial moraine of gravel and finer stones. Over time the moraine was washed away but under each boulder a pillar formed creating these curious forms. If you visit this site the best view is from the road driving up to the village. On the inside of a right hand bend you will see a single, sloping parking space, stop here and you can take the first shot above. The path from the car park in town descends quickly but near the top you can take the other picture shown above. If you descend further I could discover no better views and the climb back up is steep.

Returning to the subject of wines, Franciacorta was excellent but Lidl's prosecco at under €5 a bottle is almost as good. This explains why we drove into Switzerland later with a few more bottles than Swiss law permits. The Swiss, not being part of the EU operate a strict customs regime with limits on alcohol importation but they seem to be hottest on enforcing this on their citizens and tourists are often left alone as we were

We didn't venture far into Switzerland at first, stopping at a site in the Italian speaking part of Switzerland beside Lago Poschiavo.

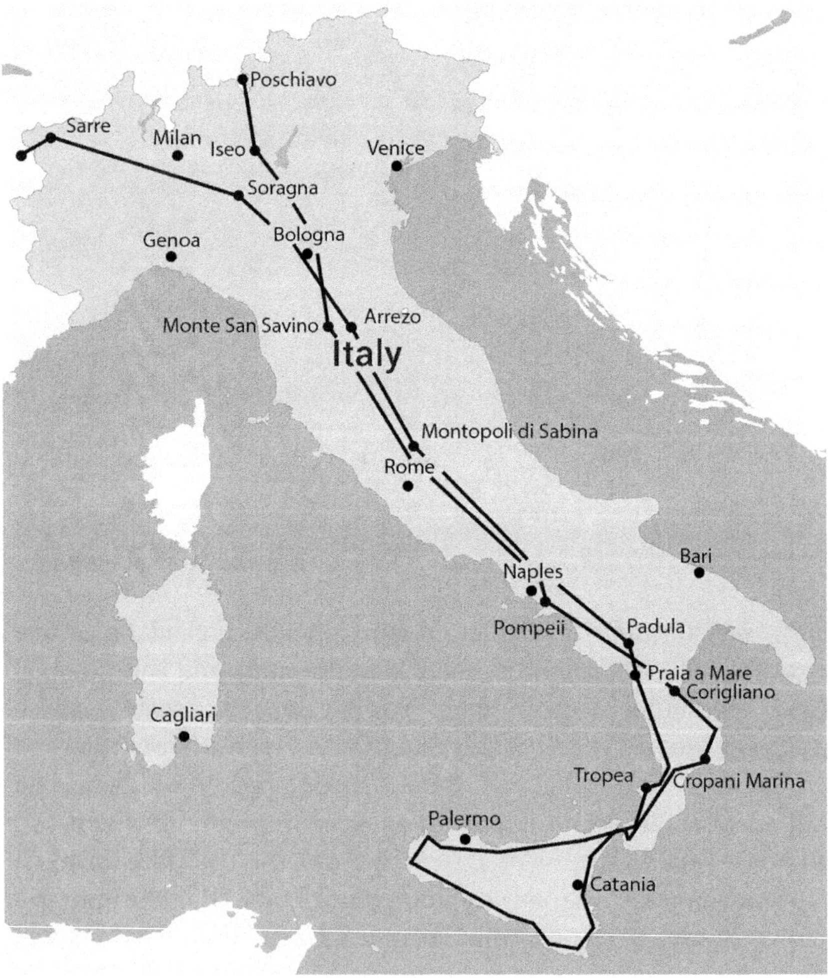

Getting here proved interesting. Our route took us over the *Passeo dell Aprica* an unimpressive 1181m on the map but a challenging drive on the ground. The road was narrow and single track in places but the descent was striking. We dropped over 700m in ten kilometres and unlike many passes there were no hairpin bends until we got near the bottom. The road clung to the side of the valley and the road went steeply down it. Second gear for ten kilometres with occasional use of the brakes. If you come this way try this road.

Our traverse of Switzerland continued the next day and it was like driving through a landscape decorated with postcards. Almost wherever you looked chocolate box views of villages and mountains appeared.

But the year was drawing to a close. We first noticed this at Lago d'Iseo when leaves started falling around us from the trees. Today's highpoint, literally and metaphorically, was the *Passeo del Bermina* (2328m), and if it sounds Italian it is because we were still in the part of Switzerland where Italian is widely spoken. The climb up the pass reminded us again autumn was arriving, the trees were golden in colour.

On the next page is the view before the top of the pass with snow on the peaks.

The view from the pass. The lake is a reservoir.

Not having planned to come through Switzerland we were light on the Swiss map front and the Swiss like the UK have resisted the temptation to join the euro. Needing to get Swiss money and buy a map of Switzerland we stopped in St Moritz. The cash machine we found worked faultlessly as no doubt everything does in Switzerland but it only seemed capable of dispensing 100 Swiss Franc notes. The machine was conveniently next door to a shop where we could buy a map. The assistant didn't blink an eye as I handed over what was almost an £80 note but then the map took a sizeable chunk out of it. This transaction was a useful introduction to Swiss prices.

We stopped for the second night in Switzerland at Camping Panorama at Surcuolm. The entry in CamperContact said it accepted ACSI cards but we found it didn't and I feared the small change left after buying the map would be used up paying when we left the following morning. It almost was; the charge for the night was £37.

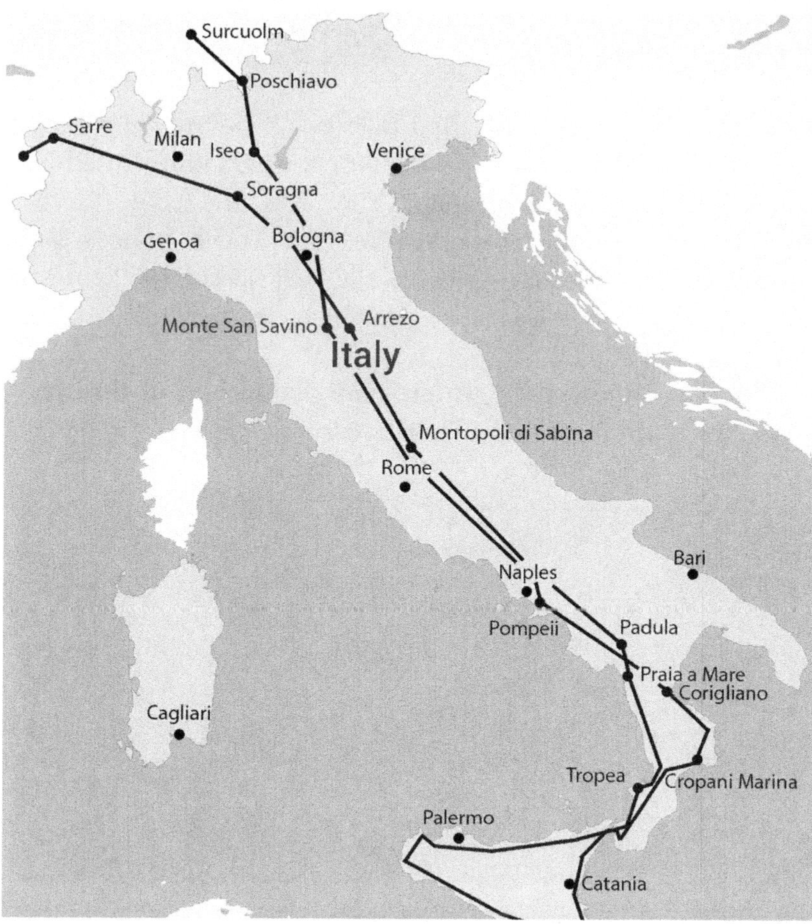

This was the view from the aptly named Panorama Camping. The peaks in the distance are over 10,000 feet.

The next day we went over *two* passes but before we reached the first of them, the *Oberalppass*, we crossed a long dotted line drawn on our expensive map. This was the route of the extraordinary Gotthard Base Tunnel, the world's longest and deepest railway tunnel. Opened only in December 2016 it carries mostly freight but a few passenger trains zoom through at up to 250 kph.

After the *Oberalppass* we crossed the second of the day's passes, the stunning 2224m *Sustenpass*.

We stopped for lunch on the *Sustenpass* surrounded by snowy peaks. Afterwards heading west all day until after skirting around the Brienzersee (more chocolate box views) we turned south at Interlaken and headed into the big mountains.

Although it was not where we were heading we made a side excursion on the way towards Grindelwald to see the Eiger.

I wanted to come here because I first saw the Eiger as a child while camping with my parents. This must have been fifty years ago and the image in my mind remains vivid, strengthened no doubt from accounts read and films seen of climbing on the notorious North Face.

After paying homage to the Eiger, which was impossible to photograph as the sun was shining from behind it we returned to the main valley and headed to Camping Breithorn, which had been recommended to us. Disappointingly, when we arrived everything was shut. Someone from a permanent pitch said the owners would return but seemed non-committal on when this would be. The toilets were locked so we headed back to Lauterbrunnen and Camping Jungfrau.

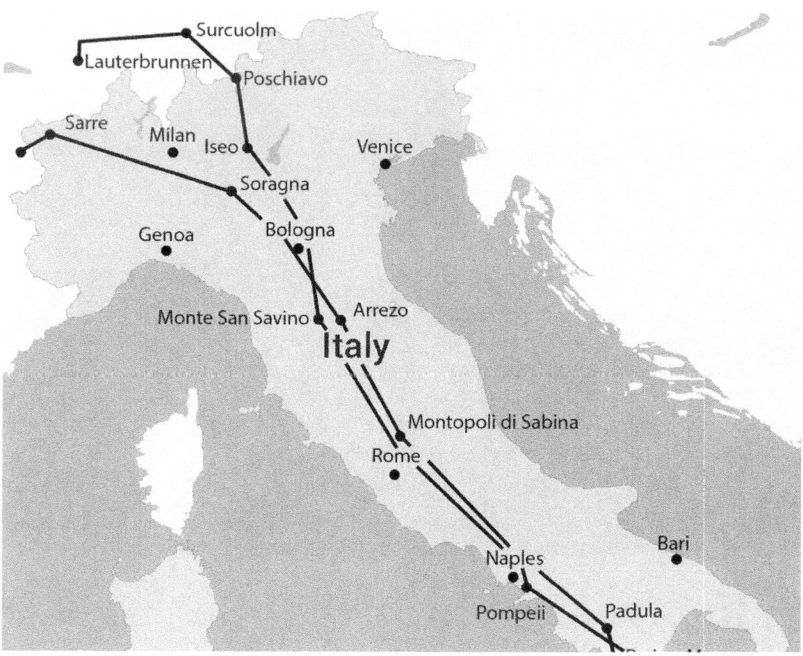

This was easily the most luxurious campsite yet seen. There was even a free to use dishwashing machine and the toilet blocks were so clean you could safely perform open heart surgery in them.

They like their waterfalls in Switzerland. The 297m Staubbach Falls overlook the site and are illuminated at night.

There is a lot to see in this region and we briefly considered making the expensive (£100 per person) visit to the 2,970m

Schilthorn which has a revolving restaurant, the *Piz Gloria*, on it. The peak featured in the James Bond film On Her Majesty's Secret Service and "007" is emblazoned on the restaurant just in case you didn't know.

Fiscal realism won the argument so instead of a dizzying and dizzyingly expensive cable car ride we walked up the valley from the campsite to visit the Trümmelbach Falls.

The falls are invisible even when you are standing below them.

In the shot above (chocolate box photo #236) you can see a gap between the mountains in the background above the farmhouse, but at the valley floor level there is no obvious gap. This is because the falls run through a narrow water-worn cleft in the rock. Inside this cleft they have cut tunnels and built airy walkways so you can see the ten main falls. The shot below is typical of the interior. It isn't a place if you don't like heights.

We went geocaching afterwards and found a couple close by. One contained two trackables I pocketed and I dropped off one I found on Dartmoor and a new one of my own. Travelling Terrier #1 had been released into the wild! One of the trackables we found here originated from Québec and the other from Belgium. For those not familiar with geocaching, trackables are metal tags with a unique number which you collect, record and move on to another geocache. One I've found had visited Australia and North America before landing in the UK. The geocache they are found in is typically a plastic box hidden in a crevice or hole in a tree and is located using GPS coordinates plus a written description.

Before we leave Switzerland here is chocolate box photo #237.

A waterfall, a chalet, the Swiss flag and the Staubbach Falls in the background.

After our geocaching we visited the camp shop. This was like a supermarket and we bought a few presents and a money box for ourselves in the shape of a large red cow. Another CHF100 note was damaged during the transactions leaving us very little change to put in the money box.

Camping Jungfrau wasn't as expensive as I feared. We were given a 20% low season discount and another 10% for the ACSI card bringing the total to slightly over CHF 40 (£32) a night. Without the discounts it would have been about £50. I recommend staying here even if you only go for one night for the experience and you get two free chocolates and a campsite sticker when you check out. We ate the chocolates almost immediately but kept the sticker as a souvenir.

Switzerland is wonderful but it is as expensive as its reputation maintains. A few things we found were the same as at home. Fuel was about £1.20 to £1.25 a litre and a bottle of Swiss wine we bought was £6.00. So you can have a cheap time in Switzerland if you keep driving and drink only Swiss wine. Sadly, if you stop in a motorhome for the night you must use a campsite. Wild camping is strictly forbidden and the local Swiss will quickly reach for the telephone if they think you are going to stay where you shouldn't. We were sad to say goodbye to Switzerland but my wallet was relieved.

France

The escape from Switzerland was as twisty as I expected and a long drive too. This was entirely self-inflicted. There is an extensive network of motorways in Switzerland but to use them you need to buy a *vignette*. For vehicles under 3.5t like us we would have to buy an annual vignette to use the motorways at a cost of about €35. Vehicles over 3.5t have to pay a daily charge. Although the *vignette* isn't too expensive I wanted to see if we could cross the country without using motorways. You can as we confirmed but I would buy a *vignette* if we ever returned which we must because it is a most beautiful country and English widely spoken. This was well illustrated by an episode when we visited the Trümmelbach Falls. We fell into conversation with a Swiss gentleman (in English) and then he spoke to two men who worked at the Falls. He started each conversation in German but quickly changed to English because this was the common language between them. They were east European I think. The number of foreigners working in Switzerland is a concern to the Swiss but they need them to keep the place running.

Emerging from Switzerland we stopped just inside France near Besançon at the *Museums Maisons Comptoises* at Nancray. It is only a grass car park for the museum but there was a service point and it was wonderfully quiet and dark at night.

This was followed by a lazy day of driving. I let the SANEF toll tag take the strain and we did over 300 km on the *autoroute* ending the day at a pleasant *aire* by the river Yonne near Auxerre.

The French, upon whom we should take pity as they suffer under the tyrannical yoke of the EU know how to site an *aire*.

It wasn't free, €7.60 a night including electricity if we wanted it.

I won't go into details about our flight across France, the map below shows the route and the places we stayed at are recorded at the back of this book in Appendix 2. We did it in three hops, driving for four or five hours each day.

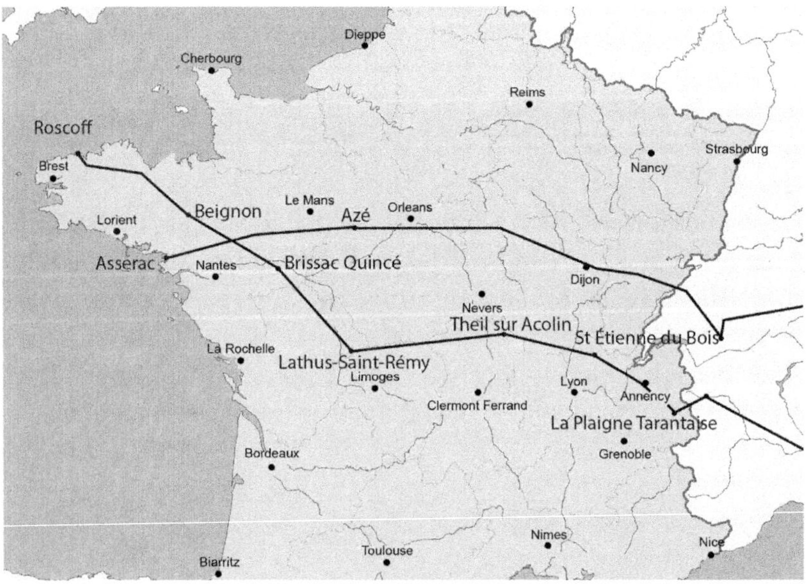

Our destination, as you can see from the map, was southern Brittany and Camping Le Moulin de L'Eclis near Asserac, a pleasant site set northwest of Nantes behind a typical beach of the region backed by dunes and trees.

The pull north remained strong so after two days of gentle walks near the campsite we moved up the coast to another *aire* at Le Faou, south of Brest and within the Amorique Regional Park. The *aire* was one of the Camping-car Park group, a French organisation which has taken over existing *aires* and several former municipal campsites and fitted them with automated barriers. We have found them excellent and though not the cheapest where they are well positioned, like this one, they are a useful alternative to more remote spots. The weather had been good for a long period but it was changing and we experienced heavy rain but we were parked on gravel so the mud kept its distance. Le Faou is a small town but a walk up the main street in between showers was pleasant. From here we moved close to the most westerly point of mainland France and another *aire* where we enjoyed excellent coastal walking in improving weather. I found the beach deserted and could let Charlie off the lead.

Unfortunately I shouldn't as he promptly found a Portuguese Man O'War.

He was stung though not badly and his lip remained swollen on one side for about a week afterwards. Subsequently, we saw several more of the creatures, which are not jellyfish despite their appearance. They are classed as a *siphonophore* and are not a single animal but a colony of individual organisms (polyps) working together collectively with different polyps having different functions.

As the time of the ferry approached we needed to take Charlie to a vet for his obligatory worming and to be certified fit to travel. His lip didn't look too bad and it wasn't until we returned home he developed scabs where the tentacles touched him.

The vet we chose was in Landerneau, a town we have visited before. It has an unusual bridge across the river with houses and shops built on it and a large veterinary practice within walking distance of the excellent *aire*, a former municipal campsite we used on our first visit.

After his passport was stamped we made one further move, to yet another *aire* of the Camping-car Park group close to Roscoff and a place with good walking and a few geocaches to search for. The northern Brittany coast here is rocky with massive boulders and remote beaches to explore. Some boulders even have seats built into them.

We caught the afternoon ferry from Roscoff, arriving home in the dark at around ten o'clock. We enjoyed every moment away. Italy and above all Sicily is worth the long drive.

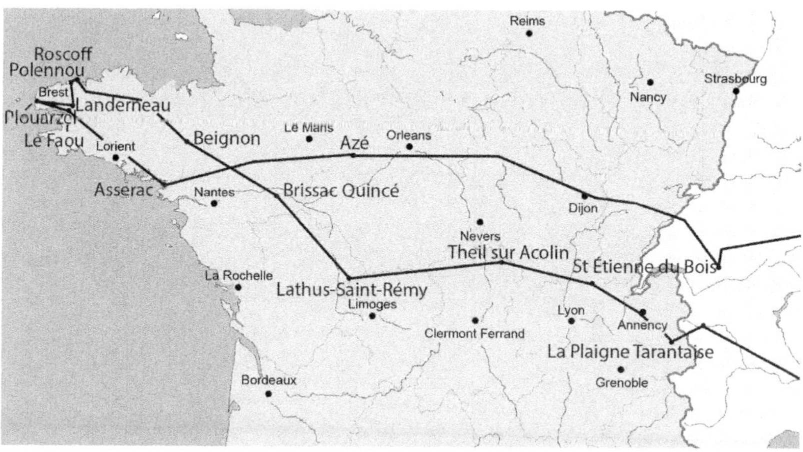

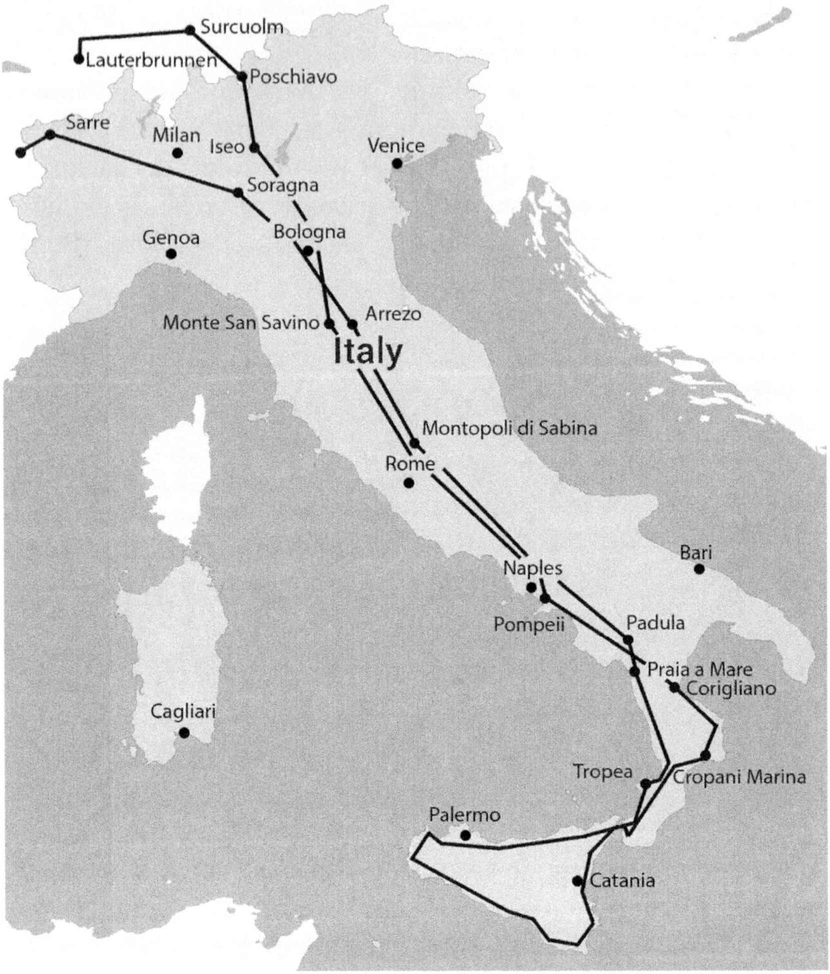
Surcuolm
Lauterbrunnen
Poschiavo
Sarre
Milan
Iseo
Venice
Soragna
Genoa
Bologna
Monte San Savino
Arrezo
Italy
Montopoli di Sabina
Rome
Bari
Naples
Pompeii
Padula
Praia a Mare
Corigliano
Cagliari
Tropea
Cropani Marina
Palermo
Catania

Appendix 1 Motorhomes

A motorhome, campervan, motorcaravan or in the language of North America an RV, can at its simplest be a van with a mattress thrown in the back with a bucket for a toilet (optional) and a portable gas stove for cooking (also optional). At the other end of the scale it could be a vehicle the size of a bus costing hundreds of thousands of whatever currency you like to choose. All have features in common, they are self-propelled in the sense of having an engine and don't need to be towed like a caravan, they have beds and in all but the smallest vehicles a toilet/shower and a kitchen. Numerous options can be added, heating, satellite television and awnings to give shade for example, but the basic motorhome remains a mobile house you drive to new places and in which you can put your head down for a night's sleep.

Our Motorhome

Our motorhome is a Murvi Morocco, made a few miles from where we live in South Devon. It is six metres (twenty feet) long, sleeps two and has an excellent large kitchen and a toilet compartment big enough to have a comfortable shower in. Storage space is limited but this encourages us to reduce clutter and take only what is essential. I have fitted a large storage box on the rear to carry our deck chairs, the insulated cover for the windscreen (great when it is hot) and numerous smaller items such as the ground sheet and the hose for filling with fresh water.

After trialling a few options we sleep under a duvet, as we do at home. It is easy to wash the cover and we get a comfortable night's' rest.

Which Motorhome?

The smallest motorhomes are little bigger than standard cars and they have the great advantage of being easy to drive and parked anywhere a car can. The downside is their kitchen and toilet facilities, if present, are basic although this isn't always a problem and small campers remain popular. The classic surfer's VW is a good example of this type. For us, being soft I guess, we chose almost the smallest motorhome you could buy with a full sized kitchen and toilet/shower. You can get ones shorter with these facilities but this will be at the expense of even less storage space.

There is no such thing as the perfect motorhome. One widely voiced maxim is "they are all a compromise" referring to the trade-off between the various features of a motorhome. Within a given size of vehicle there is a decision to be made on how to divide up the available space. A large sleeping area with a permanently fixed bed means less space for other features. To get around this and make a larger "living room" the bed can be made to fold away. This immediately gives more space but the bed needs to be made up every night. If you buy a large motorhome it is possible to have both a fixed bed and a large space for lounging and entertaining but apart from being more expensive the compromise is such a vehicle can be a challenge to drive on narrow roads and park in confined spaces such as those you might find in a mountain village. An alternative bed configuration is the drop down bed where a fully made up bed winds up into the roof of the vehicle and is lowered when required. Motorhomes are made in all different sizes and internal layouts because not everyone's requirements are the same. Our model wouldn't suit a lot of people and many of the motorhomes I see on the road wouldn't suit us.

As this isn't a book about choosing a motorhome I will leave the subject at this point. I can only suggest if you plan on buying a motorhome try not to follow the route all too many have been down and buy one only to discover there is something about it you not only dislike but decide is so bad a feature you can't live with it and a different vehicle is needed. This is an expensive mistake but one people make. If you have been camping or caravanning before you will have a reasonable idea about living with your loved ones in a confined space. If you haven't then renting a motorhome first would be wise. Renting is expensive but it is a lot cheaper than the loss you will make changing your motorhome for another shortly after you bought it.

Appendix 2 Where We Stayed

With a few exceptions we only ever stay on campsites or *aires*. The latter we find using the CamperContact app called All Motorhome Parkings. These are referred to below by their site code number. So CC10222 is site code 10222 on the CamperContact website. There are several other websites listing places to stay but the CamperContact app is easy to use and versions are available for both Android and iOS. The app includes reviews of most *aires*, machine translating them where necessary into almost readable English.

We used ACSI (www.campingcard.com) for finding campsites. Their books together with the accompanying discount card are extremely useful. They do not cover all possible sites, particularly in popular areas where the site owners do not need to offer discounts. But this suits us as we usually avoid the busy places. As their guidebook reference numbers change annually they have not been used but where "ACSI" appears the campsite name and local town are shown and these should be enough to find them in the books using the index. For a few sites I have included a web address, for example Camping Dei Trulli in Alberobello, which is non-ACSI.

A third source of stopovers is the Camping-car Park group, https://campingcar.com a French company with a growing network of aires around France with automated barriers. Entry is gained with a card on which you put credit, online or at one of the machines the aires have where you can join and be issued with a new card. These sites I have marked with the abbreviation CCP.

Google maps is useful for finding campsites. If you look at the area you are interested in and type "camping" into the search bar the known sites will appear and details can be found by clicking on each one.

We also used the Sicily Camping Tour map and more details of this can be found in the Sicily section below.

Where We Stayed - 2016

France

10 May, 2016 *Aire* at Pouencé; CC1471
11 May, Aire at Nieuil l'Espoir; CC1689
12-13 May, Parc Verger Campsite, www.parcverger.com
14 May, Aire at Saint Alvère, CC22223
15-16 May, Private house, Montesquiou.
17 May, Camping Saint Martin, Sorèze, ACSI
18 May, Camping Beauséjour, Sérignan Plage, ACSI
19 May, Saint Jean du Gard, CC2415
20 May, Vignerons de Chusclan, CC2429
21-22 May, Banon, CC2333
23 May, Annot, CC2242
24 May, Roubion, CC24944
25 May, Jausiers, CC2337
25 May, Barcelonnette, CC11807 (for water only)

Italy

26 May, Olivetta San Michele, CC20717
27-29 May, Camping Pian de Boschi, Pietro Ligure, ACSI
30-31 May, Agriturismo dei Peri, Castelnuovo Magra, CC4514
1-2 June, Aire, San Roman in Garfagnana, CC9379
3-5 June, Camping Toscana Village, Montopoli, ACSI
6 June, Volpaia, CC4458 (for lunch only)
6-7 June, Camping Orlando, Cavriglia, ACSI
8 June, Aire, Radda in Chianti, CC4457
9-10 June, Podere il Casale near Pienza, CC47567, http://podereilcasale.com/en/
11 June, Santa Fiora, CC4198
12 June, Colle di Tora, CC11017
13-15 June, Camping Parco Degli Ulivi, Pieschici, ACSI
16-19 June, Camping Baia e Cala Campoi, Vieste del Gargano, ACSI

20 June, Camping Pineta al Mare, Specchiolla di Carovigno, ACSI
21-23 June, Camping dei Trulli, Alberobello, www.campingdeitrulli.it
23 June, Agriturismo Padre Pio Giovane, CC20088
24-26 June,Camping Podere Sei Poorte, Monteciccardo. ACSI www.podereseipoorte.it
27-29 June, Camping Gaiole, Lake Corlo. ACSI site. www.campinggajole.it
30 June-3 July, Camping Valle Verde, Predazzo, ACSI site. http://campingvalleverde.it

France

5 July, Aire du Camping-car Collet, Montgenèvre, ACSI 2350
6 July, Ferme de la Condamine, Bresignan CC12541 and France Passion
7 July, We should have stayed at Camping de L'Ardeche, Vallon Pont d'Arc, ACSI
8-10 July Camping Chantemerle, Florac, ACSI
11 July, Aire by the Lac de Pareloup, Salles-Curan, CC30484
12 July, Municipal aire, Lagrasse, CC2470
13 July, Aire, Espéreza, CC20236
14 July, Aire, Les Angles, CC12061

Spain

15-17 July, Camping El Berguedà, Guardiola de Berguedà, ACSI
18-19 July, Camping Voraparc, Espot, www.voraparc.com

France

20 July, Camping Baptistou, Montréjeau, CC28629
21 July, Aire, Miélan, CC22664
22-24 July, Camping Domaine Lacs de Gascogne, Seissan, ACSI.
25 July, Private house, Near Auch

Spain

26 July, *Aire*, Errenteria, CC15155

Where We Stayed - 2017

France

23 August, Aire, Beignon, CC19710
24 August, Aire, Brissac Quincé, CC3971
25 August, Aire, Lathus St Rémy, CC15257
26 August, Aire, Thiel sur Acolin, CC21411
27 August, Camping du Sevron, St Étienne du Bois, ACSI
28-29 August, Camping de Montchavin, La Plaigne Tarantaise, ACSI and CC51735

Italy - Mainland

30 August, Camping Monte Bianco, Sarre, ACSI
31 August, Aire, Soragna, CC6468
1 September, Camping Villaggio Le Ginestre, Arezzo, ACSI
2 September, Aire, Montopoli di Sabina, CC4862
3 September, Aire, Padula, CC48476
4-5 September, Camping International, Praia a Mare, ACSI
6-7 September, Camping Marina del Convento, Tropea, ACSI

Sicily

As the purpose of this trip was to visit Sicily I have listed below the places where we stayed in more detail. ACSI books and CamperContact were used as usual to find places but we used information from a map I picked up published by Sicily Camping Tour. SCT are a group of sites, some were in ACSI but not all, and on presentation of the card which comes with the map you get a discount. The organisation has a website: http://www.sicilycampingtour.com/

8-9 September, Camping Villagio Marinello, ACSI, Oliveri/Marinello
www.villaggiomarinello.it Nice beach.

10 September, Camping & Village Rais Gerbi, Finale di Pollina, www.raisgerbi.it
Good site when it rains - hard standing pitches. Beach of boulders.

11 September, Camping La Playa, Isola delle Femmine. ASCI.
Unattractive rocky beach but SCT map and card available here.

12-13 September, Camping La Pineta, San Vito Lo Capo. ACSI.
Beach too far away. Pitches a bit chaotic. Camping El Bahira a little to the south probably much better.

14 September, Area Play Time, Castellammare del Golfo, CC7956.
Expensive for a basic sosta. No drinking water available but grey and black waste can be disposed of. The campsite further down the same road would be preferable but it is small and pitches close together.

15-19 September, Camping Helios, Triscina di Selinunte, SCT listed site, not ACSI.
Good beach and clean site.

20 September, Camping Valle dei Templi, Agrigento, SCT listed site.
www.campingvalledeitempli.com

21 September, Eurocamping Due Rocche, Falconara/Sicula. ACSI.
Good beach but facilities tatty and not cleaned regularly. Friendly reception with good English.

22-26 September, Camping Scarabeo, Punta Braccetto. ACSI. www.scarabeocamping.it
Good beach, fish, bread and vegetable vans visit. The best site we stayed on in Sicily.

27 September, Camping Sabbiadoro, Avola. ACSI. www.campeggiosabbiadoro.it
Immaculately kept site full of plants. Clean beach but access road narrow with sharp bends. An N&B Arto managed to get in but anything bigger might struggle.

28 September, Camping Jonio, Catania. ACSI.
Small site built on lava rocks. Set in the town, minimal dog walking locally.

29 September-2 October, Camping La Focetta Sicula, Sant' Alessio Sicula/Taormina. ACSI. Friendly reception, good English spoken. Good beach but water shelves quickly into deep water. Supermarket, fish shop and village with ATM just outside the site.

Coordinates of Messina port: N38.2059252, E15.5608937.

Italy - Mainland

3 October, car park for visiting the Riace Bronzes in Reggio Calabria: N38.11445, E15.64968
3 October, Camping Casa Vacanza, Cropani Marina, ACSI.
4 October, Camping Village Thurium, Corigliano, ACSI
5-6 October, Camping Zeus, Pompeii, ASCI.
7 October, Aire, Monte San Savino
8-9 October, Camping Covelo, Iseo, ACSI

Switzerland

10 October, Camping Cavresc, Poschiavo, ACSI
11 October, Panorama Camping, Surcuolm, ACSI

12-13 October, Camping Jungfrau Holiday Park, Lauterbrunnen, ACSI

France

14 October, Aire, Museum Houses Comtoises, Nancray
15 October, Aire, Gurgy, near Auxerre,
16 October, Private Aire, Azé, Vendôme
17-18 October, Camping Le Moulin De L'Eclis, Asserac, ACSI
19-20 October, Commercial Aire, Le Faou. CC12996 and CCP.
21-22 October, Aire, Plouarzel, CC3475
23 October, Aire, Landerneau, CC1250
24-25 October, Polennou, Cléder, CCP.

Appendix 3 Information

Guide Books

We are fans of the DK Eyewitness Travel books. They are generally up to date, well printed and have lots of clear illustrations. One feature we have found invaluable in their country guides is at the start of each section they list the highlights in each region together with a good map showing where these highlights are to be found. We used these frequently to plot our route. We sometimes use this feature perversely, deliberately choosing an area on the map where there were no obvious highlights. This is a sure-fire way to avoid the crowds and we were rarely disappointed with what we found.

For Italy we used two DK books, the main one on Italy and their thinner volume covering only Sicily. We also carried the DK France guide.

The Rough Guides are well produced and worth carrying but though once a fan of the Lonely Planet series I rarely use them now. In my opinion they are often poorly printed, with near illegible maps and are aimed more at the back packer looking for nightlife and cheap accommodation. Yet, all these books are worth looking at if you have the time before you leave as each carries information not included in the others.

Maps

The Michelin Road Atlas for Italy is not as well printed as their laminated equivalent for France but is adequate for day to day navigation. For general route planning a big map of the whole country you can unfold is essential and the Michelin maps take up little room but have enough detail to be useful for navigation.

For larger scale maps those produced by Marco Polo are well produced and we used their map of Sicily. It has good detail but is physically large and using it in a small vehicle a challenge.

Google maps are invaluable both in their normal map view and satellite view. I used it several times in real time on walks.

Language

Not my strong point but I've found the various BBC Active audio books best but there is a wide choice available from other companies.

Communication

I find a broadband connection invaluable and a data only sim card in a Huawei E5577 MiFi keeps us connected. Only rarely did we not have a signal, especially when using an external antenna. A MiFi is a device which connects to a broadband service like a mobile phone but then generates a local wifi signal which other devices can connect to and share the connection. You can do the same with most mobile phones, turning on a local hotspot but a good MiFi will allow you to connect an external antenna to give considerably improved reception in marginal areas. I used a Netgear MiMo antenna in Italy but since returning I have fitted a permanent antenna on the roof of the motorhome. This is a Poynting MiMo LTE vehicle antenna and my tests have confirmed it gives a considerably better signal than the Netgear antenna. The speed of upload has improved markedly. This is useful as I upload my images each day to cloud storage.

The best broadband provider to use changes weekly. A local card will inevitably give a fast signal but in both France and Italy I found a Vodafone data only card bought in the UK reliably made a 4G connection.

Appendix 4 The Hundred Years' War

The Hundred Years' War, which lasted over a hundred years and wasn't so much a war as a series of battles followed by interludes of inactivity had its origins in the Norman Conquest of England. The Normans continued to rule from their base in England the lands they owned in France. Over time the French kings strengthened their grip on what were seen as English possessions until eventually only Gascony in the far southwest of France remained. Things started to go wrong in the early fourteenth century and a detailed description of how it all unravelled would take a book to explain and many books have been written on this subject. But a Horrible Histories version of the period might run along the following lines.

The mother of the reigning English king (Edward III) was Isabella of France, who was the daughter of the late Philip IV of France, which made Edward a grandson of a former French king. Meanwhile, back in France, the French passed a law in 1316 preventing a woman inheriting the throne so when Charles IV of France died without a son the trouble-making Isabella claimed the French throne on behalf of her son, Edward, who was a nephew of Charles. The French would have nothing with this scheme, claiming Isabella could not pass on a right she was not allowed to hold herself as a woman. So the French chose someone else (another Philip) and for a few years the English accepted the position. Then the French started meddling in England's war against Scotland, who were allies of the French and this so enraged Edward III he went to war with France and invaded in 1337. Things started well with English victories at Crecy, Poitiers and Agincourt but the French had greater resources, fighting at home so to speak and began to fight back after a revival of the French spirit led by Joan of Arc. Subsequently the French inflicted crushing victories over the English at the battles of Patay, Formigny and Castillon. Battles few of us in England today seem to remember. In 1453 following the battle of Castillon the war was over. England remained technically at war with France for another twenty years but was no longer a threat. This was because we took to fighting each other the following year in the War of the Roses. A conflict which had some of its origins in the discontent felt by English nobles at losing their French estates.

The Battle of Poitiers occurred early on in this long drawn out skirmish with nearly a hundred years to go before the final whistle. The protagonists were Edward, Prince of Wales, the eldest son of Edward III and John II of France. Edward started by leading a *chevauchée* in August 1356. A *chevauchée* was a form of medieval warfare where a force moved through the countryside damaging as much of the enemy's' economy as possible by burning and looting, the latter being popular with the troops. The word comes from the French for a "promenade" though it also means "horse charge" and both translations are appropriate. Providing the attacking force could keep moving they stood a chance of evading any enemy force fielded against them.

Edward's force made good progress northwards from their base in Gascony but they lost momentum at Tours on the river Loire when they failed to take the castle. A timely or untimely depending on the side you were on downpour prevented them burning the city around the castle. The delay caused by this failure gave John time to depart with a force to intercept Edward, who he eventually caught up with outside the village of Nouallé southeast of Poitiers. Edward, later to be known as the Black Prince from the colour of his armour was aware the French king had superior forces and was prepared to negotiate a truce. A representative of the pope, Cardinal Talleyrand Perigord interceded on Sunday 18th September, 1356 to broker a peace. The French were not prepared to strike terms with "pillagers and looters" and agreed only to delay the inevitable battle until the following day rather than fight on a Sunday in what became known as the "Peace of God".

When the battle did start the French should have won the day but their forces were badly led and without reference to their king the French Marshals mounted disorganised attacks on different routes against the well defended English positions. The French elite cavalry were the first to fall, cut down by Welsh archers and things rapidly unravelled as first the archers then the English *coutilliers* (cutlass bearers) massacred the French forces in the natural traps of the marshy bends of the Moisson river and the surrounding woods and thickets where they hid in wait for their targets.

The French king fought on heroically to the last, reaching a point where only he and his son plus a few retainers were surrounded on all sides by their enemies before surrendering.

After his capture King John dined with the Prince of Wales and he was eventually taken to England where he was kept while protracted negotiations took place over his ransom. The practice of ransoming high value prisoners was well established and many significant fortunes were made this way. With a king the ransom demand was always going to be huge and after further battlefield skirmishes and the signing of the Treaty of Bretagne a figure of three million crowns was agreed. The sum could not be raised immediately but the king was allowed to return to France four years after his capture, in exchange for a large number of hostages, including Louis, his son. This might have been the end of things but an impoverished France struggled to raise the ransom and Louis remained in captivity for several years. Unable to negotiate his release the enterprising lad escaped instead. On hearing this King John returned to England for reasons not fully understood now. It may have been chivalric honour, which was at its peak during this era and offering himself in return for his escaped son repaired the reputation his families' honour. Alternatively it is possible he had grown tired of ruling France, a country in turmoil and broke after paying his ransom and he preferred the pleasures of London where as an honoured prisoner he had freedom to travel and entertain while in 'captivity'. Unfortunately, if the latter was his reason he was not to enjoy any pleasures for long as he fell ill and died within six months of returning to England.

France took a long time to recover from the defeat at Poitiers and King John's ransom emptied the French Treasury of golden *écues* (crowns) leading to the minting of the first francs, a name derived from the French for "free" and a currency which was to endue for several hundred years before being supplanted by the euro.

Appendix 5 The Author

John Laidler was born in Carlisle, Cumbria. After starting as an apprentice with a local engineering firm and subsequently graduating with a degree in Mechanical Engineering from Newcastle Polytechnic he spent the next thirty something years doing various jobs including a spell as a beekeeper and running a business selling beekeeping equipment. He lives with his wife in South Devon and has two sons and a daft dog.

By the same author: "**Two Go to Spain**"
Available on Amazon as an ebook and paperback.

www.john-laidler.co.uk

Printed in Great Britain
by Amazon

73206125R00190